working?

EMPLOYMENT

POLICY

IN

CANADA

Stephen McBride

Rock's
Mills
Press

Published by
Rock's Mills Press

Copyright © 2017 by Stephen McBride.
Published by arrangement with the author. All rights reserved.

Library and Archives Canada Cataloguing in Publication data is available on request. Contact us at customer.service@rocksmillspress.com.

CONTENTS

Illustrations

Acronyms

AI	Artificial Intelligence
CIC	Citizenship and Immigration Canada
ESA	Employment Standards Act
ESDC	Employment and Social Development Canada
FAFIA	Feminist Alliance for International Action
HRSDC	Human Resources and Social Development Canada
IMP	International Mobility Program
IRCC	Immigration, Refugees and Citizenship Canada
IRPA	Immigration and Refugee Protection Act
LMIA	Labour Market Impact Assessment
LMO	Labour Market Opinions
LSA	Labour Standards Act
NIEAP	Non-Immigrant Employment Authorization Program
OECD	Organisation for Economic Co-operation and Development
OHS	Occupational Health and Safety
OPSEU	Ontario Public Service Employees Union
PNP	Provincial Nominee Program
SAWP	Seasonal Agricultural Workers Program
TFWP	Temporary Foreign Worker Program
YES	Youth Employment Strategy

Acknowledgements

In preparing this book I have benefited from the assistance and insights of many students, colleagues and friends and am grateful for funding from the Social Sciences and Humanities Research Council of Canada (SSHRC) and the Canada Research Chairs Program.

In particular I would like to thank for research and/or editorial assistance: Mohammad Ferdosi, Sorin Mitrea, Jacob Muirhead, James Watson, Scott Leon, Nour Afara, Oldrich Bubak, and Samantha Manley; and for kindly providing feedback on individual draft chapters: Marjorie Griffin Cohen, Bryan Evans, John Shields and Heather Whiteside.

Jen Rubio was an enthusiastic and supportive editor and her encouragement and energy was invaluable to completing the manuscript much more quickly than would otherwise have been the case!

Most of all I would like to thank my wife Jan Keeton, who in addition to all her usual support, carefully read and commented on the entire manuscript.

It goes without saying that any remaining errors are the sole responsibility of the author.

1

From Full Employment to Flexible Employment

There is currently much dissatisfaction with employment and work in Canada. Many employers see a scene in which labour shortages exist side-by-side with pools of unemployed workers. But employers claim that these workers either have the wrong skills or are in the wrong place, or they want too much money for work performed. For the workforce, the downsizing of the manufacturing sector and diminished opportunities in a budget-constrained public sector is eliminating the well-paying, often unionized jobs that were the pathway to a secure middle-class lifestyle. The future is bleak for workers in these sectors who lose their jobs and—equally worrying for others—it is unclear how their children will be able to attain a similar level of economic prosperity and security that they have enjoyed. For the majority of Canadians who lack adequate pensions, the end of working life spells economic difficulty.

For young workers entering the labour market, acquiring and maintaining a good job is a fraught process; there are few satisfactory paths to a career in a time of so-called flexibility and precarious working conditions. Pre-employment practices such as unpaid internships have achieved a degree of notoriety. Some now refer to a whole sub-strata of the labour market as the "gig economy," characterized by a combination of precarious, insecure, and temporary job opportunities.[1] In fact, such analyses are hardly new. In a report called *Good Jobs, Bad Jobs: Employment in the Service Sector* the Economic Council of Canada (1990) had warned of the growth of a low-wage sector with insecure or precarious conditions of work. Its solution was to intensify job training to heighten skill levels that might qualify those individuals for better employment opportunities. Whether or not this was the right diagnosis or prescription is a matter for debate. However, the problems identified

1 Workers in the gig economy: "could be in contingent or alternative employment arrangements, or both, ... Contingent workers are those who don't have an implicit or explicit contract for long-term employment. Alternative employment arrangements include independent contractors (also called freelancers or independent consultants), on-call workers, and workers provided by temporary help agencies or contract firms. See www.bls.gov/careeroutlook/2016/article/what-is-the-gig-economy.htm

by the Economic Council not only persist, but arguably have worsened, and can be discussed in almost the exact language used as they were in 1990; this indicates a failure of employment policy generally to deal with labour market problems.

Given the importance of employment for economic well-being and the social and cultural well-being that depends on it, employment should be at the centre of politics and public policy. Yet it is not. Employment policy is a relative backwater. How many of us can name the minister responsible? And a case can be made that existing policy exacerbates rather than solves the problems that so many face in the contemporary labour market. This book describes, analyses, and explains this situation.

A brief word about my definition of work or labour. In order for any kind of economic activity to occur, work must be performed. Those performing it must be mobilized, organized, and their skills and energies applied to the production process. By production process I mean all the stages of economic activity including design, production, and marketing, in all sectors of the economy including services. How much labour power, and what type of labour will be used varies enormously by economic sector and level of technological development. It also varies over historical time. But the application of labour is a constant. For small producers the labour may be their own. For larger producers, labour power must be obtained from others in some way. In a capitalist labour market this involves purchasing an employee's time and skill through an employment relationship that involves payment of wages or salaries and, sometimes, benefits. Other systems such as slavery are possible; however, for the most part, these days the exchanges and relations between employers and employees take place in the labour market.

Just as firms and employers need to hire workers to carry out their economic activities, most people must sell their labour power in order to make a living. Not everyone needs to do this. Some people are for various reasons unable to work or otherwise participate in the labour market and must therefore depend on others or the state for sustenance; some would like to participate, but are prevented from doing so because of discrimination or other reasons; others may be independently wealthy and have no need to work themselves, in effect living off the efforts of others.

A statistic called the *Labour force participation rate* gives some purchase on how many people rely on the employment relationship to make their living. It measures the proportion of the population ages 15 and older (often capped at the official retirement age, such as 65, if there is one) that is economically active in the sense of supplying labour for the production of goods and services. The labour force participation rate includes people who may be temporarily unemployed as long as they are actively looking for work. It typically excludes people who are in full-time education, given that they may be preparing to enter the labour force but are not currently part of it, along with anyone who is neither working nor seeking work. In Canada, for the last few decades the labour force participation rate has been in the 64–68 percent range. This means that most Canadians of working age depend on the money they make from their employment. Additionally, those too young to work will normally be dependent on the incomes generated by the work of their parent(s); and those who have retired from work may receive work-related pensions in addition to a state pension, the Canada Pension Plan (CPP) that is also geared to contributions made during one's working life.

What happens in the labour market is therefore of major significance to employers and employees. For the former, obtaining the right kind of labour, in sufficient quantity, and at the right price, will be a determinant of economic success. For the latter, obtaining the right job will confer economic security, the satisfaction that may derive from the creative activity of work and social relationships forged in the workplace, along with the means to pursue leisure or cultural activities outside the workplace. Failure to obtain adequate employment is likely to lead to economic insecurity, social isolation, or exclusion, personal unhappiness, and assorted health ill-effects that are associated with unemployment and precarious employment.

The conclusion to be drawn from this very brief introduction is as follows: work and labour are essential human activities; and our way of organizing them (through the labour market in today's world) has major ramifications for personal and social well-being, and possibly for the sustainability of our political system. In short, the labour market is an important place. Like all markets it is not free, in the sense of being unregulated. Rather, regulations and policies pertaining directly to the labour market and, more broadly, to the economy and society in which it is embedded, condition the way it operates. Preparation for employment, the amount of employment provided, and the terms and conditions under which employment occurs all emerge from this market and are shaped by the legislative, policy, and regulatory environment in which it functions. Given its importance to our economic, social, psychological, physical, and cultural well-being, we need to pay more attention to how it functions, and how it sometimes malfunctions.

The Canadian Labour Market in Context

In common with other western countries Canada enjoyed a long period of post-World War II economic boom. In fact, the period saw its share of ups and downs, but recessions tended to be short-lived and shallow, and most economic indicators trended consistently upward. Exactly what was responsible for this long-boom remains a matter of debate—it was certainly not all policy driven. However, there was a widespread tendency to attribute economic success and relatively full employment to the implementation of a set of ideas and policies derived from the work of the British economist John Maynard Keynes. These policies were articulated in terms of achieving full or high levels of employment and provision of a steadily expanding welfare state. Keynes' ideas began to become popular during the Great Depression and were adopted widely in western countries in the post-war world.

Since the 1970s these ideas have been displaced by the neoliberal approach—which will be referenced throughout this book; neoliberal thinking places much greater reliance on markets and has sought to reduce and restructure the state. The result is that the state has less capacity to modify market outcomes. At one level, neoliberalism consists of a number of mutually reinforcing policy goals, underpinned by a theory that emphasizes individualism, the sanctity and efficiency of private property rights, the rule of law, and a free market with a minimal but strong state (Harvey 2007; Gamble 1988). Its program includes policies promoting these aims, such as privatization and deregulation, enhanced capital mobility and free trade, an anti-inflation rather than full-employment focus, and a limited and fiscally constrained state.[2] Applied to labour market and social policy neoliberalism is defined by the promotion of individual responsibility, private delivery of services, attachment of strict conditions and obligations to receipt of benefits (e.g. workfare), tougher qualification requirements, and lower benefit

2 For an application to Canada see McBride and Whiteside 2011, chapter 4.

levels for recipients of social programs intended to "activate" them and encourage their (re-)attachment to the labour market.[3] It is based on the notion that individual deficiencies are the cause of unemployment.

Keynes considered most of the mass unemployment of the 1930s to be caused by systemic rather than individual factors, notably by a lack of effective aggregate demand. [Aggregate demand can be described as the quantity of goods and services demanded in an economy at a given price level, and is comprised of spending on consumption, investment, government, and net exports.] Unemployment happens when effective aggregate demand falls below the capacity of the economy to supply goods and services. According to orthodox economic theory, then and now, there was an automatic tendency for supply and demand to be in equilibrium, or balanced, at a level of full employment.[4] That is, with all labour and manufacturing capacity fully employed, there would be sufficient demand to absorb this production. The mechanisms of adjustment were wages, prices, and interest rates. As long as markets were free to make these adjustments, they would balance supply and demand. Shocks and imbalances might occur, but the market would bring balance back to the system, at least in the long-run. It was this claim, of course, which drew Keynes' famous riposte: "in the long-run we are all dead." As a result, in the short-run, something needed to be done about the mass unemployment of the 1930s, which was the context for his most important theoretical writings. This was particularly important because, according to Keynes, there was no good reason to suppose that the economy would move back into equilibrium at full-employment levels. Instead, it might stay stuck with a balance between demand and supply, but without the effective level of demand to pull into use the full productive potential of the economy. Unless something were done to close the gap between potential output and actual levels of effective demand, then stagnation—with accompanying high levels of unemployment—could persist for long periods. Government should therefore act to raise the level of aggregate demand. This

3 The neoliberal package is not fixed but evolves over time and show considerable variety according to jurisdiction. However the concept is worth retaining since there is continuity of fundamentals over the entire period it has been dominant: budgetary austerity, implementation of regressive taxation, deregulation and re-regulation, privatization, liberalization, a determination to keep inflation under control even if at the expense of high unemployment, individual activation (as with welfare to work or "workfare+programs" rather than social compensation in the face of systemic problems such as unemployment, and free trade and capital mobility.

4 In its modern version, orthodox economics suggests that unemployment will stabilize at its natural rate (or the Non-Accelerating Inflation Rate of Unemployment), which could be considered the best achievable rate of unemployment.

could be done either by increasing its own spending, or by intervening in the private economy such that exports increased, or consumption or investment spending was adjusted upwards to the necessary level.

Marx considered labour to be a fundamental expression of human creativity, something intrinsic to the human condition. Under capitalism, however, the ability and capacity of individuals to labour—which Marx termed "labour power"—became a commodity and its bearers subject to exploitation and alienation. In Marx's schema labour power was a unique commodity because only it had the capacity to create new value (added value) in the production process. This additional value ("surplus value" in Marxist terminology) was appropriated by the owner/employer, with the result that workers under capitalism are inevitably exploited (defined as being paid less than the value of what their labour power produces). Because in selling their labour power, workers submit to the authority of the employer over all aspects of the production process, including ownership and disposition of the end-product, workers also experience alienation—from the process of production (which is controlled by their employer), to a sense of identity that could but does not under these conditions result from the expression of creative powers through labour, from other workers because relations are for the most part not cooperative, and from the final product of what they are working on, since it belongs to their employer (see Rinehart 1998).

For Marx, the relations between workers and employers are inherently conflictual—a condition of class struggle exists between the two sides of production though its intensity will vary over time. The conflict is about terms and conditions of the employment relationship and some moderation of the stark picture of exploitation and alienation may be possible, for example in periods when labour scarcity strengthens the hand of labour. However, short of eliminating capitalism itself the basic relationship persists. In this struggle it is in the interests of capital to keep labour weak. One way of doing this is through ensuring an oversupply of labour in relation to the number of employment opportunities available, thus driving down labour's bargaining power and wages, and its ability to win other concessions. Marx referred to an "industrial reserve army" as an endemic feature of capitalism. By this he meant a section of the potential labour force, not currently employed (at least to the same level as the main part of the labour force) but which can be called into the work force whenever the need arises. At various times and places this category might include agricultural workers, women, the young, the old, immigrants, temporary migrant workers, social assistance recipients, and overseas workers whose labour power can be accessed through outsourcing production to offshore locations and, courtesy of free trade agreements, importing the products that might formerly have been produced domestically. From this perspective capital will resist the idea of full employment. Indeed, this was expressed very early in the debates about the adoption of Keynesian full employment policies in the UK. The first problem for capital from such policies was an authority problem. As *The London Times* put it in January 1943: "The first function of unemployment ... is that it maintains the authority of master over man" (sic [cited in Gonick 1987, 82–83]; see also Kalecki 1943). Second, an inflation problem, affecting many sectors of society, but particularly those with accumulated wealth, was also identified.

In this context, Keynes' emphasis on the need for full-employment, and his willingness to tolerate budget deficits to achieve it led to charges that he was a socialist. On the contrary, his proposals were designed to save the free enterprise system from the consequences of its own instability and tendency to depressions: "the world will not much longer tolerate the unemployment ... inevitably associated with present day capitalist individualism" (Keynes 1936, 380–81). What Keynes sought to change was not the ownership of firms, nor what they produced, but rather the volume that they were able to produce and sell. Some of this might be achieved through having an impact on investment spending, but more commonly it would operate through increased consumer or government spending. Monetary policy could play a role in inducing additional spending through interest rate adjustments, but it was expected that fiscal policy—government spending—would shoulder much of the burden. In times of recession, such spending would result in budget deficits. Some of the spending could be discretionary, such as with increasing the flow of infrastructure spending. Other parts would be built through expenditures that would be triggered by a recession itself. One example would be benefits to the unemployed. As their numbers increased in a recessionary period, spending would automatically increase. And such spending would stabilize the economy by sustaining levels of aggregate demand at levels much higher than would have been the case in their absence. These measures, and others like them (such as the income support programs of Canada's slowly developing welfare state in the post-war period), were the "automatic stabilizers" of the Keynesian era. A similar rationale was behind additional measures, such as tolerance or encouragement of trade union organizing. Other things being equal, high levels of union membership would drive wages up and thus overcome the demand deficiency to which capitalism was prone.

In Canada, adoption of the Keynesian model was complicated by the country's economic openness, reliance on exports, and resource dependency. In addition its institutional structures (see Chapter 2) made policy coordination difficult. Easy implementation of Keynesian policies assumed a type of national economic management that was compromised if a country's borders were, in economic terms, too open. For example, if a country had a high propensity to import goods and services from elsewhere, and if there were no trade barriers to prevent this, government spending to increase effective aggregate demand might leak out of the country to the benefit of producers elsewhere. One of the negative effects of contemporary free trade agreements is that they eliminate policy instruments that could be used to stimulate domestic demand without leakage of this sort. Hence they tend to lock-in one economic policy model and inhibit alternatives. Nevertheless, early in the post-war period, Canada did make an effort to meet the new priorities despite its relative trade openness, and the 1945 White Paper on Employment and Income (Canada, Department of Reconstruction, 1945) promised government policy predicated on "high and stable levels of employment" (rather than the full-employment pledge made in some other countries). The White Paper contained a "synthesis of the traditional staples-led approach to economic development with the Keynesian theory of demand management and fiscal stabilization" (Wolfe 1984, 55). Whether or not the adoption of Keynesianism was responsible for the post-war boom,[5] the two were closely associated, in Canada and elsewhere in the western world; there is no doubt that policy likely played a significant role.

There is no consensus about when precisely the post-war boom ended. However, it is safe to say that it was entering crisis by 1975 with several factors, including other policy shifts, the Bank of Canada's adoption of monetarist doctrines, and the federal government's adoption of wage and price controls serving as markers.[6] We shall re-

5 On this see Campbell 1987.
6 On these developments see McBride 1992, Chapter 4.

turn to policy below; for now, it is worthwhile to compare the labour market at the close of that period, in 1974, with that of today. This is important for two reasons. First, we need to dispel the notion that the past was a "golden age" and that everything is worse now. By some indicators, the situation today actually looks better than it did in the mid-1970s. Second, while the past was no golden age, in other areas there has been a dramatic deterioration in labour market conditions. These deteriorating conditions help account for the difficulties faced by so many today.

The Labour Market: A Snapshot Then and Now

On three key indicators it is possible to argue that the labour market was either in better position in 2016 than it was in 1974, or at least is no worse. These are the labour force participation, employment, and unemployment rates, summarized in Chart 1. The employment rate refers to the number of persons employed expressed as a percentage of the total working population. The unemployment rate is the percentage of the labour force who are available for but without work. The labour force participation rate is the share of the working-age population that is employed (working) or unemployed (and looking for work).

Chart 1: Key Labour Market Indicators, 1974 and 2016

	1974			2016		
	Overall	Men	Women	Overall	Men	Women
Employment Rate	55.9	71.0	41.4	61.1	64.9	57.5
Labour Force Participation Rate	60.0	75.6	44.8	65.7	70.3	61.3
Un-employment Rate	6.8	6.4	8.6	7.0	7.7	7.0

Source: Statistics Canada

This chart shows that the employment and labour force participation rates were higher in 2016. There was little difference in the rate of unemployment. For women there have been significant improvements in all three indicators; for men, employment and labour force participation rates diminished, while their unemployment rate increased. For now, we can note that the basic data in the chart presents a useful corrective to simple nostalgia for the Keynesian era.

That said, any snapshot of the situation on two different dates fails to reveal what might have happened in between. We will analyse this issue in later chapters. Here we can observe that unemployment went up in the 1980s and the 1990s, when it averaged 9.5 percent. Moreover, in the 2000–2016 period, which includes the pre-crisis boom as well as the post-crisis recession unemployment averaged just over 7 percent (Statistics Canada: Table 282-0004, "Labour force survey estimates [LFS], by educational attainment, sex and age group, annual [persons unless otherwise noted]," CANSIM). In terms of the unemployment rate, therefore, performance after 1974 was markedly inferior in the 1980s and 1990s, and somewhat worse than the 1970s in the period after 2000. In the case of the other two indicators—the employment rate and the labour participation rate—the trend in both these cases has been steadily upward, though with some declines in the recessions of the early 1980s and 1990s. Nonetheless, if we look beyond the basic figures, we begin to see a very different picture.

What follows here are snapshots of some features of working life that collectively indicate why the labour market is in worse shape today than formerly, notwithstanding the statistics just cited. These features include unemployment insurance, trade union coverage, precarious work, low wages and real incomes, and inequality.

Unemployment insurance, since renamed Employment Insurance (EI), was introduced with a number of purposes. One of these was to provide increased security for those in the labour force who might become unemployed. The unemployment rate in both our snapshot years was very similar. However, by 2016 the size of the labour force had almost doubled. Yet many more people were receiving unemployment insurance payments in the mid-1970s (719,000 was the figure for December 1976), compared to four decades later, when it was 568,800 (data available at Statistics Canada). This fits with other studies that show decreased coverage for unemployed workers and lower salary replacement rates. For example, during the period between 1990 and 2001, a Canadian Labour Congress study (2003) showed a 50 percent decline in the ratio of beneficiaries to unemployed (this is known as the B/U ratio). According to David Gray and Colin Busby (2016, 3):

The B/U ratio reached a peak of 84 percent in early 1990, after which it declined sharply to a trough of 44 percent in late 1997 ... Despite this drastic decline over a seven-year interval, it has been remarkably stable since then: in the neighbourhood of 44 percent. It also appears to have returned to a cyclical pattern ...; it rose to 47 percent during the 2009 recession, then dipped to 38 percent in early 2014, and subsequently recovered to 42 percent in 2015.

We will look more closely at the employment insurance issue in later chapters but, for now, we can note that if the system was designed to produce greater security within the labour market, then the labour market of the 2010s is a less secure place than it was previously. The majority of unemployed persons no longer receive benefits.

The same general conclusion can be drawn from the decline of trade unions. Unions are protective institutions for the employees belonging to them. Wages and employment benefits can normally be negotiated more effectively on a collective than on an individual basis. Once negotiated, collective agreements provide a set of rules governing the workplace and confer rights on workers. The unions provide quasi-legal assistance in filing grievances against alleged managerial breaches of those rules and rights. The absolute number of union members in Canada has grown substantially, from about 1.5 million to 4.75 million, but the percentage of the labour force belonging to unions has declined, from around 35 to 30 percent. In the private sector, this decline is quite dramatic, with fewer than 20 percent belonging to trade unions. Increasingly, employees face their employers with no labour organization at their side. In contrast to the private sector unionization trends, of course, the public sector remains heavily unionized, with over 70 percent belonging.

Against this general background, the decline of full-time, full-year work has led to precarious and insecure employment for many. According to *It's More than Poverty: Employment Precarity and Household Well-Being* (Lewchuk et al 2013), at least 20 percent of those working are in precarious forms of employment, representing an increase of nearly 50 percent in the last 20 years. Conversely, in 2011 only half of the employed people between the ages of 25 and 65 in the GTA-Hamilton labour market were in a standard employment relationship (23) and the category of "'self employed without employees'" had increased by almost 45 percent over the same period. In the Toronto Census Metropolitan Area, the number of people who described their job as temporary had increased by 40 percent since 1997 (24). Leah Vosko (2004, 53) advanced four qualitative criteria for assessing whether a job is precarious: control over the process, degree of certainty of continuing employment, degree of regulatory protection or whether the worker has access to social and labour protections, and income level. Thus control, certainty or predicability, along with rights, income and employment status are determinants of precariousness. Consistent with the argument that problems stemming from work insecurity are serious, an international and Canadian literature review of work published in the 2000s found that precarious work was characterized by a number of negative results for those involved in it. These included: exclusion from the state-provided benefits that standard workers enjoy; deterioration in health and safety conditions at work (Quinlan et al 2001); falling between the cracks of social policies designed for the Standard Employment Relationship (SER) (Rittich 2004, 33; Vosko 2004, 90); less coverage by trade unions and, if unionized, perhaps subject to special and less favourable contracts (Quinlan et al 2001, 358; Bergstrom 2003, 29); impacts on health in general (i.e. besides issues of occupational health) including the psychological stress of non-standard employment and the physical affects of working shift work (Winson and Leach 2002, 142; Bergstrom 2003, 19; Quinlan 2003, 3); loss of self-worth and other psychological impacts (Winson and Leach 2002, 133); family separation and loss of social ties partly because of working unsociable hours (Winson and Leach 2002, 150; Lowe 2000, 129; Chaykowski 2005, 10); and adverse community impacts as individuals become disengaged (Winson and Leach 2002).

Nationally, part-time employment as a percentage of total employment had doubled from 6 to 12 percent.[7] The CIBC's Canadian Employment Index (Tal 2015) similarly recorded a decline in work quality. Based on an index where 1988 equalled 100, the index had declined by almost 15 percent in 2015. The index combines data on the distribution of part- and full-time jobs, the proportions of self-employed versus paid employment, and the sectoral composition of full-time paid

7 Based on 1976 Census Data Statistics Canada (1980), "Canada's Female Labour Force: The Changing Face of Labour." Statistics Canada Demography Division. Series on 1976 Census and for 2013 (statcan.gc.ca/tables-tableaux/sum-som/l01/cst01/labor12-eng.htm).

work. In 2016, Tal noted continued deterioration in the labour market: part-time jobs accounted for 90 percent of jobs created in 2015 and 2016; the share of low paying jobs in the prime working age bracket of 25 to 54 had increased over time; and the share of workers paid less than the average wage had risen to 61 percent – a development characteristic of a widening wage gap.

Data from 2014 show that just over a quarter of workers were considered low waged (that is, defined as half of median hourly wages), with the incidence of low wages varying by gender, age, and part-time status. Thus women were 1.5 times more likely to be receiving low wages than men, young workers 2.5 times more likely than middle-aged or older workers, and part-time workers 2.5 times more likely than full-time workers (Thomas 2016). One component of the low waged are those receiving statutory minimum wages. The constant dollar value of the minimum wage is similar to what it was in the late 1970s. In 2013, 6.7 percent of employees were paid the minimum wage, compared to 5.0 percent in 1997. Young workers, less educated workers, and those working in the service sectors were most likely to be at the minimum wage. The industries with the highest proportion of minimum wage workers were the retail trade sector and the food and accommodation sectors (Galarneau and Fecteau 2014).

In general, real wage rates have not done particularly well in the neoliberal era. From 1981 to 2011 there was only a 4.7 percent increase in real hourly wages (2010 dollars) for men aged 25 to 54 employed full-time. For women, the comparable figure was 20.2 percent. In concrete terms, the *median* hourly real wage rose from just under $19 in 1981 to just under $21 in 2011 (2010 dollars), or about 10 cents per year. Interestingly the comparable *average* hourly wage has shown a higher rate of growth (from approximately $20.75 to $23.50) due to the rise in the earnings of those at the top of the income distribution (Morissette, Picot, and Lu 2015).

Chart 2 (see next page) represents these trends.

Income inequality has significantly increased during the neoliberal period. A widely used measure of income inequality is the Gini index as shown in Chart 3.

14

Stephen McBride

Chart 2: Real Hourly Wages of Full-Time Workers Aged 17 to 64, 1981 to 2011

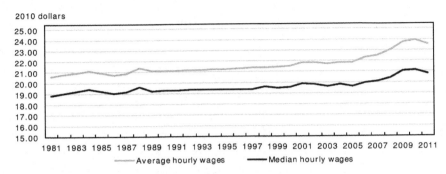

Note: Estimates for 1982, 1983, 1985, and 1991 to 1996 are based on interpolations of data. Real hourly wages are obtained by dividing hourly wages by the Consumer Price Index (CPI).

Sources: Statistics Canada, 1981 Survey of Work History, 1984 Survey of Union Membership, 1986 to 1990 Labour Market Activity Survey, 1997 to 2011 Labour Force Survey, and Consumer Price Index (Allitems).

Chart 3: Income Inequality Has Been Increasing in Canada
(Gini index using adjusted after-tax income, where 0 represents exact equality and 1 represents total inequality.)

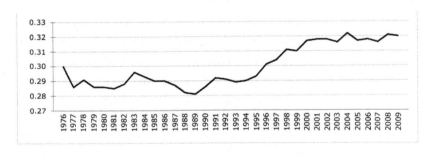

Source: Conference Board of Canada (conferenceboard.ca/hcp/hot-topics/caninequality.aspx)

Other measurements show similar trends. In Canada, only the fifth quintile—the group of richest Canadians—has increased its share of national income since 1999 (Battams, Spinks, and Sauve 2014, 12). Another study concluded that, "In 2013, the average after-tax income of the richest 10 percent of Canadian households was 20 times that of the average income of the poorest 10 percent, the second highest ratio of any period on record since 1976" (Klein and Yalnizyan 2016, 5).

Meanwhile households incurred more debt: "In 2013, total debt as a percentage of disposable income averaged 165.5 percent in 2013, up from 110 percent in 2000" (Battams, Spinks, and Sauve 2014, 20), and from 86 percent in the early 1980s (www.bankofcanada.ca/wp-content/uploads/2012/02/boc-review-winter11-12-bailliu.pdf). It has continued to rise, to 167.6 percent, in 2016 (see for example http://business.financialpost.com/news/economy/canadas-household-debt-is-now-bigger-than-its-gdp-for-the-first-time/wcm/6255f0de-6743-4de5-a12f-2393638200af).

These numbers warrant a closer look at the conditions inside the labour market. For now, this brief sketch has had two objectives. The first was to show that not everything about the labour market is worse than it was; the 1970s did not represent a golden age of employment. Second, there is no doubt that many areas have seen deteriorating conditions. The perception that today's labour market is a more hostile place is grounded in reality. While it was not a golden age, we may be able to learn from the experience of the 1970s labour market and the policies that shaped it; we can also learn other lessons from the way it was dismantled by succeeding policies.

The Policy Framework: From a Full to a Flexible Employment Regime

This section outlines the policy transition from a post-World War II period—often depicted as the Keynesian welfare state era, or the era of full-employment managed by a benevolent state—to one of a neoliberal emphasis on the primacy of market forces. In addition to a description of this transition, I also introduce a number of alternative explanations for the trends. These include the notion that the change has been driven by increased conflict within the workplace between employers (capital) and labour. In these conflicts, it has been the former—capital—that has generally prevailed.

Others argue that the changes have less to do with the preferences of social actors like employers and more to do with necessity in the form of globalization. Globalization, in this view, is an uncontrollable process that mandates certain types of adaptation, including those affecting work—with the price of failure being economic decline. Employers, therefore, may be driving the shift to flexible employment;

however, they are seen as having little choice if they are to survive in an increasingly competitive global economy.

Providing an ideological rationale, and sometimes adduced as a causal factor, is the set of ideas associated with neoliberalism. These include the idea that state intervention in the economy obstructs the efficiency of the market and should therefore be kept to a minimum. In this context, therefore, employers are given considerable leeway to structure their workforces as they see fit, regardless of the diminished protection to their employees.

Similarly, privatization and deregulation are seen as primary means to constrain the state, along with reduced spending in general, reduction of public debt, and balanced budgets. The fact that the preferred method of achieving the latter is through restraints on spending rather than through increased revenues via taxes indicates that the overarching goal is not a balanced budget per se, but rather a reduced role for the state. Neoliberals, however, tend to favour a strong but limited state (Gamble 1988). The strong state is maintained in areas like law and order, defence and protection of property rights, so the goal of spending restraint will fall in areas like social programs—the kinds of programs that augment the incomes of the population, particularly the less affluent, by provision of in-kind free or subsidized benefits such as education, health, pensions, and income security. With respect to the labour market, neoliberals argue that various problems, including unemployment, result from "rigidities," including increased security for workers whether achieved through negotiated settlements with employers or through state regulation. Removal of these rigidities will, they argue, let the labour market function efficiently ("flexibly"), enabling these systemic problems to be overcome.

Between the end of World War II and the mid-1970s, the Canadian labour market was relatively secure and exhibited relatively full employment. "Relatively" here is in comparison to the situation in the earlier twentieth century as well as the subsequent situation in the 1980s and beyond. Security refers to low unemployment levels, increased protection due to unionization, and the lower incidence of part-time or temporary work (as compared to full-time, on-going work).

Governments, of course, are always engaged in juggling economic priorities. Yet amid the short-term fluctuations it is possible to discern broader trends. In the 30-year post-war period it is evident that government's articulation of economic goals prioritized employment issues.

This might be expressed either as "high and stable" levels of employment or as a commitment to bringing about full employment. After 1975, other aims became prominent. While governments still talked of jobs or employment, they became a lower priority. From the mid-1970s, inflation issues achieved dominance in government pronouncements that establish the broad goals of policy, such as federal Throne and Budget speeches. From the 1980s, after the inflation threat subsided, fiscal issues of budget deficits and the need to reduce government debt came to occupy the top place in these speeches.[8]

This was a rhetorical shift. But it was accompanied by developments in the real world of work. The labour market was restructured such that it became a less secure environment for workers, and a more flexible space for employers. Insecurity of the workforce and flexibility for employers share an umbilical connection. In broad terms, therefore, it is fair to say we have moved from full employment to flexible employment.

Flexibility sometimes works to the advantage of employees who may benefit from flexible work hours or part-time work if they have family or other commitments that make the normal working day or week unattractive, and if they have some influence on how their working time is to be structured. More commonly, however, flexibility serves employers' interests and needs. It is employers who determine the allocation and conditions of working time. Guy Standing (1999) has analysed this shift to flexible employment in considerable detail and points out that for workers the term really translates into "insecurity". Thus, the opposite of flexibility from labour's point of view is not inflexibility or rigidity but, rather, security. He identifies seven forms of labour market security (Standing 1999, 52):

> *Labour market security*: adequate employment opportunities, through state-guaranteed full employment;
>
> *Employment security*: protection against arbitrary dismissal, regulations on hiring and firing, imposition of costs on employers, etc.;
>
> *Job security*: a niche designated as an occupation or "'career,'" plus tolerance of demarcation practices, barriers to skill dilution, craft boundaries, job qualifications, restrictive practices, craft unions, etc.;
>
> *Work security*: protection against accidents and illness at

---

8 For details on this transition in articulated goals see McBride 1992, Chapter 4.

work, through safety and health regulations, limits on working time, unsociable hours, night work for women, etc.;

Skill reproduction security: widespread opportunities to
gain and retain skills, through apprenticeships, employment
training, etc.;

Income security: protection of income through minimum
wage machinery, wage indexation, comprehensive social security, progressive taxation, etc.;

Representation security: protection of collective voice in the
labour market, through independent trade unions and employer associations incorporated economically and politically
into the state, with the right to strike, etc."

The degree to which workers enjoy these types of security depends
of course on their relative power vis-à-vis capital and the state. In this
book the first of these, labour market security runs throughout but
is paid special attention in Chapters 1 and 3. Chapters 4 and 5 deal
with skill reproduction security among other issues. Employment, job,
work, and income security receive attention in Chapters 6, 7 and 8;
and representation security in Chapter 9. Provision of security, or of its
opposite, flexibility/insecurity, is influenced by the mode of regulation
of the labour market. Three forms can be distinguished: regulation by
the state, by the market, and by "voice" (that is in direct negotiations or
bargaining between employers and workers or their representatives).
Although each of these regulatory modes has its own characteristics,
Standing's basic argument is that the thirty years after World War II
(the period of full employment) was also a period of state regulation of
the labour market that tended to extend labour's rights and security.
Today, the predominant mode is market regulation (or deregulation)
and the corollary is insecurity for workers.

The broad macroeconomic shift after 1975 from Keynesianism to
neoliberalism can be seen in the labour market arena. Here the shift
was from state to market regulation and the result was one of rising
unemployment (tolerated if not induced by states in the battle against
inflation). This in itself weakened labour. State policies encouraged or
permitted flexibility rather than security. With this shift, "fear changed
sides" (Standing 1999, 81) and all the forms of security that had characterized the post-war era —however incompletely—were diminished
by a mixture of state measures and employer strategies, all designed
to maximize advantage in the new context. We will examine some

of these measures and strategies in later chapters. Their cumulative impact was to weaken security for workers and increase flexibility for employers.

In analysing the turn to flexibility Guy Standing once again (1999, Chapter 4) provides a reliable overview of its dimensions and types. Over recent decades employers have sought to make their employment relations, labour forces, and employment cost structures much more flexible than they were in the preceding post-World War II period. States have assisted them in doing so.

This is partly the result of reorganization of production, and employment, by large multinational enterprises. Rather than remaining integrated entities responsible for an entire chain of production—a responsibility that tended to increase the possibility of unionization and hence regulation of wages and benefits by negotiation with labour— the process of production is broken into component parts. Some of these component parts are geographic. Other components are functional, wherein smaller entities within the overarching enterprise (or outside firms or suppliers) are bound to the controlling enterprise by various contracts and must assume responsibility for controlling their own costs. In this context, wage flexibility can take many forms. These include the substitution of piece rates for time rates, shorter call-out periods and/or increased overtime hours, altering the hours to qualify for time-and-a-half or double-time overtime rates, substitution of bonuses or sign-on or incentive payments for embedded increases in the salary grid, increased differentiation between starting and existing employees, and increased differentiation between categories of workers generally.

Differentiation may benefit some employees, typically higher-level managers and highly skilled workers who receive higher wages and salaries and increased occupational, that is private benefits. In turn, this may undermine the reliance of these groups on state-provided universal benefits and thus their political support for them. Those workers negatively affected by differentiation lose bargaining power as formerly solidaristic groups are detached and, if state benefits are simultaneously constrained, their power position is further weakened.

Quite apart from the outsourcing of some labour functions and costs to suppliers, large enterprises also have an interest in restructuring—increasing the flexibility of employment functions and controlling the costs in their direct jurisdiction. In addition to wages, there are various benefits provided by employers that are a source of income and security for employees. For employers they represent costs and—to the extent they confer security on employees—a potential loss of power or control. Achieving more flexibility with regards to such benefits is good for employers; it reduces their costs and/or increases their control (or both). The range of items that may be covered is long, sometimes involving obligations to the state as well as direct to employees. The list includes pension and benefit plans to which employers contribute, costs of training and supervising workers, adhering to state-mandated employment standards, and the payment of payroll taxes or social security contributions to finance state-provided benefits. Adjusting these costs, transferring them to private or state providers (as with certain types of training), lobbying for reduced state benefits and consequent reduced contributions to them, may all provide business with relief from what it sees as excessive obligations. Other types of flexibility include greater leeway in hiring and firing. This increases employers' ability to obtain an optimum size workforce that can be quickly adjusted in light of market conditions. For workers it means decreased employment protection, all the more effective in achieving labour discipline as the unemployment insurance system was also pared back.The option to substitute certain types of labour for others is also important. Thus part-time or temporary workers can either be hired directly or procured from alternative suppliers, such a temporary agencies (see Vosko 2000), or outsourced through homeworking arrangements managed by a sub-contractor, or obtained as a result of temporary migrant worker programs operated by private providers under the rubric of state programs. Not all flexibility mechanisms involve low-wage workers. Various staff functions involving high wage-earners with specialized skills can be sub-contracted to consultants.

These are only examples of the types of strategies that employers have implemented in the pursuit of flexibility. Whether these have been driven primarily by optional strategies on the part of capital, necessitated by the pressures of globalization, and/or informed by a political strategy of neoliberalism will be of interest throughout the book. However, at this point all we need note is that notwithstanding some improvements with respect to earlier years in some areas, the overall trend within the labour market has been from relative security for workers to relative insecurity. This trend is closely connected to the drive for flexibility, mostly for employers, in labour market conditions. We turn now to a more detailed examination of this situation, beginning with chapters that address the employment policy-making system in Canada, and the overlaps between economic and social policy.

References

Battams, Nathan, Nora Spinks and Roger Sauve. 2014. The Current State of Canadian Family Finances 2013–14 Report Ottawa: Vanier Institute. vanierinstitute.ca/wp-content/uploads/2015/11/FFIN_2014-06-09_Report-2013-2014.pdf.

Bergstrom, O. 2003. "Introduction," in O. Bergstrom and D. Storrie, eds. *Contingent Employment in Europe and the United States.* Northampton: Elgar.

Campbell, Robert. 1987. *Grand Illusions: The Politics of the Keynesian Experience in Canada, 1945–75.* Peterborough: Broadview Press.

Canada. Department of Reconstruction White Paper on Employment and Income. Ottawa: 1945.

Canadian Labour Congress. 2003. Falling Unemployment Insurance Protection for Canada's Unemployed. Ottawa: Canadian Labour Congress.

Chaykowski, R. P. March. "Non-Standard Work and Economic Vunerability." Document no. 3: Vulnerable Workers Series. Ottawa: Canadian Policy Research Networks.

Cranford, Cynthia, Leah Vosko, and Nancy Zuckewich. 2003. "The gender of precarious employment in Canada." *Industrial Relations/Relations Industrielles* 58(3):454–79.

Economic Council of Canada. 1990. *Good Jobs, Bad Jobs: Employment in the Service Sector.* Ottawa: Economic Council of Canada.

Galarneau, Diane, and Eric Fecteau. 2014. "The Ups and Downs of Minimum Wage." Statistics Canada statcan.gc.ca/pub/75-006-x/2014001/article/14035-eng.htm.

Gamble, Andrew. 1988. *The Free Economy and the Strong State.* London: Palgrave Macmillan.

Gonick, Cy. 1987. *The Great Economic Debate: Failed Economics and a Future for Canada.* Toronto: Lorimer.

Gray, David and Colin Busby. 2016. "Unequal Access: Making Sense of EI Eligibility Rules and How to Improve Them." Toronto: C.D. Howe Institute Commentary NO. 450 cdhowe.org/sites/default/files/attachments/research_papers/mixed/Commentary_450.pdf

Harvey, David. 2007. *A Brief History of Neoliberalism*. Oxford: Oxford University Press.

Kalecki, Michael. 1943. "Political Aspects of Full Unemployment." *Political Quarterly 14* (October–December).

Keynes, John Maynard. 1936. *The General Theory of Employment, Interest and Money*. London: Macmillan.

Klein, Seth, and Armine Yalnizyan. 2016. "Better is Always Possible: A Federal Plan to Tackle Poverty and Inequality." Vancouver: Canadian Centre for Policy Alternatives Technical Paper. policyalternatives.ca/sites/default/files/uploads/publications/National%20Office/2016/02/Better_Is_Always%20Possible.pdf

Brenda Leach and Anthony Winson. 2003. *Contingent Work, Disrupted Lives: Labour and Community in the New Rural Economy*. Toronto: University of Toronto Press.

Lewchuk, Wayne et al. 2013. "It's More than Poverty: Precarious Employment and Household Wellbeing." Reports of the Poverty and Employment Precarity in Southern Ontario Research Group. https://pepsouwt.files.wordpress.com/2013/02/its-more-than-poverty-feb-2013.pdf

Lowe, Graham. 2000. "Rethinking Contingent Work." *Workplace Gazette* 2 (3): 126–29.

McBride, Stephen. 1992. *Not Working: State, Unemployment, and Neo-conservatism in Canada*. Toronto: University of Toronto Press.

McBride, Stephen and Heather Whiteside. 2011. *Private Affluence, Public Austerity:Economic Crisis and Democratic Malaise in Canada* Halifax: Fernwood.

Morissette, René, Garnett Picot, and Yuqian Lu. 2015. "The Evolution of Canadian Wages over the Last Three Decades." Statistics Canada Analytical Studies Branch Research Paper Series. www.statcan.gc.ca/pub/11f0019m/11f0019m2013347-eng.pdf.

Quinlan, M., C. Mayhew, and P. Bohle. 2001. "The Global Expansion of Precarious Employment, Work Disorganisation and and Consequences for Occupational Health: A Review of Recent Research", International Journal of Heaqlth Services 31:2, 335–414.

Rinehart, James. 1998. *The Tyranny of Work: Alienation and the Labour Process*, 3rd edition Toronto: Harcourt Brace Jovanovich Canada.

Rittich, K. 2004. *Vulnerability at Work: Legal and Policy Issues in the New Economy*. Ottawa: Law Commission of Canada.

Standing, Guy. 1999. *Global Labour Flexibility: Seeking Distributive Justice*. London: Macmillan.

Tal, Benjamin. 2015. "Employment Quality – Trending Down." CIBC Employment Quality Index (March 5).

Tal, Benjamin. 2016. "On the Quality of Employment in Canada." *CIBC In Focus*. 28 November 28.

Thomas, Jasmin. 2016. "Trends in low wage employment in Canada: incidence, gap and intensity, 1997–2014." Centre for the study of living standards Report 2016–10. csls.ca/reports/csls2016-10.pdf.

Vosko, Leah F. 2000. *Temporary Work: The Gendered Rise of a Precarious Employment Relationship*. Toronto: University of Toronto Press.

Vosko. Leah. 2004."Confronting the Norm: Gender and the International Regulation of Precarious Work." Ottawa: Law Commission of Canada.

Wolfe, David. 1984. "The Rise and Demise of the Keynesian Era in Canada 1930–82," in Michael S. Cross, and Gregory S. Kealey, *Modern Canada, 1930-1980s*. Toronto: McClelland and Stewart.

2

The Institutional Dimension of Employment Policy in Canada

Introduction

Most employment occurs in the private sector; but whether employment is public or private, it takes place within a legal and policy framework established by the state. Later chapters will address the state policy and regulatory initiatives that influence employment. First, however, let us establish the institutional arrangements that govern this important area. I will discuss the role of government in Canada at its various different levels, given that employment policy consists of mixed federal-provincial jurisdiction. In addition, in this era of globalization, we must also take into account certain international influences that apply to employment policy.

Institutions are by and large permanent features of the political landscape. For this reason, government policy should be accommodated to what is possible within them. However, institutional arrangements are not immutable: they can change to accommodate the needs of particular policies. This can sometimes be a formal development. A classic example is the 1940 constitutional amendment that made unemployment insurance a federal responsibility. Arrangements that are less formal can arise within a relatively fixed institutional structure to facilitate desired policies. An example here would be the establishment of labour force development boards in the 1980s and early 1990s that were attempts to incorporate key social actors—particularly business and labour—into the training policy apparatus. The objective was to obtain buy-in and expertise of these important labour market players in order to establish training programs that would better serve the needs of the economy than those devised by government alone.

My analysis here takes key institutions into account, both their relative permanence and the possibility that they may change. As such, my argument is informed by a theoretical perspective known as "social structure of accumulation" theory. This theory holds that capitalist economies experience "long waves" of relative stability and prosperity followed by periods of crisis and renewal and change. During the upside of the cycle, a set of institutional arrangements are in place. These arrangements simultaneously sustain accumulation and at the same time provide a degree of social stability and cohesion. Periodically, however, crises arise that may call into question the economic system itself and/or the institutional arrangements that sustained it in times of prosperity. This may be because structural developments within the economy produce a crisis where capital accumulation, taken to be the *sine qua non* of the system, becomes increasingly problematic. Or, perhaps, it may be framed as a situation where a given institutional structure and its associated policies consist of an obstacle standing in the path of continuous accumulation and growth. Either way, in a crisis and as part of any recovery process, institutions themselves can be subject to change in order to better accommodate the needs of the system (O'Hara 2006; Kotz 1994; McDonough 1999; Gordon et al 1994).

So it seems logical to expect a close connection between institutions and employment policies at any given time. (In my usage here, institutions are both formal structures and less formal organizations or arrangements within government, or between government and social actors.) This poses the question of whether the combination of policies and institutions in Canada today is functional or dysfunctional, or whether the less-than-ideal labour market conditions briefly outlined in Chapter 1 are the result of other factors. This chapter outlines the federal-provincial, societal, and international dimensions of Canada's institutions that create employment policies and that will be used in later chapters.

In the wake of globalization, there are international influences; however, jurisdiction over most aspects of employment policy resides firmly at the nation-state level. In the case of a federal country like Canada, of course, that leaves open the issue of which level of government, federal or provincial, wields jurisdiction over what policy areas. This issue is of perennial concern in Canadian policy studies. Canada is a highly decentralized federation and the lines of authority are seldom completely clear. Without attributing primary causality to the complexities of Canadian institutions they clearly play some role in inhibiting possible responses to employment issues.

Linking Institutions, Ideas, and Policies

There is a wide variety of public policies that can influence employment outcomes. The choice of actual policy depends partly on the paradigm informing public policy in general, and on the accumulation needs of the system as seen by key actors. Choosing a policy will be implemented in an institutional context that may facilitate or, alternatively, obstruct its achievement. If the latter, this may give rise to pressures for institutional change or, alternatively, be presented as a reason certain policy options are off the table.

The classical liberal and neoliberal paradigms mostly rely on market mechanisms. They require strong but limited political institutions to guarantee the primacy and smooth operation of market relations. Fiscal and monetary policy are designed to allow market forces to operate freely; they are also directed to price stability rather than employment-related goals. This does not imply a completely "laissez-faire" policy stance (that is, leaving everything to the market). On the contrary, the settings of fiscal and monetary policy—depending on the economic circumstances and the preferences of policy-makers—may serve to stimulate or restrain the level of economic activity. In addition, a level of state intervention may be necessary to structure markets as a means of liberating them from what may be seen as wrong-headed or excessive regulation. For the purposes of this book, examples can be found in measures to achieve greater labour market flexibility by eliminating or reducing regulations designed to protect employees in various ways. In essence, flexibility involves reducing the rights of employees and corresponding obligations on employers; it also involves reducing the supports and benefits to those temporarily outside the labour market. These measures are intended to reduce the costs to employers of hiring workers, and thus to serve as an incentive to job creation by employers. They also induce workers to be more flexible in what kinds of work and conditions they will accept by undermining the ability to remain outside the labour force.

In the Keynesian approach, the big levers of fiscal and monetary policy could be adjusted to keep aggregate demand at full-employment levels. But with significant pockets of seasonal work—and this is particularly true in a regionally diverse country like Canada—these policies needed supplementation by others, such as training, winter-works projects, regional development, and social welfare. Even during the

Keynesian era, the conviction grew that not all unemployment could be explained in terms of demand deficiency. The consequence of this was increased reliance on supplementary measures. Later, in what turned out to be the transition from Keynesianism to neoliberalism, efforts were made to integrate Keynesian demand-side policies with a supply-side orientation in training. The attempt to use neo-corporatist tripartite institutions to achieve this failed (McBride 1992, 58–64).

Fiscal and monetary policy clearly condition the economy. Moreover, depending on the goals, the specific instruments and setting of these policies may provide a robust platform for employment. This platform can be either a direct result of the policies (Keynesian model) or the indirect consequence of establishing a conducive context for market forces to flourish and thus provide employment (neoliberal model). Trade and investment policy may be part of an active industrial policy featuring significant state intervention (federal and/or provincial) to create strong industrial sectors. Alternatively, as in the neoliberal era, trade and investment policy may be predicated on striking down barriers to international and inter-provincial trade in line with the theory of comparative advantage. In this case, the international agreements act as constraints on nation-states' ability to devise industrial policies. Comparative advantage theory, which underpins free trade agreements, holds that free trade is welfare enhancing and that jurisdictions should focus on those economic activities in which they are most efficient. Sources of comparative advantage, sometimes reconceptualized as competitive advantage, could include natural endowments such as natural resources, or achieved advantages such as a highy qualified workforce attractive to investors. Canada's historical development has been attributed to its depency on a succession of "staple" products and its inability to fully break from this development model (Drache 1991), a problem some have argued has been exacerbated by modern free trade agreements (Stanford 2008).

Federal–Provincial Relations, Institutions and Areas of Employment Policy

Macroeconomic Context

Chapter 3 will look in more detail at how employment policy stands at the nexus of economic and social policy. Institutionally, a glance at the list of relevant policies reveals that, in most cases, either one or the other level of jurisdiction is predominant. Monetary policy—derived from the federal power over currency and banking—is predominantly federal (though each province controls securities regulation). Fiscal policy is mixed, in that both federal and provincial governments have the right to tax and spend. However, the federal jurisdiction over taxes is larger (see Malcolmson et al 2016, 66–69), giving rise to concepts and practices like "federal spending power" in the post-war period. Then, because of its strong fiscal position, the federal government was able to forge federal–provincial "shared cost programs" in areas of provincial responsibility, and to attach federal conditions to how the money would be spent. Trade policy is federal; but as a result of judicial decision, in areas where trade policy affects provincial jurisdiction (as latter-day trade agreements frequently do), it involves a degree of federal-provincial coordination (Kukucha 2008). Investment policy is mixed. Provinces certainly have jurisdiction in that area, derived from the "property and civil rights" provisions of the constitution. But the federal government is also active.

Labour Market Policies

In the areas of labour, social, education, and training, Rodney Haddow and Thomas Klassen (2006, 67–88) have provided a useful typology for delineating federal-provincial interaction. The typology consists of areas where the federal government has the sole jurisdiction (for example, unemployment insurance), or is paramount (immigration); areas where the provinces have sole authority or are paramount (education and, by extension, training; workers' compensation; social assistance); areas of parallel jurisdiction based on what category of employees are subject to the legislation or regulation (occupational health and safety, industrial relations, employment standards); and areas where there are overlaps (active labour market measures under the employment insurance system).

This helps clarify a very complex institutional situation. However, this summary is not watertight; curious exceptions exist. Nevertheless, even in this simplified version it is clear that labour market policies are jurisdictionally intertwined. Even where one or the other level of government can act with relative autonomy, the effects of those actions will be felt elsewhere. For example, if the federal government alters the generosity of the employment insurance system, there will be a resulting impact on provincial social assistance programs. Changes in employment standards for provincially regulated workers (85 to 90 percent of the total Canadian workforce) have an impact on federally regulated workers living in the same communities. If entanglement and interconnectedness are features of the broad employment policy domain, coordination and cooperation offer themselves as possible solutions. However, these have been difficult to achieve in practice.

Industrial Relations

Industrial relations policies help shape the relationship between capital and labour (at least that portion of labour that is organized into trade unions). Milestones in industrial relations legislation in Canada include the federal 1872 Trade Unions Act: here, unions were released from the threat of prosecution for criminal conspiracy. Subsequent legislation in 1875–76 legalised peaceful picketing. However, this legislation did little to compel the recognition of unions by employers. As such, the existing power asymmetries of the labour market that favoured capital persisted (Woods 1973, 39–42). There were attempts in the early part of the twentieth century to establish a voluntary conciliation system, with some elements of compulsion. These were mostly federal initiatives that culminated in the Industrial Disputes Investigation Act (IDIA), 1907. This Act provided that either party to a dispute could request an investigation by a conciliation board. Its findings were not binding on the parties, although there was provision for publication of the board's findings, presumably to allow for public opinion to influence the dispute (Woods 1973, 56–64).

In 1925, a judicial decision allocated the bulk of the industrial relations jurisdiction to the provinces. However, in what became a pattern in this policy sphere, the provinces emulated the federal approach, in this case by passing legislation enabling the Industrial Disputes Investigation Act to apply to them. As a result, between 1907 and 1944, the IDIA approach constituted the Canadian policy toward industrial disputes.

A wartime federal order-in-council, P.C. 1003, established a new legislative environment for post-war industrial relations. This legislation was the product of working-class pressure under wartime conditions of full-employment. However, the legislation did not represent an unqualified victory for labour. The new industrial relations system was bureaucratic, containing elaborate certification procedures, legally enforceable contracts, no-strike provisions for the duration of contracts, and liability of trade unions and their members if illegal strikes took place. On the other hand, it did guarantee the right to organize and to bargain collectively. It also forced employers to recognize unions once certain conditions were met; it defined unfair labour practices; and it provided remedies under the law for violations. As with the IDIA, this federal initiative established the pattern across Canada; most provinces passed very similar industrial relations legislation (McBride 1987). Versions of the legislation were extended to public-sector workers, though the timing and provisions varied more than the initial framework that applied to private sector workers. The result of provinces' modelling of their own systems on the federal system, was the emergence of something like a national industrial relations system, in spite of provincial predominance in the policy area.

PC1003 has often been seen as a Canadian version of the U.S. Wagner Act, and therefore of indirect international influence. The legislation certainly did incorporate aspects of the Wagner Act's approach to labour-capital relationships (Woods 1973, 64–70, 86–92). But Canada's post-war legislation also built on the IDIA tradition by including provisions for compulsory conciliation and mediation before strikes could occur, banning strikes for the duration of collective agreements, and placing a number of other restrictions on the way unions could operate.

The implementation and enforcement of the legislation is typically in the hands of labour relations boards. These are arms-length (from government) administrative tribunals that oversee decisions about the certification and decertification of unions, hear complaints about unfair labour practices, and provide mediation and conciliation services during negotiations (Haddow and Klassen 2006, 80).

Employment Standards, Health and Safety, Workers Compensation, Equity[9]

In these areas, most Canadian workers are covered by provincial jurisdiction. Federal coverage extends to the federal public service, as well as workers in banking, broadcasting, inter-provincial transportation,

9 This section is based on the summary in Haddow and Klassen (2006, 67–78).

shipping, and other industries that are subject to federal legislation.

Employment standards establish a floor, or minimum, beneath which employers may not go. These standards cover issues like minimum wages, hours of work, vacations and statutory holidays, and termination of employment. They are of greatest interest to non-unionized workers (this is because unionized workers' collective agreements typically exceed those minimum standards). There are some exclusions from coverage and the details of the standards vary considerably between provinces. The federal government enacts its own employment standards, but defers to the provinces on minimum wages; here, federal workers are subject to the minimum wage in the province of their work. Issues of pay and employment equity follow the same jurisdictional lines, as does regulation of occupational health and safety. In the case of health and safety there are often specific provisions for certain industries, as well as variation among provinces. Worker's compensation is unusual: it is essentially an insurance program operated by tripartite public boards or agencies, but funded by employers whom, in return, are protected from private lawsuits in the case of industrial accidents. This is because the workers are covered by, and receive compensation from the workers' compensation system. The boards administering the system operate at arm's length from government and set the premiums, benefit levels, and so on. About 80 percent of all workers are covered, but the categories of workers covered vary by province. The federal level of government chose not to set up its own workers' compensation system, so federally regulated employees fall under the jurisdiction of the province in which they work.

Unemployment Insurance

In 1940, as a result of a constitutional amendment, unemployment insurance (UI) became an exclusive responsibility of the federal government. The long delay in establishing an unemployment insurance system, compared to many other countries, has been variously attributed to jurisdictional disputes between federal and provincial governments on the one hand, and to the ideological hegemony of business on the other. In Leslie Pal's view (1988, 151–52), the constitutional problem was a genuine obstacle. For James Struthers (1983, 209–10) the jurisdictional issue served as a useful excuse for inaction. More important was the dominance of an ideology which placed exclusive emphasis on the needs of a capitalist labour market (Struthers 1983, 6–9). The impact of two world wars and fears of social disturbances following the second world war served to push aside the lingering dominance of this ideology as early as 1940 (Struthers 1983, 213; see also Campeau 2005 Chapter 3).

The fact that UI became an exclusively federal matter meant there were few institutional complications as long as it remained focused on income support for the unemployed. Of course, changes in eligibility could affect the provincial social welfare rolls, but for much of its history the UI system was institutionally unproblematic. This began to change with the turn to neoliberalism. The federal government became interested in using the fund for active measures (originally termed "developmental uses"). By 1989 Canada's new Labour Force Development Strategy was aimed at increasing use of UI funds for vocational training. For this reason, intrusions into provincial jurisdiction also increased, at least until the devolution of training to the provinces through LMDAs from 1996 onwards.

Training and Active Labour Market Policy

Training represents one of those areas where institutions have adapted to meet perceived needs as these needs changed over time. Prior to the 1960s, training received little attention from the federal or provincial governments. Insofar as training policy could be said to exist, it consisted of limited support for apprenticeships and active encouragement of the importation of already-trained workers through immigration (Doern and Phidd 1983, 504).

Training policy, for the most part originally confined to apprenticeships, was a minor sub-set of the education portfolio. This clearly fell under provincial jurisdiction. Later, as the importance of training increased and came to be seen as an adjunct of Keynesian economic policy, the federal government became more involved. This involvement consisted largely of funding provincial training institutions, but there were also contributions made for those undergoing training. Until the mid-1960s the federal role had consisted of minor conditional grant programs. The most significant of these were the Vocational Training Coordination Act (1942), and its successors, the Technical and Vocational Training Act of 1960 (Paquet 1976) and the Adult Occupational Training Act (1967). These were based on federal financial support for teaching institutions and contributions towards the costs of training the unemployed. Given the federal government's overall responsibility for macroeconomic policy and its specific constitutional responsibility for unemployment insurance, the latter was an obvious area for federal activity. The operational side of federal support consisted of funding for apprenticeships and other training programs, including some programs that were aimed at students, with others aimed at the already employed. Specific programs targeted academic upgrading (sometimes known as basic training for skill development), language training for immigrants, specialized skill training, and apprenticeships.

Under federal-provincial agreements, the provinces retained control over the location, structure, and administration of training facilities. Over time, provinces came to depend on federal training purchases for the upkeep of their community college institutions. However, the federal government became increasingly dissatisfied with these arrangements, given the lack of federal visibility as well as disparities in provincial participation in the programs (Dupre et al 1974, 37–46). Notwithstanding federal dissatisfaction, however, the programs did stimulate the creation of public training facilities, provided training to considerable numbers of Canadians, and marked an important stage in the extension of labour market policy.

Gradually the bigger and better resourced provinces identified gaps in, or had other priorities not well served by, these federal programs. As such, they began to establish their own parallel programs. Demands grew for decentralization of labour market policy. This was particularly true of Quebec, which saw the area as a crucial element in its (nationalist) economic development strategy. Federal interest in partially privatizing training exacerbated tensions with provinces that perceived a threat to the viability of their public training institutions. A new generation of federal-provincial training agreements in the 1980s attempted to address these issues, but there was major provincial dissatisfaction (McBride 1992, 152–54; Klassen 2000). In the aftermath of the 1995 Quebec referendum on sovereignty—but also motivated by the federal government's neoliberal deficit reduction priorities—the federal government moved to withdraw from most training and other active labour market measures. This was associated with restructuring the unemployment insurance system and using its funds to promote more active adaptation on the part of the unemployed. The traditional income support that unemployment insurance represented had increasingly come to be seen unfavourably as "passive."

Decentralization was accomplished by non-constitutional means. A period of constitutional fatigue followed the referendum, as well as previous decades of constitutional negotiations covering the Constitution Act of 1982. This was followed later by failed efforts at constitutional reform in the Meech Lake Accord and Charlottetown Agreement and referendum. The favoured instruments were federal-provincial Labour Market Development Agreements (LMDAs). Here, the federal government offered to transfer funds to deliver active measures (such as training, wage subsidies, self-employment assistance) to unemployed persons who qualified for employment insurance payments. Federal staff could also be transferred to the provinces. Federal authorities retained decision-making over funding levels and eligibility criteria. Two major types of LMDA emerged. Under one type (typically involving smaller provinces) there were some key features: systems of joint management were established; staff were not transferred; and program delivery typically remained with federal officials or contractors. Agreements with larger provinces tended to reflect their desire for greater control over the policy area and included both staff transfers and program delivery.

Reviewing the impact of the decentralization, Donna Wood and Thomas Klassen (2011, 10) noted that, including LMDAs, some 49 bilateral agreements governed active labour market policy. Furthermore, while there are differences between them, there is at the same time relative symmetry (4). This is clearly not a streamlined system, though the intensity of federal-provincial conflicts were much reduced by decentralization. Nonetheless, institutional problems remain: Wood and Klassen (2011, 12) maintain that there is a need to reduce executive (especially federal) dominance and provide a place for societal actors to provide input. There is also a need to increase transparency, research and opportunities for mutual learning, as well as to reduce fragmentation and the remaining program incoherence. Elsewhere, Wood (2015) examined mechanisms for intergovernmental coordination in the area, consisting of regular meetings between Ministers of Labour and Administrators of Labour Legislation (CALL, which deals with labour relations and health and safety), the Forum of Labour Market Ministers (FLMM; this body focuses on workforce development, employment and mobility of labour), and Ministers of Social Services (MSS; a body that addresses social assistance, poverty, disability, and welfare). Wood concluded that the outputs of CALL are "slim"; moreover, there is a "lack of engagement by ministers and deputy ministers plus weak and rotating secretariats in the FLMM and MSS policy domains" which result in many policy issues being "ignored or avoided" (Wood 2012, 141).

Social Assistance

Social assistance resides at the provincial level, although there have been significant cost-sharing agreements. As part of its Keynesian turn, the federal government expanded its financial support for social assistance under the Canada Assistance Plan, in effect from 1966–96. This was paralleled by other social policy transfers in health and education. In the mid-1990s, these arrangements underwent neoliberal restructuring as the federal government's policy priority changed: deficit control displaced building national social security standards. The previously separate transfers were rolled into a single block-funding scheme (the Canada Health and Social Transfer, CHST, subsequently restructured in 2004 to create two new transfers: the Canada Health Transfer and the Canada Social Transfer, or CST). The federal conditions that had accompanied the CAP included the following: provinces should provide assistance to every person in need and they should take into account people's needs in setting assistance rates; provide an appeal mechanism to enable challenges to eligibility decisions; they should not discriminate on the basis of province of origin; and they should not require work as a condition for receiving assistance (Anderson 2004). With the exception of a prohibition on residency requirements, these conditions were eliminated. This increased the amount of provincial variation in program design and delivery (Boychuk 1998; Haddow and Klassen 2006, 86); there is now a patchwork of programs reflecting provincial priorities and resources.

Immigration

In Canada's federal system, immigration is an institutionally complex policy area with shared or "concurrent" jurisdiction between various levels of government. Depending on the historical period, this has involved the interaction of numerous institutions—a situation that makes a coordinated approach difficult to achieve. For this reason, the attribution of goals or priorities necessarily involves the simplification of what can be a highly contested process. In terms of federal-provincial relations, "immigration falls under the leadership of the federal government but responsibility is shared with the provinces and territories" (Auditor General 2009, 6). Broadly speaking, the "federal government takes charge of the selection process while provincial governments are responsible for the provision of settlement services" (Hiebert 2006, 45). Today, federal institutions involved in various aspects of the immigration system include Citizenship and Immigration Canada (CIC), Employment and Social Development Canada, and the Canada Border Services Agency. At the provincial level institutional actors include "provincial regulatory bodies [for regulated professions], postsecondary educational institutions and credential assessment services ... In addition, community-based service organizations—and, of course, employers—are key players" (Alboim and McIsaac 2007, 3). Adding to the institutional mixture, since the Charter of Rights and Freedoms came into effect, the courts are also involved with the scrutiny of immigration rules and decisions (Nijboer 2010).

Since immigration is one area of shared jurisdiction, there are a variety of bilateral agreements in place outlining the responsibilities of the provinces and federal authorities respectively. Under the Canada-Quebec Accord Relating to Immigration and Temporary Admission of Aliens, Quebec has full responsibility both for the selection of immigrants (except for some in the Family Class and in-Canada refugee categories) as well as for providing settlement services. Both of these activities are supported by a federal grant. Agreements with the other provinces and territories leave the federal government in charge of most immigration matters, but there are arrangements in place with all provinces and territories. This system provides for a Provincial Nominee Program (PNP) that permits the provinces and territories to nominate immigrants for permanent residence who will fit local labour market needs. Under PNPs, the province—using a points-based system—is effectively the nominator. In other cases, it will be employers who, having demonstrated that they cannot fill their labour needs from domestic sources, can nominate workers to fill vacancies.

The public opinion context in which these institutions currently operate is rather more favourable to immigration and immigrants than is the case in many foreign jurisdictions (Challinor 2011, 13). However, immigration policy can serve a number of goals. These include humanitarian aims, foreign policy, social and economic goals. No surprise that there is considerable debate about priorities as well as the details of policy.

That said, for much of the country's history, federal authorities predominated and "economic goals formed a central orientation of immigration policy" (Green and Green 1999, 426). However, it is not self-evident which economic goals were prevalent at any given time. A minimal but useful distinction is that immigration policy can be divided into long-term and short-term goals. Here it can be argued that the former, are designed at "achieving demographic benefits (those relating to size and age composition of the inflow), benefits from general immigrant characteristics such as flexibility, and investment and trade flow benefits"; short-term goals are more narrowly focused on "achieving benefits from meeting immediate shortages in the labour market" (Green and Green 1999, 427). Institutional arrangements have evolved in this context.

The State and Social Actors

A second feature of the institutional context pertains to the relationship between social actors and the state. Considered from a comparative perspective, these relationships are structured in different ways ranging from the informal and ad hoc, to the highly structured and institutionalized.

There have been periods in which Canadian governments have paid little attention to social actors on employment issues, except perhaps to receive lobbying delegations from various interest groups. This arm's length system of expression of group interests is often called pluralism. The main idea here is that while many groups compete for governments' attention, no one group is privileged; as such, government makes its decisions taking into account various interests, either autonomously or on the basis of what it perceives as the common denominator among them. The reality may be different, as many critics have argued,[10] but the form is one in which no particular interest is formally integrated into the policy process.

In other periods, though, there have been efforts to closely integrate and institutionalize these relationships to better obtain their advice and cooperation. For the most part, these initiatives have stopped short of sharing government's decision-making authority with private actors. In some other countries, notably in parts of western Europe

10 The classic statement on this is that of Schattschneider (1960, 35) who wrote that, "The flaw in the pluralist heaven is that the heavenly chorus sings with a strong upper class accent."

and Scandinavia, institutionalization of decision-making between business, labour, and the state has been normal and generally goes under the name of corporatism or neo-corporatism.[11] Modern corporatism typically refers to tripartite cooperation between the state, labour, and business, and has been deployed in a number of contexts—sometimes to accomplish national economic management, sometimes to achieve sectoral objectives such as a better training system (Schmitter and Lehmbruch 1979; Wiarda 1997).

In liberal countries, neo-corporatism originated as a means of sustaining full-employment while restraining inflation through voluntary wage controls. The main Canadian expressions were the federal Anti-Inflation Program in the mid-1970s and Ontario's Social Contract initiative in the early 1990s (see Panitch 1980; McBride 1983, 1996). Earlier expressions of the incorporation of key labour market interests into institutions can be found in the inclusion of business and labour representatives on the commissions administering the unemployment insurance system. Despite the inclusion of social actors, the powers of the commissions have been described as "marginal" and "limited," thus offsetting the effects of integrating them (Haddow 2000, 37). Similar points might be made about the tripartite membership of Workers Compensation Boards. There are traces too of the corporatist approach in the design of Canada's industrial relations system, possibly because of the influence of long-time Prime Minister Mackenzie King who—rhetorically at least—was an advocate of the corporatist approach (Whitaker 1977; see also McBride 1995).

In the late 1980s, neo-corporatist institutions were developed as a means of enlisting the support of key economic agents in the construction of a competition state; that is, a state that would be competitive in the new global economy. Increasingly, training, retraining, and labour adjustment were identified as the policy areas crucial to increased competitiveness as well as areas in which a social partnership approach would be helpful. In the end, most foundered in the face of business indifference or opposition to actual power-sharing (McElligott 2001, 125–26).

In Ontario, the Premier's Council (1990) drove what was termed the "progressive competitiveness" approach (Albo 1994). This also had indigenous roots in Québec and British Columbia. Elsewhere it was

11 The prefix "neo-" or sometimes "societal" has been used to distinguish these institutions from the kind of corporatist state, based on fascist ideology and coercive practices, found in Germany, Italy and other parts of Europe in the 1930s.

the product of federal pressure, if present at all (Haddow and Sharpe 1997, 6–9). Federally it was expressed in the Labour Force Development Strategy until around 1995 when a strategy of labour market deregulation replaced it. Similarly, after the defeat of the Rae New Democratic Party (NDP) government in 1995, the Ontario Training and Adjustment Board (OTAB) was abolished. By this time, equivalent boards in most other provinces were defunct. In Québec, the inclusion of stakeholders in a variety of boards and commissions came to constitute the "Quebec model." Even where the Commission of Labour Market Partners continued, representing employers, labour, academia, and community organizations, there is the view that the Quebec model is now very fragile in the face of neoliberalism (Graefe 2012).

However, for several years under the Labour Force Development Strategy, funding for developmental uses of the unemployment insurance fund was administered on the advice of a Canadian Labour Force Development Board (CLFDB). This Board was dominated by business and labour representatives (Mahon 1990). The CLFDB was made up of 22 voting members; of these, eight were from and chosen by business, eight were from and chosen by labour, two from the education and training community, and one from each of four equity groups. Though technically advisory, the federal government initially indicated that in spending developmental UI funds, it would treat consensus advice from the CLFDB as virtually binding. By 1995 this privilege had been revoked by the government and the Board itself was abolished in 1999. Beyond developing consensus between the labour market partners, reinforced by the accountability of board members to their constituencies through "reference groups," the CLFDB was intended to act as an advocate for training. It was also involved in establishing provincial and local equivalents in a number of provinces. In some of the larger provinces—notably Quebec, Ontario, and British Columbia—parallel developments resulted in the creation of provincial boards designed to provide advice or to deliver labour market programs.

Another development in labour-business-government cooperation, promoted by the federal government, was sectoral councils that sought to build on common interests, particularly regarding training and adjustment issues, that were specific to a particular industrial sector (Gunderson and Sharpe 1998). Examples included the Canadian Steel and Employment Congress at the national level. Though some of these institutions linger, most have been abandoned.

International Influences

Tracing policy connections is made more complicated by the increased interdependence of states and economies in the wake of globalization. Some policies that contribute to employment outcomes, such as monetary, trade and investment, have become partially internationalized. Similarly, international organizations often have strong views on what kind of labour market policies constitute "best practices" and should be pursued by individual states. Sometimes these are imposed as part of international agreements. This typically happens when a state gets into economic difficulties and requests assistance from bodies such as the IMF, World Bank, or, as in the case of EU countries since the 2008 financial crisis, from the Troika (composed of the IMF, the European Commission, and the European Central Bank). As part of what are sometimes called structural adjustment programs (Greer 2014), or memorandums of understanding between debtors and lenders (Ayhan and McBride 2015), structural labour market reforms are imposed, with a view to making employment relations more flexible.

Alternatively, moral suasion or pressure is exercised, as with the Organisation for Economic Cooperation and Development's (OECD) *Jobs Study* and subsequent *Jobs Strategy*. The OECD applied strong pressure to its members and, by implication, other countries as well, by proselytizing a liberal flexibility model of labour markets, often in the face of empirical evidence suggesting its benefits were highly exaggerated (McBride and Williams 2001; McBride, McNutt and Williams 2008). One aspect of the institutional context of Canadian employment policy is, therefore, international.

Canada has not been on the receiving end of any structural adjustment programs, so international policy influences are less direct and subject to voluntary compliance. In terms of exerting influence on Canadian employment policy, probably the most important international body has been the OECD. Andrew Jackson (2008) has provided an excellent account of how domestic institutions—centred on the Department of Finance—and the OECD interact. The interactions are almost continuous at the level of officials who participate in a wide variety of meetings with their peers in other OECD member states, and with OECD officials, in pursuit of "best practices" in numerous policy fields. These activities have been described as "meditative," in the sense of being devoted to knowledge creation, backed by an extensive OECD research capacity. The emphasis is on policy learning, discovering "what works" and what may be applied in the home country. These are supplemented by "surveillance" or "inquisitorial" activities (see Mahon and McBride 2008, 3–22).

An example of the latter is the preparation of regular "country studies" or *Economic Surveys* of individual nation-states in which the policy stance is described and evaluated. The process is one in which the OECD prepares a draft document and then sends a team to visit the country. During its visit, the team questions government officials and holds a series of additional meetings with key interest groups before preparing a final draft report. This report is discussed with the national government and subsequently published. Depending on its contents, the report may provide ammunition to either the national government or its critics.

In the case of Canada, Andrew Jackson has noted that the Department of Finance is the key interlocutor. Even though many of the Economic Surveys focused heavily on employment issues, the responsible government department—Human Resources and Development Canada at the time Jackson was writing—tended to be excluded or its influence marginalised (Jackson 2008, 175–76). This is an indication that any "best practices" identified were likely to be imbued by the neoliberal ideology embodied in the Department of Finance and its OECD equivalent, the Economics Department of that organization, rather than being evidence-based. It is hard to assess the actual independent influence the OECD wields, but, according to Jackson (2008, 183), it seems to have varied by sub-area, being most pronounced in the area of cuts to the unemployment insurance system, and less influential in other areas where Canadian policy may have converged with OECD recommendations (but where the roots of that convergence were largely domestic).

Conclusions

Canada is a highly decentralized federation (McIntosh 2000) and federal-provincial cooperation varies by area (Wood 2015). The same, of course, is true of many policy domains in Canada. In general, however—at least in the economic and labour market policy areas—intergovernmental relations have been described as "uncoordinated and conflictual" (Haddow 2012, 223).

One question about this is whether the condition of the Canadian labour market, sketched in the previous chapter, can be attributed to institutional failure or dysfunction. Without excessively anticipating the analysis to be presented in the rest of the book, two points can reasonably be made at this stage.

First, adopting or implementing a coherent plan to deal with employment is made more complicated by the maze of overlapping and sometimes contradictory structures. From an efficiency, equity, or functional perspective it is unlikely that anyone would consciously adopt the architecture that has emerged in Canada in this policy area. Second, however, these structures do not seem to have prevented the adoption of a broad paradigmatic approached to employment. Thus, the post-World War II promotion of Keynesian full employment policies proved possible, even if it was much more complicated than in a unitary political system. Nor was the shift to a neoliberal, flexible, employment orientation significantly obstructed by these institutions. Institutions may have been a contributory factor to the current labour market and employment situation, and their impact on the details of policy certainly needs to be taken into account but, as will be argued in the remainder of this book, interests, economic structures, and ideas loom larger in understanding the trends and impacts.

References

Albo, Greg. 1994. "'Competitive Austerity' and the Impasse of Capitalist Employment Policy," in Ralph Miliband and Leo Panitch, eds., *Socialist Register 1994: Between Globalism and Nationalism*. London: Merlin Press.

Alboim, Naomi, and McIsaac, Elizabeth. 2007. "Making the Connections: Ottawa's Role in Immigrant Employment." *Institute for Research on Public Policy Choices*, 13(3).

Anderson, John. 2004. "Paul Martin and the Liberal Social Policy Record," in Todd Scarth, ed., *Hell and High Water: An Assessment of Paul Martin's Record and Implications for the Future*. Ottawa: Canadian Centre for Policy Alternatives.

Ayhan, Berkay, and Stephen McBride. 2015. "Global Crisis and Social Policy in Semi-Peripheral Europe: Comparing Ireland, Portugal and Greece," in Stephen McBride, Rianne Mahon, and Gerard W. Boychuk, eds., *After '08: Social Policy and the Global Financial Crisis*. Vancouver: UBC Press.

Boychuk, Gerard W. 1998. *Patchworks of Purpose*. Montreal: McGill-Queens University Press.

Campeau, Georges. 2005. *From UI to EI: Waging War on the Welfare State*. Vancouver: UBC Press.

Challinor, Ashley E. 2011. "Canada's Immigration Policy: A Focus on Human Capital." *Migration Policy Institute*. Available online.

Doern, G. Bruce, and Richard Phidd. 1983. *Canadian Public Policy*. Toronto: Methuen.

Drache, Daniel. 1991. "Harold Innis and Canadian Capitalist Development," in Gordon Laxer, ed., *Perspectives on Canadian Economic Development*. Toronto: Oxford University Press.

Drache, Daniel, ed. 1992. *Getting on Track: Social Democratic Strategies for Ontario*. Montreal: McGill-Queen's University Press.

Dupré, Stefan, David M. Cameron, Graeme H. McKechnie, and Theodore B. Rotenberg. 1973. *Federalism and Policy Development: The Case of Adult Occupational Training in Ontario*. Toronto: University of Toronto Press.

Gordon, David M., Richard Edwards, and Michael Reich. 1994. "Long Swings and Stages of Capitalism," in David M. Kotz, Terrence McDonough, and Michael Reich, eds., *Social Structures of Accumulation*. Cambridge: Cambridge University Press.

Graefe, Peter. 2012. "Whither the Quebec Model? Boom, Bust and Quebec Labour," in John Peters, ed., *Boom, Bust and Crisis: Labour, Corporate Power and Politics in Canada*. Halifax: Fernwood.

Green, Alan G., and Green, David A. 1999. "The Economic Goals of Canada's Immigration Policy: Past and Present," *Canadian Public Policy/Analyse de Politiques* 25(4): 425–51.

Greer, Scott. 2014. "Structural Adjustment Comes to Europe: Lessons for the Eurozone from the Conditionality Debates." *Global Social Policy* 14(1): 51–71.

Gunderson, Morley, and Andrew Sharpe, eds. 1998. *Forging Business-Labour Partnerships: The Emergence of Sector Councils in Canada*. Toronto: University of Toronto Press.

Haddow, R. 2000. "The Political and Institutional Landscape of Canadian Labour Market Policy-Making," in Tom McIntosh, ed., *Federalism, Democracy and Labour Market Policy in Canada*. Montreal: McGill-Queen's UP.

Haddow, Rodney, and Andrew Sharpe. 1997. "Canada's Experiment with Labour Force Development Boards: An Introduction," in Rodney Haddow and Andrew Sharpe, eds. *Social Partnerships for Training*. Montreal: McGill-Queen's University Press.

Haddow, Rodney. 2012. "Federalism and Economic Adjustment: Skills and Economic Development in the Face of Globalization and Crisis," in Herman Bakvis and Grace Skogstad, eds., *Canadian Federalism*, 3rd edn. Toronto: Oxford University Press.

Haddow, Rodney, and Thomas Klassen. 2006. *Partisanship, Globalization, and Canadian Labour Market Policy: Four Provinces in Comparative Perspective*. Toronto: University of Toronto Press.

Hiebert, Daniel. 2006. "Winning, Losing, and Still Playing the Game: The Political Economy of Immigration in Canada." *Journal of Economic and Social Geography* 97(1): 38–48.

Jackson, Andrew. 2008. "'Crafting the Conventional Wisdom': The OECD and the Canadian Policy Process," in Rianne Mahon and Stephen McBride, eds., *The OECD and Transnational Governance*. Vancouver: UBC Press.

Klassen, Thomas R. 2000. "The Federal-Provincial Labour Market Development Agreements: Brave New Model of Collaboration?," in Tom McIntosh, ed., *Federalism, Democracy and Labour Market Policy in Canada*. Montreal: McGill-Queens University Press.

Kotz, David M. 1994. "Interpreting the Social Structure of Accumulation," in David M. Kotz, Terrence McDonough, and Michael Reich, eds., *Social Structure of Accumulation*. Cambridge: Cambridge University Press.

Kukucha, Christopher. 2008. *The Provinces and Canadian Foreign Trade Policy*. Vancouver: UBC Press

Mahon, Rianne. 1990. "Adjusting to Win? The New Tory Training Initiative," in Katherine A. Graham, ed., *How Ottawa Spends*. Ottawa: Carleton UP.

Mahon, Rianne, and Stephen McBride. 2008. "Introduction," in Rianne Mahon and Stephen McBride, eds., *The OECD and Transnational Governance*. Vancouver: UBC Press.

Malcolmson, Patrick, Richard Myers, Gerald Baier, and Thomas M.J. Bateman. 2016. *The Canadian Regime*, 6th edn. Toronto: University of Toronto Press.

McBride, Stephen. 1987. "Hard Times and the 'Rules of the Game': A Study of the Legislative Environment of Labour-Capital Conflict," in Robert Argue, Charlene Gannage, and D.W. Livingstone, eds., *Working People and Hard Times: Canadian Perspectives*. Toronto: Garamond Press.

McBride, Stephen, and Russell A. Williams. 2001. "Globalization, the Restructuring of Labour Markets and Policy Convergence," *Global Social Policy* 1(3): 281–309.

McBride, Stephen, K. McNutt, and R. Williams. 2015. "Policy Learning? The OECD and Its Jobs Study," in R. Mahon and S. McBride, eds., *The OECD and Transnational Governance*. Vancouver UBC Press.

McBride, Stephen. 1983. "Public Policy as a Determinant of Interest Group Behaviour: The Canadian Labour Congress' Corporatist Initiative, 1976–1978," *Canadian Journal of Political Science* XVI: 501–17

McBride, Stephen. 1995. "Coercion and Consent: The Recurring Corporatist Temptation in Canadian Labour Relations," in Cy Gonick, Paul Phillips, and Jesse Vorst, eds., *Labour Gains, Labour Pains: Fifty Years of PC1003*. Halifax: Fernwood.

McBride, Stephen. 1992. *Not Working: State, Unemployment and Neo-Conservatism in Canada*. Toronto: University of Toronto Press.

McBride, Stephen. 1996. "The Continuing Crisis of Social Democracy: Ontario's Social Contract in Perspective," *Studies in Political Economy*, 50: (Summer): 65-93.

McDonough, Terrence. 1999. "Gordon's Accumulation Theory: The Highest Stage of Stadial Theory." *Review of Radical Political Economics* 31(6): 27–32.

McElligott, Greg. 2001. *Beyond Service: State Workers, Public Policy, and the Prospects for Democratic Administration*. Toronto: University of Toronto Press.

McIntosh, Tom. 2000. "Governing Labour Market Policy: Canadian Federalism, the Social Union and a Changing Economy," in Tom McIntosh, ed., *Federalism, Democracy and Labour Market Policy in Canada*. Montreal: McGill-Queens University Press.

Nijboer, Harriet. 2010. *Federal Provincial Relations on Immigration: Striking the Right Balance*. Unpulished Masters of Law Thesis, Faculty of Law, University of Toronto.

Office of the Auditor General of Canada. 2009. *Fall Report to the House of Commons*. Ch. 2: "Selecting Foreign Workers Under the Immigration Program." Ottawa: Minister of Public Works and Government Services Canada.

O'Hara, Phillip Anthony. 2006. *Growth and Development in the Global Political Economy*. Routledge: London.

Ontario Premier's Council. 1990. *People and Skills in the New Global Economy*. Toronto: Queen's Printer.

Pal, Leslie A. 1988. *State, Class and Bureaucracy: Canadian Unemployment Insurance and Public Policy*. Kingston and Montreal: McGill-Queen's University Press.

Panitch, Leo. 1980. "Recent Theorizations of Corporatism: Reflections on a Growth Industry," *British Journal of Sociology* 31: 159–87.

Paquet, Pierre. 1976. "The Development of Canadian Policy in Occupational Adult Education and Manpower," in Canadian Association for Adult Education, *Manpower Training at the Crossroads*. Ottawa: National Library.

Schattschneider, Elmer Eric. 1960. *The Semisovereign People: A Realist's View of Democracy in America*. New York: Holt, Rinehart and Winston.

Schmitter, Philippe. C., and Gerhard Lehmbruch, eds. 1979. *Trends Toward Corporatist Intermediation*. London: Sage.

Sharpe, Andrew, and Rodney Haddow, eds. 1997. *Social Partnerships for Training: Canada's Experiment with Labour Force Development Boards*. Kingston: Queen's University School of Policy Studies.

Stanford, Jim. 2008. "Staples, Deindustrialization, and Foreign Investment: Canada's Economic Journey Back to the Future." *Studies in Political Economy* 82(1): 7–34.

Struthers, James. 1983. *No Fault of Their Own: Unemployment and the Canadian Welfare State, 1914–1941*. Toronto: University of Toronto Press.

Whitaker, Reg. 1977. "The Liberal Corporatist Ideas of Mackenzie King," *Labour? Le Travail: The Journal of Labour History* 2: 137–69.

Wiarda, Howard J. 1997. *Corporatism and Comparative Politics*. Armonk, NY: M.E. Sharpe.

Wood, Donna E. 2015. "Comparing Intergovernmental Institutions in Human Capital Development," in Loleen Berdahl, André Juneau, and Carolyn Hughes Tuohy, eds., *Canada the State of the Federation 2012: Regions, Resources and Resiliency*. Montreal: McGill-Queens University Press.

Wood, Donna E. and Thomas R. Klassen. 2011. "Improving the Governance of Employment and Training Policy in Canada." Mowat Centre Employment Insurance Task Force.Toronto: Mowat Centre.

Woods, Harry D. 1973. *Labour Policy in Canada*.Toronto, Macmillan, 2nd edition.

3

Employment and the Labour Market: The Nexus of the Economic and the Social

Most adults earn their living, or a substantial portion of it, through wages derived from the sale of their labour power in the labour market. As a result, they are highly dependent, not only on their own skills and attributes, but also on the capacity of that market to generate suitable employment opportunities.

Though states and markets are often counter-posed in expressions such as the state *versus* the market, this is not a useful way of analysing modern political economy. In reality, states and markets are intertwined, though often in different ways in different jurisdictions. Certainly, markets are not naturally occurring phenomena, but rather are structured by state policies governing contracts, property rights, currency values, not to mention a host of other things.

Employment, being concerned with the production of both material goods and services, falls under the rubric of states' economic policies. These policies affect markets, including labour markets. But this does not mean that employment opportunities—whether viewed quantitatively or qualitatively—are a principal object of economic policy. Economic policies have various goals. Employment may be central to them, as arguably was the case in the Keynesian period, or marginal, as is more common today under neoliberalism. In the latter case, healthy employment outcomes are supposed to flow from overall economic performance, perhaps as influenced by the framework established by policy measures. But employment per se is not a specific policy objective.

Whether employment is central to or tangential to overall economic policies, the issue is also addressed by social policies. Such policies have a variety of functions and aims. Conceived broadly, social policy includes education, health, pensions, as well as various income supports of a general or targeted nature.

One minimum aspect of social policy is ensuring that those who find themselves outside the labour market for whatever reasons—disability, loss of job, age—are able to survive. This might involve providing some public income support to those who need it. But direct public involvement is not necessarily the chief method of doing this. States may insist that families look after their own non-working members, or devolve the responsibility to charitable organizations, perhaps with the assistance of public funds or tax concessions.

Other aspects of social policy have multiple goals. Education policy is partly about citizenship and personal development, discovery and transmission of knowledge for its own sake, and so forth. When viewed through the prism of the needs of the labour market, education has a role in preparing people for labour market participation by providing them with either general or transferable skills, or with skills specific to particular types of employment. The case is similar with health policy, which serves the needs of the sick and engages in preventative health measures, but which also plays a role in maintaining the capacity of the workforce. Pensions meet the needs of those whose working life is over, and various supports may be provided to those unable to work (such as the disabled) or those unable to find work (unemployment insurance).

However, configured, there is obviously a close connection between economic and social policy. The latter can be conceived variously as a contributor to the success of economic policy, or as a residual policy area that kicks in when individuals find themselves without work. Alternatively, social policy measures can be conceived as giving some individuals a chance to subsist outside the labour market and hence provide a glimpse of how a non-market economy might be organized. Examples might include the more generous versions of basic minimum income proposals that have attracted attention in recent years.

In explaining employment's location in the nexus between economic and social policy, we will first reprise some general ideas that have influenced how states in liberal democratic societies have constructed economic and social policy. Then we need to look at real world examples of how these ideas—and the practices upon which they are based—might be configured differently. Placing Canada in this comparative context will help the analysis of Canadian employment policies in later chapters.

Ideas about Managing Economic and Social Policy

As is to be expected, the main paradigms or ideologies on which political decision-makers have drawn have different views on how to manage economic and social affairs. These ideas influence the adoption of particular economic and social policies. However, some qualifications are in order. Even within similarities produced by ideological orientations, practices may be modified by constellations of interests and institutional influences so some variation within each ideologically based approach to economic and social policies is to be expected. This may apply when comparing jurisdictions at a particular moment in time, or equally it may apply within a single jurisdiction where there may be variations over time. So variation may be observed between countries with systems rooted in different ideologies, as well as within those based on similar ideas. As well, structural or historical circumstances may produce a degree of convergence, notwithstanding the ideational preferences of policy-makers.

Nevertheless, ideas derived from ideological predispositions are important. Classic liberals, including neoliberals, emphasize individualism and the freedom of individuals to act without undue restraint. In economic terms individuals are seen as self-reliant, rational, self-interested actors seeking to maximize benefits for themselves. In this view, the interaction of such individuals within a framework of law and, in economic terms, in a free market, produces socially optimum outcomes. This is Adam Smith's famous "hidden hand" of the market which transforms the pursuit of individual self-interest into results that serve the general benefit of all. The role of the state is to ensure a context in which markets can operate freely and supply necessary public goods that markets might not deliver effectively. In such a world, so long as freedom of opportunity exists, outcomes will be both fair and efficient. Individual failure might trigger social support, but it would be residual, and often limited, so as not to create a disincentive to individuals to better themselves and encourage them to end dependence on state assistance. There are of course other trends within liberalism, such as that represented by Keynes, which place the emphasis for much individual misfortune—such as unemployment—on systemic factors, and thus advocate a more collectivist response. In practice, there is often little to differentiate this type of "positive" or "welfare" liberal from social democrats.

Today, conservatives share many classic liberal values but traditionally have expressed a degree of collectivism. When Margaret Thatcher
famously claimed that "there is no such thing as society," she deviated
from classic conservatives. For them, unlike for Mrs. Thatcher, there *is*
such a thing as society. It may be hierarchical, individuals may not be
equal, but maintaining the bonds that link individuals in a social order
has some priority and may involve a greater degree of state intervention and structured cooperation between sectors of society than would
be seen as appropriate under a liberal view. This might involve the construction of social programs, often contributory, to preserve hierarchy.
Both contributions and benefit levels reflect income and status differentials. Such programs are designed to ensure both social stability and
preserve hierarchy by linking benefits firmly to the social status of the
contributor.

For socialists and social democrats, collectivism was traditionally
linked to egalitarianism and a sense of social solidarity. For most social democrats, equality referred only to equality of opportunity; but at
times the conditions to ensure such an outcome led them far further
in the direction of state intervention than liberals or conservatives. Ensuring the existence of a level playing field for individuals might entail
going well beyond legal rights and involve provision of free or highly
subsidized education, health, and other social programs justified on
the basis that they were necessary to enable individuals to participate
effectively in a competitive liberal society and economy. For much of
the twentieth century the programmatic implication of this orientation
was the building of a comprehensive welfare state, an endeavour that
was also consistent with the solidaristic sentiments of most socialists
and social democrats.

Comparative Political Economy of Economic and Social Policy

The literature on existing political economies has noted that the
welfare state comes in different varieties and, indeed, that there are
identifiable varieties of capitalism itself. The most famous typology of
the welfare state was advanced in Gøsta Esping-Andersen's work, *The
Three Worlds of Welfare Capitalism* (1990). Although there are criticisms of the typology, some of which are noted below, the schema has
proven to be highly influential and, in a modified version, it is still in
use.

Esping-Andersen's work addresses the classical political economic question of the relationship between the market (and property) and the state (democracy), and how this relationship influences labour market outcomes and class structure (1990, 93). He identifies three primary ideal types of welfare state regimes: liberal, conservative/corporatist, and social-democratic; each of these is characterized by a cluster of social policy variables (1990, 26–29).[12] These welfare regimes are built upon somewhat different relationships between the state, the market and the family,[13] and vary according to their de-commodifying and stratification outcomes.[14] By decommodification, Esping-Anderson means the provision of benefits that reduced citizens' dependence on the market.

The first type is the "liberal welfare state," of which the U.S. and Canada are examples, and in which social benefits are typically modest and recipients are often stigmatized. The effect of such a regime is to reinforce the primacy of the market. "Conservative welfare states," exemplified by a number of continental European countries, are less concerned with reinforcing market forces than with the preservation of class and status differentials. Such regimes exhibit a range of state-provided benefits which, however, have little redistributive effect, and which—as a result of religious influences—are committed to the preservation of traditional family roles and relationships. The "social democratic welfare state" is infused with the ethos of universalism and promotes high levels of equally available benefits. The consequences of different welfare state regimes for full employment are as follows. Only the social democratic type is: "genuinely committed to a full-employment guarantee, and entirely dependent on its attainment . . . Neither

12 This typology has been expanded to include "The Southern Model" (Ferrera 1996) including the welfare states of Italy, Spain, Portugal, and Greece which did not conform to any of the other models.

13 Although the family was not considered to the same extent initially. See next section.

14 De-commodification entails the extent to which an individual's welfare is detached from their position in the labour market (1990, 105); stratification concerns the distribution of state assistance based on class position. For example, in the Nordic countries in the period when Esping-Anderson was writing, "manual workers come to enjoy rights identical to salaried white-collar employees or civil servants; all strata and classes are incorporated under one universal insurance system" (113). Conversely, in liberal welfare states, which tended to rely much more heavily on market mechanisms, means-tested assistance and modest social insurance cater mainly to "a clientele of low-income, usually working-class, state dependents," while those successful in the market purchase private insurance. Finally, welfare policies in the conservative model were geared towards the preservation of status differentials where rights were attached to class and status. Conservative welfare states were strongly committed to the preservation of the traditional family model, and tended to intervene only when "the family's capacity to service its members is exhausted" (ibid, 112).

of the two alternative regime-types espouse full-employment as an integral part of their welfare state commitment. In the conservative tradition, of course, women are discouraged from working; in the liberal ideal, concerns of gender matter less than the sanctity of the market" (1990, 28). Esping-Andersen argued that once they became crystallized, such regimes functioned as "independent causal variables" which "systematically influence social and economic behaviour." In particular, "nations' capacity to maintain full-employment over the post-war period was decisively influenced by the welfare state" (1990, 141–42).

These three ideal-types varied widely in their structure and policies both in time and place, and the adoption of one or the other model was generally explained by the nature of coalitions between different social classes and the balance of power in the state and civil society (Ferragina and Seeleib-Kaiser 2011). While this theoretical framework has largely held up against criticism, it has evolved since the 1990s, as the theoretical implications of including gender and family in the model have been explored.

In 1993, Ann Shola Orloff contended that the *Three Worlds* typology did not adequately consider the roles of gender and family in citizens' relationship to the labour market (see also Hook 2015, 14). Orloff argued that womens' experiences with state social provision differed markedly from those of men, especially in the realms of paid and unpaid labour. In this view, welfare states should also be evaluated by the extent to which they are "women-friendly" (Orloff 1993, 304). According to Hook (2015), two main theoretical camps emerged from Orloff's critique. The first dismissed the *Three Worlds* typology and focused exclusively on gender and family (Lewis, 1992; Lewis and Ostner, 1994; Sainsbury, 1996). The second camp sought to incorporate gender and family and bring consideration of women's unpaid work into the state-market nexus (Orloff 1993; Korpi 2000; O'Connor et al 1999).

These critiques resulted in Esping-Andersen reformulating his framework to include a measure of "familialism" alongside de-commodification and stratification. Familialism means the extent to which families are supposed to absorb social risks, and to which they are the primary source of welfare (Hook 2015, 16). This gave rise to a number of modifications to the original schema. According to Esping-Andersen (1999) the conservative welfare states are familialist, while the liberal welfare state is non-familialist and the social-democratic welfare states are de-familialist (due to the state lessening families caregiving responsibilities through state spending) (ibid).

Others (e.g. Kuitto 2011) applied the concepts of de-commodification and de-familization to the structure of welfare spending. Spending on cash benefits or transfers (pensions or unemployment benefits) was seen as more likely to have a de-commodifying effect, while spending on services (childcare facilities) would be more likely to fulfill the defamilization dimension (Kuitto 2011, 350). According to this theory, welfare regimes can be defined in part by the composition of their social spending between spending on transfers on the one hand, and spending on services on the other.

While most accounts comparing welfare states now include a gender component, there is still an ongoing debate concerning how well the *Three Worlds* model holds up under the neoliberal epoch. One of the central political claims Esping-Andersen made is that through the medium of the welfare state capitalism can be modified to a certain extent to de-commodify and de-stratify workers.

The growth in the importance of the services sector, combined with the relative decline of manufacturing, has had consequences for welfare states. The implications of this are mediated by the dependence of the welfare state on whether the state privileges the market, the family, or assumes responsibility for employment and labour supply (Oesch 2015, 95). According to Esping-Andersen (1999) there are three potential trajectories. The first privileges the market, and results in high job growth in the service sector, but pay at very low wages. The second prioritizes a state response which creates service jobs within the public sector, especially in the sectors of childcare, health, and education. Finally, the last trajectory lets wages follow developments in the economy more generally therefore pricing out interpersonal services for a large portion of the population, requiring them to be carried out in the home (Esping-Andersen 1999, 111–12 [cited in Oesch 2015, 97]). These trajectories correspond to liberal, social-democratic, and conservative welfare states respectively (Iversen and Wren 1998). The liberal response leads to large wage inequality, while the social-democratic response creates expanding fiscal demands on the state; finally, the conservative response can lead to high unemployment among the lowly educated, as well as a highly gender segregated labour market. Whatever the trajectory, however, with the decline of the traditional working class and its patterns of voting, and the rise of neoliberalism, the dynamic of welfare politics has been considerably altered.

Welfare state outcomes tend to overlap with another classification scheme, put forward in Peter Hall and David Soskice's *Varieties of Capitalism: The Institutional Foundations of Comparative Advantage.* The focus here is on the strategic interactions between multiple actors within political economies, particularly on how firms coordinate relationships to maintain and enhance their comparative advantage. Hall and Soskice identify five spheres in which firms develop relationships: 1) industrial relations; 2) vocational training and education; 3) corporate governance; 4) inter-firm relations; and 5) employee relations (2001, 7). Political economies can then be grouped according to the ways in which firms coordinate with the state, labour institutions, and other firms. According to this typology, political economies fall into one of two camps: the liberal market economies (LMEs), or the coordinated market economies (CMEs). Here, we are less concerned with the means by which coordination is achieved than by the fact that it is; another key issue here is how the way this is done contrasts with the liberal market economy type, to which Canada belongs.

Liberal market economies leave "coordination" to market-based mechanisms and competitive market arrangements both between firms and within the labour market. The US is the archetypical example of an LME. Firms in these systems are heavily dependent on their valuation in equity markets, and are evaluated on their share prices and current profitability. This promotes certain types of behaviour on their part, including "flexible" employment practices to cut costs. Since this "flexibility" makes hiring and firing easier depending on the business cycle, individuals are encouraged to invest in general skills, rather than firm-specific skills (Hall and Soskice 2001, 30).

Social policy in LMEs is usually considered to interfere with markets by either enforcing regulatory regimes, or raising labour costs by tightening labour markets (ibid. 50). As a result, market-based solutions are generally preferred to state intervention, unless state intervention provides institutional infrastructure for enhancing advanced sector firms' comparative advantage (Iversen and Soskice, 2015). LMEs are virtually always accompanied by liberal welfare states, which emphasize low levels of benefits to maintain fluid labour markets.

In contrast, CMEs such as Germany and the Scandinavian countries typically have a higher union density, and tend to set wages through industry-level bargaining, due to the overall level of co-ordination (as opposed to competition) in the economy. CMEs are more likely to pursue production strategies that depend on a labour force with very specific skills and high levels of firm commitment. These high levels of commitment are underwritten by longer employment tenures, industry-negotiated wages, and protective labour organizations (Iversen and Soskice 2015, 27). Furthermore, corporate governance and firms' ability to secure capital investments are based less on stock prices or current profitability, and revolve more on diffuse knowledge networks and firm reputation. While Iversen and Soskice do not explicitly equate CMEs with any particular type of social model, it is highly likely that they will be conservative or social-democratic welfare states depending on the composition of their class-coalitions and centralized strength of organized labour. These connections between economic and social policy fit in to what Hall and Soskice term "institutional complementarities" (ibid. 17). What they mean by this term is that political economies pursue social policies that augment the comparative advantages provided by the economic system, and vice versa. For example, Hall and Soskice (2001) usefully summarize Aoki's 1994 argument: "long-term employment is far more feasible where financial systems provide capital on terms that are not sensitive to current profitability," acknowledging an important institutional interdependence (18). Therefore, once these institutional complementarities are established, the system may become resistant to change.

Although institutional complementarities are a part of the cohesive connection between social and economic policy, this notion has come under fire from multiple critics who claim that this typology assumes resilience of welfare regimes. For them the reality may be convergence or at least erosion of differences under common pressures of globalization and neoliberalism. Schelke (2012) points to the contradictory notion that many reforms over the last two decades have gone against the logic of supposed complementarities. Examples include the creation of temporary and casualized employment even in the CMEs. This raises the possibility of convergence between LMEs, CMEs, and their corresponding welfare state regimes due to processes of globalization and neoliberalism.

Certainly, pressures from international organizations have been towards convergence. The clearest example of this in the labour market/ social policy area has been the OECD's promotion of flexibilization and liberalization under the rubric of its 1994 *Jobs Study* and subsequent Jobs Strategy initiative. OECD recommendations, of course, are not binding on member states, but the "best practices" identified under the Jobs Strategy were pursued with unusual vigour and consistency for over a decade (McBride and Williams 2001; McBride, McNutt and Williams 2008). Contrary to the idea of discrete welfare state regimes or varieties of capitalism, the OECD advocated a "one–size-fits-all" approach based partly on neoliberal theoretical premises and partly on an interpretation of the US 1980s and 1990s labour market as a success story that could be emulated everywhere. Thus deregulation and welfare state restructuring were advanced as the solution to high levels of unemployment and other labour market issues. The fact that there was little evidence to support the proposition that adoption of this model led to superior labour market outcomes did little to deter the OECD from its enthusiasm. Adoption of the OECD recommendations was far from uniform amongst OECD members. Some members attempted a "flexicurity" approach; here, aspects of flexibilization—for example easing employers' ability to hire and fire, combined with continuous training and supports for workers transitioning to new skills—should help retain a measure of security for workers. Yet, consistent with the notion of convergence, even those states that were relatively non-compliant were aligned with more than half of the recommendations made by the OECD, a result that would suggest a trend to the preferred neoliberal model postulated by the OECD. This is consistent with the view that the capacity of the state and organized labour to defend "non-liberal" capitalism is diminishing, and liberal capitalism is becoming the increasingly common tendency (Streeck 2001).

Another possibility is of a "dual convergence" in the face of several factors, including increased capital mobility, the shift to post-industrial employment, and the pressures towards neoliberalism from both domestic and international sources. In this dual convergence concept, countries clustered as LMEs or CMEs become more alike within each category, but not necessarily between types. For example, there is perhaps evidence that within the CME category Sweden has shifted towards the German model. There is also some evidence that greater liberalization is leading other LMEs toward the US model (Howell 2003, 108–109).

Although Canadians have justifiably considered their welfare state to be more developed than that of the United States, broader international comparisons have always placed the countries within the same welfare state regime. The same is true of the economic categorizations of the varieties of capitalism literature. Canada is firmly in the LME classification. Yet, as a decentralized federal country, there have always been variations in Canada between provinces. A 2006 study of subnational welfare systems in Canada concluded that British Columbia and Ontario were clearly liberal welfare states, but had some leaning (albeit weaker than was the case in Quebec) to European models. Alberta was closest to the US model (Bernard and Saint-Arnaud 2006). The 1995 federal reforms that devolved some program responsibilities increased the scope for further differentiation between provinces. For some provinces, this provided an opportunity to move further in the direction of the US social model. In a study of British Columbia, McBride and McNutt (2007) traced the influence of international ideational pressures, the material injunctions of federal-provincial relations in the 1990s, and the election of a hard-edged neoliberal government in 2001 to show that the BC welfare state moved in the direction of a labour market program rather than a traditional social assistance initiative. As such, it had come to more closely resemble the US social model. Re-attachment to the labour market was stressed and, to the extent it was successful, the available pool of cheap labour was increased. Thus, within the category of liberal welfare states, BC represented a (limited) example of convergence to the US, and OECD-recommended, model.

Conclusions

The fact that the *Three Worlds* and *Varieties* literatures are still discussed provides a testament to their continued relevance and contributions to the field of political economy. However, despite their importance there are a number of key critiques that an examination of the literature has produced. From the *Three Worlds* literature, it has been argued that any discussion of welfare state regimes should entail consideration of the effects that de-commodifying and (de-)stratifying policies have along gender and family lines. Secondly, the shifting political economies of the modern era and the continual advance of economic liberalism requires that the theoretical framework be re-evaluated for its continued relevance. While for the most part the framework still holds up, there are shifts indicating that all the systems have been exposed to pressure to change in the direction of liberalization.

Having placed Canada in a kind of comparative framework, the next several chapters focus specifically on Canada. The chapters deal with various employment policy areas that regulate the supply of labour and the conditions under which it is utilized. Thus we examine training, immigration, unemployment insurance, employment standards, addressing inequities, and industrial and labour relations. In each case the chapters present an historical context to contemporary developments and debates. And Canada's profile as a welfare state and as a type of capitalist economy will influence the discussion. Canada has always been a global nation, but the impact of global factors also changes over time.

References

Aoki, M. 1994. "The Contingent Governance of Teams: Analysis of Institutional Complementarity." *International Economic Review* 35(3): 657–76.

Bernard, P. and S. Saint-Arnaud. 2004. "More of the same? The Position of the Four Largest Canadian Provinces in the World of Welfare State Regimes." Ottawa: CPRN, November.

Coates, D. 2000. *Models of Capitalism: Growth and Stagnation in the Modern Era*. Cambridge: Polity Press.

Esping-Andersen, G. 1990. *The Three Worlds of Welfare Capitalism*. Princeton. NJ: Princeton University Press.

Esping-Andersen, G. 1999. *Social Foundations of Postindustrial Economies*. Oxford: Oxford University Press.

Ferragina, E., and M. Seeleib-Kaiser. 2011. "Welfare Regime Debate: Past, Present, Futures?" *Policy and Politics* 39(4): 583–611.

Ferrera, M. 1996. "The 'Southern Model' of Welfare in Social Europe," *Journal of European Social Policy* 6(1): 17–37.

Gingrich, J., and S. Hausermann. 2015. "The Decline of the Working-Class Vote, The Reconfiguration of the Welfare Support Coalition and Consequences for the Welfare State." *Journal of European Social Policy* 25(1): 50–75.

Hall, P., and D. Soskice. 2001. *Varieties of Capitalism: The Institutional Foundations of Comparative Advantage*. Oxford: Oxford University Press.

Hook, J.L. 2015. "Incorporating 'Class' into Work-Family Arrangements: Insights from and for Three Worlds." *Journal of European Social Policy* 25(1): 14–31.

Howell, Chris. 2013. "Review: Varieties of Capitalism: And Then There Was One?." Comparative Politics 36(1): 103–24.

Iversen, T., and A. Wren. 1998. "Equality, Employment, and Budgetary Restraint: The Trilemma of the Service Economy." *World Politics* 50(4): 507–74.

Iversen, T., and D. Soskice. 2015. "Politics for Markets." *Journal of European Social Policy*, 25(1): 76–93.

Kalleberg, A. 2011. *Good Jobs, Bad Jobs: The Rise of Polarized and Precarious Employment Systems in the United States, 1970s to 2000s*. New York, NY: Russell Sage Foundation.

Korpi, Walter. 2000. "Faces of Inequality: Gender, Class, and Patterns of Inequalities in Different Types of Welfare States." *Social Politics* 7 (2): 127–91.

Kuitto, K. 2011. "More than just Money: Patterns of Disaggregated Welfare Expenditure in the Enlarged Europe." *Journal of European Social Policy* 21(4): 348–64.

Lewis, J., and I. Ostner. 1994. *Gender and the Evolution of European Social Policies*. Bremen: Centre for Social Policy Research, University of Bremen.

Lewis, J. 1997. "Gender and Welfare Regimes: Further Thoughts," *Social Politics* 4(2): 160–77.

Lewis, J. 1992. "Gender and the Development of Welfare Regimes," *Journal of European Social Policy* 2(3): 159–73.

McBride, Stephen, Kathleen McNutt and Russell A. Williams. 2008. "Policy Learning? The OECD and Its Jobs Study," in Rianne Mahon and Stephen McBride, eds., *The OECD and Transnational Governance*. Vancouver: UBC Press.

McBride, Stephen, and Russell A. Williams. 2001. "Globalization, the Restructuring of Labour Markets and Policy Convergence: The OECD 'Jobs Strategy.'" *Global Social Policy* 1(3): 281–309

McBride, Stephen, and Kathleen McNutt. 2007. "Devolution and Neoliberalism in the Canadian Welfare State: Ideology, National and International Conditioning Frameworks, and Policy Change in British Columbia." *Global Social Policy* 7(2): 177–201

O'Connor, J.S., A.S. Orloff, and S. Shaver. 1999. *States, Markets, Families: Gender, Liberalism, and Social Policy in Australia, Canada, Great Britain and the United States*. Cambridge: Cambridge University Press.

Oesch, D. 2015. "Welfare Regimes and Change in the Employment Structure: Britain, Denmark and Germany since 1990." *Journal of European Social Policy* 25(1): 94–110.

Orloff, A.S. 1993. "Gender and Social Rights of Citizenship: The Comparative Analysis of Gender Relations and Welfare States." *American Sociological Review* 58(3): 303–28.

Sainsbury, D. 1996. *Gender, Equality, and Welfare States*. Cambridge: Cambridge University Press.

Schelkle, W. 2012. "Collapsing Worlds and Varieties of Welfare Capitalism: In Search of a New Political Economy of Welfare." LSE "Europe in Question" Discussion Paper Series.

Streeck, W. 2001. "Introduction: Explorations into the Origins of Nonliberal Capitalism in Germany and Japan," in Wolfgang Streeck and Kozo Yamamura, eds., *The Origins of Nonliberal Capitalism: Germany and Japan in Comparison*. Ithaca: Cornell University Press.

4

Supplying the Labour Market with the Right Skills

One of the core arguments of this book is that public policy towards the labour market has veered away from measures intended to influence the demand for labour. It is now almost wholly focused on supply. "Supply" here refers not just to the volume of labour, but also to its composition, skill characteristics, and the conditions under which it is employed.

This emphasis on the supply of labour is new if the time-frame for comparison is limited to the Keynesian post-war era. However, the components of labour supply—training, immigration, and regulation of the labour market—all have long histories.

These I will briefly review in the following chapters of this book. Understanding where current policies came from, and what factors determined their design and relative priority, can be useful not only in interpreting the past, but also in delineating current options and alternatives.

Indeed it will be useful to identify a number of themes and issues that recur both in the historical survey of policy in this area, and in the discussion of contemporary policy initiatives. Training has often been advanced as a necessary condition for ensuring that a nation's workforce is effective, efficient, and prepared to produce competitively in an increasingly global economy. In Canada, there has never been a high degree of satisfaction with the country's training system (split between federal and provincial jurisdiction), in contrast to a country like Germany, widely seen to be a best-practices model. This chapter surveys and evaluates Canada's training policy record, including the role training plays in different overarching policy paradigms that dominate policy-making in particular periods. Then there are more specific theoretical perspectives that are important in training policy development, notably human capital theory.

Training has not always been conceptualized as a purely supply-side phenomenon. Theoretical context plays a role in discussions of whether training should be regarded as aiming at equity, in the sense of acting as an avenue of self-improvement for those undergoing it, or whether efficiency motives—what is good for the economy as a whole, in practice defined as meeting the needs of employers—should be prioritized. The latter approach is often linked to considerations of supplying an adequate number of appropriately trained personnel to the labour market and, where the system seems not to do that, to complaints about skill shortages or skills mismatch. Of course equity and efficiency do not have be thought of as mutually exclusive. The idea that there may be a positive sum option in which both goals can be achieved has obvious attractions to policy makers. In its "either/or" form, however, the equity versus efficiency debate is often linked to another debate. This secondary debate is about whether the goal of training policy should be the general development of the *labour force* or, instead focused on making the *labour market* function effectively. For individuals within the labour force possession of the right kind of skill confers security. In terms of Standing's (1999) typology of security cited in Chapter 1 of this volume, this is "skill reproduction security"; but possession of it—in the form of ready access to useful training—would clearly link to the other types of security. Thus the whole area is an important issue for labour.

Generic skills are provided through the education system. According to the OECD, Canada has the highest rate of completion of post-secondary education in the OECD area at 51 percent (OECD 2012), compared to the OECD average of 31 percent. The OECD figures do not include trade or vocational certifications. Typically, these specific work-related skills are provided through training systems. In practice, there are significant overlaps between education and training (as in university level professional programs in health and law, and specific vocational skills offered in secondary schools as part of the curriculum). Here, however, the emphasis is on the training system to the extent it can be separated out from other forms of education.

Evolution of Training Policy

Chapter 2 noted that prior to the 1960s training was a priority of neither federal nor of provincial levels of the state. Essentially, the de facto training policy was something along the lines of "leave it to the market." It is true that there was some provincial government attention to apprenticeships and, depending on the absorptive capacity of the economy, immigration of ready-trained workers was encouraged by the federal authorities (Doern and Phidd 1983, 504). But the state did not really involve itself in ensuring a steady supply of skilled labour.

In the midst of the Keynesian period, beginning in the 1960s, the federal government began to pay closer attention to training through providing funding to the provinces for the construction of training facilities (Goldman 1976). This involved the use of federal "spending power" in an area that remained provincial in jurisdiction. At the time these initiatives were described as "manpower" policy and, in the mid-1960s, a federal Department of Manpower and Immigration was established. The connection between domestic training programs and immigration in supplying labour has already been noted. The name of the new department symbolized the link perfectly.

Looking back on the post-war period as a whole, Canadian training policy falls into four broad stages. First, for some years until the mid 1960s there was rather limited activity. This was followed by a period of increased state intervention in which programs multiplied; this period lasted through the late 1980s. From the late 1980s to the mid-1990s there was an attempt to create a neo-corporatist training apparatus in the name of achieving a high value-added competitive economy. It was intended that cooperation between the labour market partners—business and labour—and the state would lead to a higher priority for training and the design of better programs. This was a major goal of the Labour Force Development Strategy and institutions like the Canadian Labour Force Development Board and its provincial equivalents. Finally, labour market deregulation, expressed by devolution of responsibility to the provinces and transfer of responsibility to individuals, superseded the neo-corporatist experiment from the mid 1990s, and remains the current approach. From the early 1970s the active components of labour market policy, such as training, were accompanied by a relatively generous system of unemployment insurance. The system was almost comprehensive, and benefit levels reasonable in terms of replacement rate of wages and longevity of benefits (see Chapter 6 for details). However, the gradual erosion of the system's generosity culminated in the federal government withdrawing from most training. It offloaded responsibility for active employment measures to the provinces. This was accomplished by a radical restructuring of the (now renamed) employment insurance system. In terms of cushioning individuals from the effects of unemployment, the new Employment Insurance system

(EI) was a pale image of its predecessor. The new training system thus has a diminished level of social supports underpinning it.

Training policy is influenced by a broad range of factors. Some are structural, like the state of the economy and its occupational composition. Others are ideational, such as the broad set of policy ideas influencing public policy (as with the Keynesian paradigm in post-war Canada, and its neoliberal successor more recently). Some factors are more narrowly political, such as the priority given to other policy areas. Here we can think of immigration policy where, for example, import of skilled personnel could be used either to displace or complement domestic skills programs. Finally, institutions matter, as with the operation of the federal system and jurisdictional issues between federal and provincial governments. Indeed, the uneven coverage and quality of training in Canada is often blamed on divided jurisdiction and the failure of different levels of government to coordinate their activities (Bramwell 2011). Most of the training offered by governments in Canada requires qualification for employment insurance as a pre-condition (Mendelsohn and Medow 2010). The declining coverage of the employment insurance system (see Chapter 6) means the pool of potential trainees is lower than it was formerly, and significant regional variations in EI coverage produces a disconnect between need for training and access to it. This is a situation the introduction of Labour Market Agreements (LMAs) to provide training to non-EI eligible persons has not fully corrected (Mendelsohn and Medow 2010, 9).

Paradigms and Training

The profile of training is shaped by the underlying economic paradigm that influences policy. For example, think of the Keynesian era, where demand-side management was supposed to assure full employment, training policy occupied a subsidiary role. Under neoliberalism—where possession of the right amount and type of human capital is supposed to determine an individual's success in the labour market—training policy, other things being equal, could assume a more central role. Alternatively, other neoliberal objectives such as budgetary austerity could limit its role. In any case, in the neoliberal approach, devolution of responsibility to the individual with limited state supports mixed with elements of coercion as with workfare provisions (under which receipt of benefits was made conditional on participating in work projects or specified training activities) was a central feature.

Even prior to the neoliberal challenge to Keynesianism there was a growing perception that Keynesian demand management policies had not delivered and, perhaps, could not deliver full-employment in the Canadian context. This was because of export dependence, an unusually open economy, and regional diversity. Under Canadian conditions, pockets of regional and seasonal unemployment remained impervious to macroeconomic policies. A supply-side alternative that focused on upgrading the labour force through training was seen as a supplementary instrument to macroeconomic initiatives. In its initial stages, then, the turn to supply side policies was articulated within the Keynesian framework and was consistent with the full employment objective. Later, the focus on training was to de-link demand side pre-occupations with creating employment in favour of the dictum that if you train them (workers) then they (investors) will come, and jobs will be created. This gained traction in both federal and provincial pronouncements on the training file in the 1990s. The federal Liberal government produced a position paper calling for Canada to be positioned as an "investment magnet. Key to this is to overcome Canada's 'skills deficit'—to offer the best-educated, best-trained workforce in the world" (Canada/HRDC 1994b, 10). Similarly, former New Brunswick Premier Frank McKenna argued: "You need training first. If you have the training, the jobs will take care of themselves" (*Globe and Mail*, January 16, 1993). Potentially this involved an active role for the state in provision of training and shaping the training opportunities that would be on offer. But later the supply side approach came to stress that individuals were themselves responsible for their acquisition of human capital; a reduced role for the state, and more reliance on private providers of training, became the normal approach.

Human Capital Theory

Connected to these broad paradigms, but more restricted in scope, is human capital theory, which has increasingly come to inform training policy. The human capital approach to the labour market is largely neoliberal, given its focus on individual acquisition of skills and the individual's responsibility to carry out this activity and receive the individual benefits that result. However, there are more collectivist versions of human capital theory that see social benefits arising as a result of ensuring an adequate supply of well-trained labour that attracts investors and thus produces both growth and employment. In this version, human capital theorists could advocate for an active state role in human capital provision, since the benefits are seen as being social as well as individual.

Mostly, though, human capital theory is located in the neo-classical tradition. It is central to the neoliberal analysis of labour markets (McNabb and Whitfield 1994a, 2, 16) and thus is a good fit with the flexibilization of labour markets approach. At its core, the theory holds that the knowledge and skills possessed by individuals represent a factor of production in the same way as physical capital (buildings, raw materials, machinery, etc.). Higher levels of skill and knowledge, achieved through education and training, lead to higher productivity that benefits employers but is also expressed in higher rewards for those who possess the relevant skills (see Becker 1993), and lower rewards for those who do not.

Some versions of the theory (Friedman 1962) portray all the benefits of human capital as accruing to the individual who possesses it; in this theory, no benefits accrue to society. If this is the case, the responsibility and costs of acquiring human capital should also lie with the individual. There is no reason for society to contribute to the costs of education or training. Others see a positive relationship between investments in education and training and economic growth (e.g. Schulz 1961). Thus the returns to investments in human capital are shared between the individual and society. Public contributions to education and training can be justified on this basis, though in this model the degree of public support depends on the calculation of relative benefits between individuals and society. Ivanova (2012, 5), replicating an earlier study by Allen (1998), found that "Graduates in virtually all undergraduate programs, including humanities and social sciences, contribute considerably more to the government coffers over their working lives than their education costs." This conclusion could justify free tuition for university education as much as for the K-12 system or, at least, much reduced tuition.

Speaking generally of the capitalist economies there have been at least three waves of human capital theory with somewhat different policy implications (Marginson 1997: see especially Chapter 4). The first, in 1961, was based on the proposition that more education leads to improved productivity, which in turn leads to higher economic growth. The appropriate policy response was seen as an expansion of the public education system and equal opportunity in accessing it. The second (1980s), while retaining the focus on education, productivity, and growth, held that more selective investments in education (high technology, management studies, and generic skills) would produce a better pay-off. In the hands of neoliberal policy makers, a school with which it has the most natural affinity anyway, the third wave of human capital theory in the 1980s and 1990s holds that individual investments in human capital proceed until costs exceed the anticipated benefits and that individual behaviour based on this rational calculus produces an optimum amount and quality of human capital for the economy as a whole (Marginson 1997, 116). This serves as an argument to marketize education and training and to place a greater financial burden of acquiring human capital upon those who are presumed to benefit most from it—individuals rather than society.

During the 1980s and into the 1990s, developments in Canadian labour market policy seemed ambivalent in the face of two alternative approaches based on the general-versus-individual benefits supposedly flowing from human capital development. These can be described as "progressive competitiveness" approach relying on neo-corporatist institutions, on the one hand; and "labour market regulation" on the other, which depends on market forces. Where they differed—apart from the institutional arrangements presumed necessary to bring about an optimum investment in human capital—was on the distribution of benefits between individuals and society, or segments of society, that flow from that investment.

The progressive competitiveness strategy (Albo 1994) could be seen as being rooted in a social version of human capital theory. The origin of the turn to progressive competitiveness lies in a series of early 1980s government reports that were critical of existing training. Those reports called for training to serve the needs of employers. However, the progressive competitiveness strategy articulated a broader vision in which the common interests of labour and employers lay in upgrading the skills level of the workforce. For labour, the attraction of the argument was the competitive advantage that a highly skilled workforce might confer. According to the theory, high wages could be maintained because they would be based on a high skill, high value-added, high productivity economy. Neo-corporatist institutional arrangements—reflecting a "partnership" between business, labour and government—

were viewed as mostly likely to facilitate labour force development through establishing a sense of "ownership" over the programs. Another goal was to "lever" private sector dollars for training. The approach presumed a continued involvement on the part of the federal government, unlike the subsequent deregulation strategy that was consistent with federal withdrawal from the area. In the event, even with the active involvement of government it proved impossible to make these arrangements work. In countries where they flourished, labour and left parties tended to be stronger. In the context of Canadian political culture and the power imbalance between capital and labour, it was impossible to imagine such arrangements evolving "naturally." Even with considerable political commitment, they proved unsuccessful and temporary.

Compounding this problem was the poor track record of the Canadian private sector in providing training, even in comparison to the United States (let alone some of the European countries). Annual expenditures by Canadian employers on learning and development have declined by over 40 percent in the past twenty years, from $1249 per employee in the early 1990s to $800 in 2015 … These outlays are lower than expenditures by American companies, which invested an average of $976 per employee in 2015. Canada also lags behind OECD peers in job-related informal education. In 2009, the last time this metric was measured, only 30 percent of Canadian workers participated in some form of informal job-related training, compared with 61 percent in Sweden and 47 percent in Norway" (Advisory Council on Economic Growth 2017, 6).

Reinforcing this point, business has opposed training levies by which firms are required to spend or be "levied" a small percentage of payroll in order to finance training. Training levies occur in various countries but are rare in LMEs like Canada. In 2016 the Canadian Federation of Students called for a national training levy (Canadian Federation of Students 2016; Munro, 2014). In Quebec there was such a policy, which targeted firms with payrolls of $250,000 and over, requiring them to set aside a percentage of payroll costs for training (Munro 2014). If they failed to do this or chose not to, they had to surrender the amount to a provincial training fund. The program was successful, but only insofar as it brought Quebec's training levels to the already lack-lustre Canadian average (Munro 2014).

The neo-corporatist revival, the related concept of *labour force development*, viewed as a collective or social approach to human capital formation, and the notion that business-government-labour collaboration in training represented the route to a high-wage, high-value-added competitive economy have all fallen out of favour in recent years (see Haddow and Klassen 2006). They have been displaced by the development of the *labour market* through a deregulation of labour markets approach typified by the OECD Jobs Study's flexibility model. In Canada, the policy of successive federal governments and most provincial governments of whatever partisan stripe, have proven compliant or consistent with the OECD approach (McBride and Williams 2001; McBride, McNutt and Williams 2008). The new measures presupposed increased individual responsibility for human capital development, even where some level of public support remained.

The transformation from progressive competitiveness to labour market deregulation occurred in the early to mid-1990s. The Liberal Party's 1993 election platform had emphasized labour market policy as a tool of economic development and competitiveness. Lloyd Axworthy, then Minister of Human Resources Development, outlined an approach that linked social security, labour market policy, and education to the economy and emphasized a refocusing of the income security and labour market policy systems.

However, the implementation was not as collectivist or socially minded as the 1993 election platform had suggested. Social policy reform was designed to remove perceived disincentives to individuals to seek jobs or firms to create employment, and to promote the employability of those receiving various forms of social assistance and of those who were in transition from school to the labour market. A social safety net would be retained while searching for more efficient means of delivering programs. In practice, efficiency would mean restraint and cost-cutting. In *Agenda: Jobs and Growth* (Canada 1994), the "Green Book" began to reformulate the argument of how human capital development might confer a comparative advantage on Canada. It argued that countries would be successful in creating jobs to the extent that they were able to attract investment, international as well as domestic. To create jobs in sufficient quantities, the Green Book argued, Canada must become an "investment magnet. Key to this is to overcome Canada's 'skills deficit'—to offer the best-educated, best-trained workforce in the world" (Canada 1994, 10).

However, rather than suggesting an expansion of the education and training systems the focus was on reforms to the social security system. The document stressed repeatedly that the best form of social security came from having a job and that in the context of structural unemployment caused by technological innovation and global pressures, existing social programs were ill-suited to deliver this result. Indeed they served as an obstacle to labour market adjustment. In OECD parlance social programs represented "rigidities" that prevented labour markets from functioning properly—more flexibility was the solution.

The implication was that the market would deliver so long as it was allowed to operate unhindered. Thus the way was set for a coercive integration of social and labour market programming. The rhetorical emphasis on a high skills environment to serve as an investment magnet drifted into a redesign of social programs to limit social assistance, reduce eligibility for unemployment insurance benefits, and integrate more of the unemployed into the labour market. Most would be reintegrated into low-skilled work. There was no evidence, on the other hand, of practical policies to turn the high skills rhetoric into reality. The focus of labour market policy was to be on inexpensively increasing the employability of individuals.

Devolved Training

In May 1996, the federal government transferred to the provinces the responsibility for active employment measures, including wage subsidies, temporary income supplements, support for self-employment initiatives, partnerships for job creation, and, where provinces requested, skills, loans, and grants. Provinces that assumed responsibility for the delivery of active measures could also opt to provide labour market services—screening, counselling, placement—at the time delivered by the federal government. The federal government would no longer be involved in the purchase of training, funding apprenticeships, co-op education, workplace-based training, or project-based training (HRDC 1996a and 1996b). Consistent as this was with neoliberal thinking, there were, of course, other factors in the decision to devolve active measures, not least being continuous pressure from Quebec, and the tiny margin of the federal victory in the 1995 Quebec referendum, that made accommodating Quebec's demands for devolution a priority.

Over twenty years after the transfer, what can be said about its impact on training and training policy? Institutionally, in terms of federal-provincial relations, devolution produced a tidier division of labour. The fact that Labour Market Development Agreements (LMDAs) were long-term tended to stabilize intergovernmental relations. The agreements were somewhat asymmetrical and further fragmented Canadian labour market programming. Proponents argued that this brought decision-making closer to local conditions and reflected local priorities, and was thus a good thing. Beyond the diversity based on local factors was a common thread of neoliberal principles, such as transferring responsibility to the individual victim of unemployment.

Under the LMDAs the responsibility for training and retraining EI recipients was decentralized to the provinces. The federal authorities retained responsibility for training for specific groups including youth, immigrants, people with disabilities, and Aboriginal peoples (Bramwell 2012; Gray 2003). They also continued to control the passive components of EI including fund management, eligibility criteria, and benefit rates. Participation in many of the training programs was contingent on EI eligibility (Haddow and Klassen 2006). All of the provinces except for Ontario (which signed an LMDA in 2005) signed LMDAs with the federal government in the 1990s either for co-management or full transfer of training programs (Bramwell 2012). Under co-management, the federal government and the provinces shared in managing programs and services, but the federal government delivered Employment Benefits and Support Measures (EBSMs) through local Human Resources and Skills Development Canada (HRSDC) offices. The LMDAs are administrative rather than constitutional in nature, but clearly have resulted in a fundamental decentralizing shift in authority over Canadian active labour market and training programs (Haddow and Klassen 2006).

LMDAs transferred the service delivery and administration of formerly federal EI EBSMs. Employment Benefits programs involved some longer-term retraining and skills development. Support Measures, however, focused on employability supports such as resumé building and interview skills workshops (Gray 2003). EBSM Employment Benefits under LMDAs are only accessible by EI eligible workers; while Support Measures were open to the unemployed regardless of EI status. Employment benefits have been shown to best contribute to re-employment transitions through skills or credential upgrading. Support measures proved less effective (Boon and Ours 2004; Haddow and Klassen 2006).

Ontario was a hold-out in signing an LMDA, but in 2005 the federal Liberals negotiated two agreements with the province: an LMDA as well as a new Labour Market Partnership Agreement (LMPA) that sought to address the persistent gap in training for non-EI eligible adults. LMPAs were designed to create training programs for all low-income adults regardless of EI eligibility. These LMPAs were short lived, however, falling to cancellations by the 2006 Conservative government and disagreements over intergovernmental jurisdiction (Haddow and Klassen 2006). Nonetheless, hasty devolution had created a training gap in which many non-EI eligible unemployed were left without access to training as funds were tied to EI-eligibility (Haddow and Klassen 2006). A new round of Labour Market Agreements (LMAs) sought to remedy this situation by focusing on this group of vulnerable workers left without training opportunities (MacKinnon 2013; Fernandez 2014). Post-2006, the Conservative federal government moved towards increased devolution and decentralisation following its vision of "open federalism." New LMAs were negotiated in 2007, which included fiscal transfers in the form of block grants to the provinces along with broadly defined accountability criteria. This new period of devolution or "open federalism" follows the logic that provinces are best placed and should be free to develop active labour market policies, workforce development, and training programs according to their own priorities.

LMAs constituted progress in filling the training gap in eligibility, as they provided funding transfers for skills development and support measures for non-EI eligible people (Bramwell 2012). Apart from their targeted clientele LMAs differed from LMDAs in terms of greater provincial flexibility and autonomy, as well as less stringent federal standard controls. LMAs follow high-level federally outlined strategic objectives with accountability measures in the form of common statistical indictors, while the provinces are given latitude to design and implement their own programs (Bramwell 2012).

In response to the 2008–2009 recession, the Harper government also instituted a $500 million, two-year Strategic Training and Transition Fund to provide increased access to training and retraining without being tied to EI eligibility. The Strategic Training and Transition funding was spent through various programs at the discretion of the provinces and territories between 2009 and 2011 (ESDC 2013).

Devolution of training from the federal government to the provincial governments has been both criticised and lauded. Bramwell (2012) argues that devolution has been a largely positive development, finding that active labour market programs and training projects are more effective when administered regionally and locally. Fully devolving the training of unemployed adults to the provinces could also mitigate the problems associated with overlap and conflict due to shared provincial-federal jurisdiction (Bramwell 2012). For others, the impact was negative, especially for disadvantaged groups. Ursule Critophe (2003) demonstrated that the cost of training and responsibility for accessing suitable training had been transferred to individuals with an especially damaging impact on "equity groups," including women: "Those who can ill afford to contribute to training must now do so. In many cases they are on their own when it comes to childcare and other necessary supports to their efforts. .... They are more likely than ever to find themselves relegated to the pink-collar ghettos from which they have only slowly begun to emerge. And the organizations they created and nurtured as sources of support and expertise have been under siege in the new world of for-profit providers and short-term contracts" (Critophe 2003, 31). Similar results were reported by McFarland (2003), and Lior and Wismer (2003). Wong and McBride (2003) discovered that British Columbia's provincial youth training programs were "streamed," with no laddering effect for participants (see also McBride and Stoyko 2000). Thus existing hierarchies were left undisturbed and many programs channelled youth into low-waged, marginal employment. Other criticisms included the failure of LMDAs, conceptualized in the mid-1990s, to keep pace with the fast-changing nature of employment. As well, the funding formula tended to discriminate against some provinces, notably Ontario (Mendelsohn 2014). A more fundamental criticism would be the inability of such supply-side initiatives to address the demand-side problem—a dearth of well-paid and secure job opportunities. Among critics of the training programs this often found expression in the slogan "Training for What?" In this context training seems at best as a positional good—one that redistributes opportunities, but does not enhance them in the aggregate.

Such a perspective is reinforced by developments at the higher end of human capital formation; there was evidence of shifting the cost of higher education increasingly onto students and their families, with the clear implication that access henceforth would be governed partly by economic advantage rather than merit. During the 1990s Canada became a high tuition fee country. According to the Canadian Federation of Students (2016, 4–5), "From 2001–2014, revenues from tuition fees at colleges more than doubled (a 214 percent increase); and from 2000–2015, revenues from tuition fees at universities nearly tripled (a 268 percent increase). The consequence of this trend was a sharp increase in student debt." After they graduated, many students were unable to earn enough (a pre-tax income of $20,000 was needed) to begin repaying their debt (Government of Canada 2013–14). Many were unable to earn enough to establish independent living arrangements. Milan (2016) reported that 42 percent of Canadians between 20 and 29 years old lived in their parents' homes, a substantial increase from 27 percent in 1981. Unsurprisingly, there was a trend towards postsecondary education becoming a preserve of the affluent. The Parliamentary Budget Office (2016) observed that 60 percent of students come from the top 40 percent of income earners.

Activation, Privatization, and Funding

Labour market policy has always included passive and active labour measures. The architecture of labour market policy established in the 1990s contains a much stronger emphasis on active labour market policies, though this term has changed its meaning over the years. In the heyday of the much admired "Swedish model" the term "active labour market policy" referred to an active government role and provision of a portfolio of training programs to upgrade skills continuously, and to ensure individuals' re-entry into a full-employment labour market. Over the years, the "active" designation has become attached to individuals as the objects of government policies. These individuals need to be motivated or "activated" to move back into the labour market through some mixture of encouragement, nudging, or coercion. Notwithstanding the deployment of high skills rhetoric many of the training programs provided are very short-term and consist of job search techniques and similar interventions rather than actual skills training. These efforts at activation have deep roots and are based on the theoretical perspective that personal failings of inadequate skills or motivation are responsible for labour market difficulties encountered rather than systemic factors. In the 1970s and 1980s people could be disqualified from unemployment insurance benefits for a number of reasons, including failing to apply for the requisite number of jobs per week, failing to adjust their wage expectations downwards after a certain period of unemployment, failing to appear for interviews, and so on. Later there were major bureaucratic efforts to achieve activation, often with only limited success, as John Grundy's (2015) fascinating account of HRDC's Service Outcome Measurement System[15] in the 1990s makes clear.

There have been some successes with provincially administered programs. For example, the number of apprenticeships in Canada more than doubled between 1977 and 2002, and doubled again between 2002 and 2011 (Lerman 2014, 18). Apprenticeships are primarily clustered in the construction fields such as carpenter, electrician, and plumber, and are largely under provincial jurisdiction, though there is also funding provided by the federal government in the form of grants and tax credits. In contrast to the youth focus of European apprenticeships, most Canadian apprentices are adults and therefore do little to ease school to work transitions (Lerman 2014).

Given the short-termism of many other programs, a growing culture of disqualification, and reinforced by an agenda of austerity, it is no surprise that funding for active labour market programs such as training decreased sharply in the 1990s. Thereafter, in the 2000s, it levelled off. According to OECD figures, when measured as a percentage of GDP, funding for training decreased from 0.35 percent in 1991 to 0.1 percent in 2011. Active labour market funding temporarily increased following the 2008 crash but the long-term trend is downwards, as Chart 4 indicates.

Chart 4: Training Expenditures as a Percentage of GDP

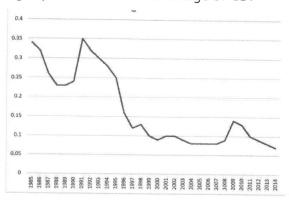

Source: OECD (2017), Public spending on labour markets (indicator).

15   The first version of this system was more accurately named "the Client Monitoring System."

From the 1990s there was a significant shift in emphasis from equity-oriented training programs, developed to assist the less advantaged,
to market-oriented training programs, developed to meet the needs of
private businesses. This shift towards market-oriented training strategies also follows the logic of neoliberal labour flexibility.

However training programs were designed, cost-cutting remained
the conditioning framework. This is indicated in the chart above as
well as by the record of the enthusiastically neoliberal provincial governments such as that in Ontario under Premier Mike Harris. The
Common Sense Revolution under Harris moved the Ontario training
regime towards a more market-oriented approach. In an effort to reduce the size of government in general, his government cut the training budget in Ontario by 17 percent in a single year (1996–1997). Active labour market programs and targeted subsidies were cut back or
eliminated altogether, such as the jobs Ontario grant which gave companies $10,000 if they trained a worker from the welfare rolls (Haddow
and Klassen 2006). The actions of the Harris government in Ontario
were at the extreme of a more general cost-cutting trend that was apparent from the earliest stages of the devolution reforms. The federal
withdrawal from training activities was accompanied by a simultaneous restructuring and reduction in the coverage and generosity of the
unemployment insurance system. Responsibility was devolved to the
provinces, training delivery increasingly privatized, use of employment
insurance funds for federal contributions to training expenditures sub-
stituted for moneys from general revenues, thus enabling austere fiscal
policies and expenditure reduction, and dilution of training quality.
Surpluses in the Employment Insurance Fund resulting from reduced
payments of benefits, while maintaining contributions or reducing
them more slowly were also diverted into general revenues and deficit
reduction under both Liberal and Conservative governments (www.
progressive-economics.ca/2008/04/09/what-happened-to-the-54-bil-
lion-ei-surplus/;   www.huffingtonpost.ca/2015/04/21/ei-fund-budget-
surplus-canada-2015_n_7113322.html).

A key feature of the federal-provincial LMDAs was language com-
mitting the governments to reduce dependency on public assistance
and to require those receiving assistance to take responsibility for iden-
tifying their own employment needs, to find appropriate programs, and
often to share the costs.

The drive to privatization had two elements. The first was an individualization of responsibility, as indicated above. The second was the privatization of functions, including work that was formerly central to the employment service such as counselling and assessment of clients.

The 1996 Employment Insurance Act had called for "results based" evaluation of the programs. This primarily featured cost-cutting criteria rather than qualitative evaluation of skills provided and acquired. Reports to the minister on the first year of experience with the new act showed the pattern. It achieved a decline of income benefits of 8.4 percent; a 14.5-percent drop in the number of initial claimants; an increase in the number of clients receiving short-term interventions such as information and counselling; and a decrease in those receiving longer-term interventions such as training. As a result, "average costs per participant in EBSMs declined from $7300 to $3900," or by 46.6 percent (HRDC 1998, ii–iii).

The roots of today's training regime lie in this context. Since the mid-1990s, amid many changes of detail, the main trends have been decentralization or devolution of responsibility from federal to provincial jurisdiction and, within an austere budget framework, addressing the needs of business while privatizing responsibility for acquiring training to individuals (Gray 2003; Bramwell 2012; Haddow and Klassen 2006). The result has been "a disciplinary and dividing practice that places steeply rising demands on people to find personal causes and responses to what are, in effect, collective social problems" (Janine Brodie [cited in Grundy 2015, 48]).

The federal government's 2013 budget introduced a Canada Job Grant (CJG) that constituted a marked shift towards a market-oriented training regime as well as devolution directly to private businesses. The CJG is a short-term grant designed to provide on-the-job skills training to the already employed, and operates by offsetting the cost of training by awarding grants to employers, to a maximum of $15,000 per worker, subject to them paying one third of the cost (ESDC 2013). That proposal quickly led to the conclusion of a new round of federal-provincial agreements[16] under the rubric of the Canada Job Fund (CJF). These agreements incorporated parts of the old LMAs dealing with provision of training to non-EI eligible persons but also included components that transfer funds to employers, subject to a contribution

16 Agreements were concluded with all provinces except for Quebec. Quebec 's programs were judged to be in line with the Canada Jobs Fund and so no specific agreement was needed.

from employers themselves, that can be used to train any category of worker (including managers and supervisors) and, in the view of critics, is likely to be mostly utilized for the already employed (CUPE 2015). There is, of course, a case to be made for "upstream" training, as training to the already employed is sometimes described. However, the details of the CJF suggest that over the term of the agreement such training will be achieved at the expense of the lower skilled and often un- or underemployed group that is excluded from EI benefits by virtue of insufficient attachment to the labour force.

Under the CJG, employers could spend $15,000 for short duration training, paid one-third each by employers, the federal government, and provincial or territorial governments. Ottawa would finance its $300 million share by cutting funds it paid to the provinces and territories for LMAs. Under LMAs those moneys were spent on groups that frequently experienced labour market problems—immigrants, Aboriginal peoples, and older unemployed Canadians. This was subsequently changed such that the federal government would pay the full $10,000 "government" grant per trainee with no provincial matching required. However, the program was still to be financed from LMA moneys (Mendelsohn and Zon 2013). Critics alleged that the CGJ pushed provincial governments aside and gave greater control over training directly to employers whose training costs would be subsidized (Ryan 2013; MacKinnon 2013). The proposed CJG fund was to be distributed per capita to the provinces and spent through the private-employers. In its stated goal, CGJ was to "put skills training decisions in the hands of employers" (Government of Canada 2014). The new Trudeau government's 2016 budget signalled small increases in funding for the LMDAs and the Canadian Jobs Fund arrangements, making the claim that these were a first step in a plan "to boost support for skills and training through these agreements. The Government will conduct broad-based consultations with provinces, territories and stakeholders in 2016–17 to identify ways to improve these agreements and guide future investments to strengthen labour market programming" (Government of Canada 2016). Similarly, increased funding was announced for union-based apprenticeship training, and the government said it sought to "incorporate greater union involvement in apprenticeship training and support innovative approaches and partnerships with other stakeholders, including employers" (Government of Canada 2016).

Apart from the subsidization issue, and the federal government's

unilateralism in proposing it, other criticisms drew attention to its focus on "short duration training" to address narrow skill shortages, while
claims of broad labour and skill shortages remain unaddressed. As well,
without a willing employer, workers would be unable to access the program directly. Ryan (2013) also argued that due to limited resources it
will likely be difficult for small businesses to access the CGJ, while large
businesses will be in the easiest position to access the funding.

Notwithstanding these criticisms and provincial unease about the
federal initiative, the LMAs have been wound down and replaced by
agreements on the CJF. The new agreements contain three elements.
In the CJG the funds flow to the employer who decides what training
is needed and purchases it for recipients chosen by the employer, who
pays one third of the cost. Under Employer Sponsored Training the
provinces (and territories) can use their own programs, but the training delivered must be employer driven. Finally, Employment Services
and Supports represent a point of continuity with the LMAs.

In a very detailed summary of what was known about the CJF in
early 2015, CUPE's researcher (CUPE 2015, 4) noted the following
concerns and issues:

"The Canada Job Fund favours employer determined training; if a
jurisdiction does not meet the required target for employer contributions, the funds will have to be returned to the federal government;
Federal funding will depend on employer take-up targets; no incentive exists for training non-employees; training providers who offer a
credential/certificate will be more likely to provide the training; the
Employment Services and Supports element, while likely to be used in
the first year of the CJF, will gradually fade away by Year 4; the ultimate
outcome will likely be a reduced transfer from the federal government,
training for existing employees, a lack of opportunities for the unemployed, those with low basic skills and the underemployed, and a return
of the challenges faced by those not eligible for EI Part II training."

It seems that the initially doubtful provinces were won over after
several rounds of negotiation and an extension in implementation
provided by the Federal government (Canadian Press 2014). Perhaps
more significantly, the LMA agreements were expiring, and in line with
asymmetrical federalism, the federal government that funded them
was in a strong negotiating position (Canadian Press 2014). Additionally, there was some compromise: originally a three-way split in cost
between the federal government, the provinces, and the private sector

was proposed, but ultimately the federal government agreed to absorb two thirds of the cost with the private sector responsible for the remaining third (Canadian Press 2014).

The trend towards devolution and the marketization of active labour market programs in Canada is pronounced. Responsibility over re/training, EBSM programming has been increasingly devolved from the federal government to the provincial governments though LMDAs and LMAs (Gray 2003; Bramwell 2012; Haddow and Klassen 2006) and, under the CJF, to employers. There has also been a distinct and accelerating shift in emphasis within active labour market programs from equity-oriented goals of assisting the less advantaged, to market-oriented training programs developed to meet the needs of private businesses (Haddow and Klassen 2006). Together these two trends intersect in a third trend towards the devolution of training decisions and funding directly to private businesses through the Canada Jobs Grant (CJG).

Skills Shortage: A Supply or Demand Issue?

One element that remains constant in discourse around training is that Canada's system fails to ensure adequate supplies of in-demand skilled labour. Most recently this is expressed in terms of an alleged skills mismatch. Much of this perception is built on widely publicized complaints from businesses, as many as 30 percent of them, that they cannot find enough skilled workers (Miner 2014, 17). Often, this is used to justify programs like the foreign temporary worker's program (see Chapter 5).

On the other hand, the Parliamentary Budget Office (2014) concluded that there was little evidence of a national labour shortage or skills mismatch in Canada. This does not, of course, imply that the training system was functioning effectively—it might just as easily be the case that there is insufficient demand for workers. The PBO examined trends in various labour market indicators, including wages that might be expected to rise under conditions of labour shortage. Its overall findings indicated that there was excess capacity in the Canadian labour market and no evidence of generalized skills shortages or mismatches, though there was some sign of tightness at the regional and sectoral levels. Similarly, a Toronto Dominion Bank report (TD 2013, 1) claimed to "debunk the notion that Canada is facing an imminent skills crisis," notwithstanding major shifts in the labour market. Noting that many of the widely expressed concerns about labour and skill shortages were anticipating future trends and developments, the TD economists cautioned that there was "good reason to look at long-term projections with considerable scepticism" (4).

Rick Miner (2014) has advanced the notion that the shortages issue referred to in the PBO and TD reports is only one aspect of a broader problem of skills mismatches. One aspect is an imbalance of demand and supply in particular skill categories. The others he identifies are geographical (equivalent to the "regional" used in the PBO report and which is widely conceded to be a reality at some times and places); another one based on under-employment (over-skilled mismatches due to highly qualified personnel being unable to find appropriate work), and a category of under-skilled/overemployment mismatches.

His analysis does tend to be based on future projections of demand for labour, from which he concludes that real labour shortages are looming and that these can be best filled by increasing labour force participation rates among underrepresented groups in the labour force—immigrants, aboriginals, persons with disabilities, young people, and older workers. He adds the proviso that these people will need to have the right skills. In light of the diminution of funding for these groups in the CJF, as opposed to better provision of training for the excluded under the now superseded LMA, this is a troubling finding.

Miner argues that underemployment is a huge problem, with almost a quarter of recent university graduates being affected (18), and that this has a number of dimensions. University graduates or other highly skilled persons are occupying positions for which they are "over-qualified"; the knock-on effect of this is that others whose qualifications would be adequate to fulfil the requirements of these jobs cannot find work because they are being blocked by better qualified people. Thus both groups are frustrated and dissatisfied and their talents are underutilized. The other aspect—of individuals holding positions for which they are not qualified—certainly exists, and might be partially addressed through internal training. This problem, however, has attracted little attention compared to the other forms of claimed skills mismatch.

However, labour market problems might be attributed to other factors, including lack of demand and wage rates inadequate to attract skilled labour. Businesses that say they cannot find enough skilled workers rarely add the qualifier, "at existing wage rates and under existing working conditions."

Conclusions

For much of its history Canada relied on the market and on immigration to meet its skill requirements. State involvement increased from the 1960s to roughly the 1980s when training was viewed as a supply-side supplement to demand-side macroeconomic policies designed to produce high levels of employment. Efforts were complicated by jurisdictional issues and largely addressed by federal spending power in that the federal authorities financed training institutions, financed some training and trainees, and provinces ran the bulk of the programs.

In the late 1980s training began to be articulated as a key ingredient of national competitiveness strategies in the face of a globalizing economy. The emphasis was on the development of the labour force. A highly educated, well-trained workforce was seen as a source of comparative advantage that would attract investment, create jobs, raise productivity, and make possible a high skills, high value-added, high wage economy. Achieving this happy outcome, however, depended on creating an institutional framework based on the "buy-in" and collaboration of labour, business, and the state. Such a framework existed in a number of European states but in the Anglo-Saxon, LMEs, such as that of Canada, the traditions were different. And it proved impossible to create sustainable institutions of this type, not least, as mentioned in Chapter 2, because business and the state were reluctant to power-share with labour. These efforts had largely been abandoned by the mid-1990s.

In a reversion to liberal, or neoliberal principles, emphasis shifted to the needs of the labour market and to the need for individuals to adapt to it by taking responsibility for their own skill development by investing in their own human capital development. This theoretical shift, articulated in terms of flexibility, was accompanied by an institutional devolution of responsibility from the federal to provincial level which, occurring as it did in a period of fiscal austerity, meant diminished resources, at least as a percentage of GDP, to the training portfolio. Much of the training provided was of a short-term, enhanced employability type rather than one that provides permanent skills. In addition, immigration changed its focus, and there was increased reliance on importation of foreign temporary migrants (see Chapter 5) who might work in the country for specific periods but, for the vast majority, would acquire no right to remain. This large category of labour fit the profile of a flexible workforce almost perfectly.

Despite contestation about the role training should play in labour market policy, considerable outlays of money and other resources, and experimentation with the different models of training, the area has largely remained in the background. It has played a supplementary role to whatever macroeconomic strategy was being pursued.

References

Advisory Council on Economic Growth. 2017. *Building a Highly Skilled and Resilient Canadian Workforce Through the Futureskills Lab.* Available online.

Allen, Robert. 1998. *Paid in Full: Who Pays for University Education in BC?* Vancouver: Canadian Centre for Policy Alternatives.

Banting, K., and J. Medow, eds. 2011. *Making EI Work: Research from the Mowat Centre Employment Insurance Task Force*, Vol. 89. Kingston: McGill-Queen's University Press.

Becker, Gary S. 1993. *Human Capital: A Theoretical and Empirical Analysis, With Special Reference to Education.* Chicago: University of Chicago Press.

Boone, Jan, and Jan van Ours. 2004. "Effective Active Labor Market Policies." *Discussion Paper No. 1335.* Bonn: Institute for the Study of Labor.

Bramwell, A. 2011. "Training Policy for the 21st Century: Decentralization and Workforce Development Programs for Unemployed Working-Age Adults in Canada." Toronto: School for Public Policy & Governance, U of T.

Canada. Department of Finance. 1994. Agenda: Jobs and Growth—A New Framework for Economic Policy. October. Ottawa: Department of Finance.

Canadian Chamber of Commerce. 2013. "Upskilling the Workforce: Employer-Sponsored Training and Resolving the Skills Gap." Available online.

Canadian Press. 2014, March 3. "Canada Job Grant: BC Signs On." Online.

Canadian Federation of Students. 2016.*Time to Think Big: The Case for Free Tuition.* Available online.

Canadian Federation of Students. 2016. Canada's College and University Students Begin National Lobby Week in Anticipation of 2016 Budget. Online.

Card, D., J. Kluve, and A. Weber. 2009. "Active Labor Market Policy Evaluations: A Meta-Analysis." CESifo Working Paper Series No. 2570; Ruhr Economic Paper No. 86. Bonn: Institute for the Study of Labor.

Conference Board of Canada. 2014. "Canadian Organizations Spending More on Staff Training: A Step in the Right Direction." Available online.

Chritoph, Ursule. 2003. "Who Wins, Who Loses: The Real Story of the Transfer of Training to the Provinces and Its Impact on Women," in M.G. Cohen, ed., *Training the Excluded for Work: Access and Equity for Women, Immigrants, First Nations, Youth, and People with Low Income.* Vancouver: UBC Press.

CUPE 2015. *The Canada Job Fund: An Overview of the Federal Transfer to*

Provinces and Territories. Ottawa: Brigid Hayes Consulting for the Canadian Union of Public Employees.

Doern, G. Bruce and Richard Phidd. 1983. *Canadian Public Policy: Ideas, Structure, Process.* Toronto: Methuen.

Employment and Social Development Canada. 2009. "Summative Evaluation of the Canada-Alberta Labour Market Development Agreement: Final Report." Strategic Policy and Research Branch. HSRDC.

Employment and Social Development Canada. 2009b. "Summative Evaluation of Employment Benefits and Support Measures in the Ontario Region." Strategic Policy and Research Branch. HSRDC.

Employment and Social Development Canada. 2012. "Formative Evaluation of Provincial Benefits and Measures Delivered under the Canada-Ontario Labour Market Development Agreement." Strategic Policy/Research Branch. HRSDC.

Employment and Social Development Canada. 2013. "Evaluation of Labour Market Agreements." Strategic Policy and Research Branch. HRSDC.

Employment and Social Development Canada. 2014. "Evaluation of Career Transition Assistance Initiative." Strategic Policy and Research Branch. HRSDC.

Fernandez, Lynne. 2014. "The 2014 Federal Budget: Austerity for the Many—Prosperity for the Few." Ottawa: Canadian Centre for Policy Alternatives.

Friedman, M. 1993. *Capitalism and Freedom.* Chicago: U of Chicago Press

Gault, C. 2014. "Canada's Private Sector Will Have Nobody to Blame for the 'Talent Crisis' But Themselves." *Financial Post*, November 21. Available online.

Goldman, Barbara. 1976. New Directions for Manpower Policy. Montreal: C.D. Howe Research Institute.

Gray, D. 2003. "National v. Regional Financing and Management of Unemployment and Related Benefits: The Case of Canada." No. 14. OECD Publishing.

Government of Canada. 2016. Budget 2016. Ottawa.

Government of Canada. 2013–14. "Statistical Review: Canada Student Loans Program." Available online.

Government of Canada. 2014. "Governments of Canada and Ontario Finalize Agreements to Help Ontarians Get Jobs." Available online.

Grundy, John. 2015. "Statistical Profiling of the Unemployed," *Studies in Political Economy* 96 (Autumn).

Ivanova, Igleka. 2012. *Paid in Full (Update): Who Pays for University Education in BC?* Vancouver: Canadian Centre for Policy Alternatives.

Haddow, R., and T.R. Klassen. 2006. *Partisanship, Globalization, and Canadian Labour Market Policy: Four Provinces in Comparative Perspective.* Toronto: University of Toronto Press.

Haddow, R., Schneider, S., and Klassen, T.R. 2003. *Contrasting Milieus and Common Constraints: The Labour Market Policy-making Capacity of Peripheral Regions in Canada and Germany* Vol. 4. Working Paper Series. Toronto: The Canadian Centre for German and European Studies, York University.

Hale, G. E. 1998. Reforming Employment Insurance: Transcending the Politics of the Status Quo." *Canadian Public Policy/Analyse De Politiques*, 429–51.

HRDC .1994. Agenda: Jobs and Growth: Improving Social Security in Canada: A Discussion Paper. Ottawa: Human Resources Development Canada.

HRDC. 1998. 1998 Employment Insurance Monitoring and Assessment Report Ottawa: Employment Insurance Commission.

Lerman, Robert. 2014. "Expanding Apprenticeship Training in Canada." Canadian Council of Chief Executives.

Lior, Karen and Susan Wismer. 2003. "Still Shopping for Training: Women, Training and Livelihoods," in M.G. Cohen ed., *Training the Excluded for Work: Access and Equity for Women, Immigrants, First Nations, Youth and People with Low Income*. Vancouver: UBC Press.

MacKinnon, Shauna. 2013. "The Canada Jobs Grant: Perpetuating Aboriginal Exclusion." Ottawa: Canadian Centre for Policy Alternatives. Available online.

Marginson, Simon. 1997. *Markets in Education*. Sydney: Allen and Unwin.

McBride, S. and R.A. Williams. 2001. "Globalization, the Restructuring of Labour Markets and Policy Convergence: The OECD 'Jobs Strategy'," *Global Social Policy* 1(3): 281–309.

McBride, Stephen, Kathleen McNutt and Russell Allan Williams. 2008. "Policy Learning? The OECD and Its Jobs Study," in Rianne Mahon and Stephen McBride, eds., *The OECD and Transnational Governance*. Vancouver: UBC Press.

McBride, Stephen and Peter Stoyko. 2000. "Youth and the Social Union: Intergovernmental Relations, Youth Unemployment and School-to-Work Transitions," in Tom McIntosh, ed., *Federalism, Democracy and Labour Market Policy in Canada*. Kingston: SPS/McGill-Queen's University Press.

McNabb, Robert and Keith Whitfield. 1994. "The Market for Training: An Overview," in Robert McNabb and Keith Whitfield, eds., *The Market for Training: International Perspectives on Theory Methodology and Policy*. Aldershot: Avery.

Mendelsohn, Matthew, and Jon Medow. 2010. "Help Wanted: How Well did the EI Program Respond During the Recent Crisis?" Toronto: Mowat Centre, School for Public Policy and Governance, University of Toronto.

Mendelsohn, Matthew. 2014. "Testimony to the House of Commons Standing Committee Human Resources, Skills and Social Development and the Status of Persons with Disabilities" (29 May).

Mendelson, M., and N. Zon. 2013. "The Training Wheels Are Off: A Closer Look at the Canada Job Grant." Toronto: School of Public Policy and Governance, U of T, Mowat Centre, and Caledon Institute of Social Policy.

Milan, Anne. 2016. "Diversity of Young Adults Living with Their Parents." Statistics Canada. June 15. Available online.

Miner, Rick. 2014. "The Great Canadian Skills Mismatch: People Without Jobs, Jobs Without People and MORE." Toronto: Miner Management Consultants.

Munro, D. 2014. "Explaining Employers' Performance on Training and Skills Development." Conference Board of Canada. Available online.

Noël, Alain. 2011. "The Effectiveness of Training for Displaced Workers with Long Prior Job Tenure." Toronto: Mowat Centre, School for Public Policy & Governance, University of Toronto.

OECD. 2012. *Education at a Glance 2012*. Available online.

OECD Statistics. 2014. Available online.

Parliamentary Budget Officer. 2014. *Labour Market Assessment 2014*. Ottawa.

Ryan, Sid. 2013. "Letter to Minister Duguid: Canada Jobs Grant." Toronto: Ontario Federation of Labour.

Parliamentary Budget Officer. 2016. "Federal Spending on Postsecondary Education." Available online.

Schulz, Theodore W. 1961. "Investment in Human Capital." *The American Economic Review* 51(1): 1–17.

Standing, Guy. 1999. *Global Labour Flexibility: Seeking Distributive Justice*. London: Macmillan.

Sharpe, Andrew. 1999. "Apprenticeship in Canada: A Training System under Siege?" Report prepared for the CLFDB National Apprenticeship Committee. Available online.

TD. 2013. *Jobs in Canada: Where, What and For Whom?* Toronto: TD Economics.

Wong, L. and McBride, S. 2003. "Youth Employment Programs in British Columbia: Taking the High Road or the Low Road?," in M.G. Cohen, ed., *Training the Excluded for Work: Access and Equity for Women, Immigrants, First Nations, Youth and People with Low Income*. Vancouver: UBC Press.

Wood, Donna E., and Thomas R. Klassen. 2009. "Bilateral Federalism and Workforce Development Policy in Canada." *Canadian Public Administration* 52.2: 249–70.

Wood, Donna E., and Thomas R. Klassen. 2011. "Improving the Governance of Employment and Training Policy in Canada." Toronto: Mowat Centre, School for Public Policy & Governance, University of Toronto.

Wood, D.E. 2013. "Comparing Employment Policy Governance Regimes in Canada and the European Union." Canadian Public Administration 56(2): 286–303.

5
Supplying the Labour Market through Importing Labour

A Globally Connected Nation and Labour Market

Historically Canada is a settler country. Waves of immigrants mixed with indigenous inhabitants, often displacing them. The settler population has long outnumbered those of indigenous descent. In that sense, Canada is a country predominantly made up of immigrants, even though many of them have been settled here for generations. There have been ebbs and flows in new immigration, but the process itself has been a continuous one. Canada has always been a global state, interconnected economically and socially to the rest of the world. Given that it is largely a nation of immigrants, this global connection is true of much of Canada's population, and therefore also of its labour force.

This chapter explores the relationship between immigration and the supply of labour in Canada. Some basic data sets the scene.

Canada has one of "the highest immigration rates in the western world, admitting approximately 0.8 percent of population annually" (Ferrer, Picot, and Riddell 2012, 1), a figure that translated into around 200,000 to 250,000 per year in the recent past. Moreover, the Trudeau government has announced plans to increase these numbers (see Chart 5) with labour shortages and demographic shortfall being the cited reasons.

Chart 5: Immigration Targets, 2016 to 2017

Economic Total	172,500	160,600	+7.41 percent
Family Total	84,000	80,000	+5 percent
Refugee and Humanitarian	43,500	59,400	-26.77 percent
Target range	280k–320k	280k–305k	+4.92 percent (higher range)
Target	300,000	300,000	No change

Source: cicnews.com/2016/10/immigration-plan-2017-canada-increased-immigrants-through-economic-family-sponsorship-programs-108621.html

Canada's immigration levels in the past half-century are consistently higher than other OECD countries. The National Household Survey estimates the foreign-born population at 6,775,700, representing 20.6 percent of the total population—the largest proportion since the 1931 Census (Statistics Canada 2016), and the highest among the G8 countries (www.statcan.gc.ca/daily-quotidien/130508/dq130508b-eng.pdf).

So it comes as no surprise that Canada has always had an active immigration policy. In the early years following Confederation, Canadian policy could have been defined as "open door"; the federal government maintained offices overseas to actively encourage immigration. The practice was rather more discriminatory than the "open door" designation suggests, however, as people of colour faced obstacles, along with criminals and the infirm. At various times in Canadian history, such obstacles to immigration included persons from "enemy" countries and other categories regarded as undesirable on religious, ideological, racial, or other grounds. Over time, policy became more complex and reflected multiple goals. Initially, with the discriminatory elements noted above, Canadian policy was designed to expand the population in a sparsely populated country as well as to augment its labour force, especially in agriculture. Here, western settlement was an important component of the first National Policy.

In 2011 the Canadian labour force consisted of about 18.7 million persons. In a detailed examination of the composition of the Canadian labour force, Kustec (2012) showed that, "Canadian-born individuals accounted for 14.4 million (77.1 percent) of the total and immigrants accounted for close to 4 million (21.2 percent). The remaining 300,000 individuals (1.7 percent) are non-landed immigrants," a category that included "temporary foreign workers, foreign students, refugee claimants who have valid work permits" (Kustec 2012, 2). Chart 6 shows the composition of the Canadian labour force in 2011. It also divides the 21 percent of the labour force who were immigrants by their date of arrival. In other words, this chart reveals the following spread of labour participants: those who arrived in the previous 5 years amounted to 3 percent of total labour force; in the previous five to ten years, 3 percent; and longer-established immigrants constituted 15 percent of the workforce.

Chart 6: Composition of the Canadian Labour Force, 2011

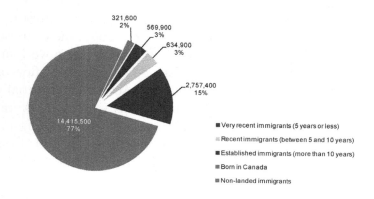

321,600
2%

569,900
3%

634,900
3%

2,757,400
15%

14,415,500
77%

■ Very recent immigrants (5 years or less)
▦ Recent immigrants (between 5 and 10 years)
■ Established immigrants (more than 10 years)
■ Born in Canada
▦ Non-landed immigrants

Source: Kustec 2012, 2.

The next section briefly reviews the development of immigration policy's various goals, including its economic role, and the way these goals have shaped the labour market. I then consider recent policies and programs, followed by contemporary issues in the immigration-labour market nexus. This includes immigrants' labour market experience and performance. Finally, I examine the turn to temporary workers to supplement traditional immigrant categories.

Canadian Immigration Policy in Historical Context

Canada's first National Policy took shape in the years after Confederation (see Eden and Molot 1993). It involved building the railways, a huge initiative with multiple development goals: uniting the country, preventing the annexation of the west by the United States, industrializing central Canada, settling the west for agriculture, and exploiting timber and minerals in the North (see McBride 2001, 36–40). Immigration was a necessary component, given that all these activities were labour intensive. This placed a premium on large numbers of mostly semi-skilled or "unskilled" workers. Thus the main immigration policy goal of the day was to recruit lower-skilled labour (Green and Green 1999, 427).

Other factors besides the imperative to acquire labour power were also at work. These included the idea of "nation-building," with the image of the nation being to establish a European nation—not to say

British nation—in northern North America. Immigration legislation and regulations therefore discriminated on the basis of country of origin and race. Perhaps the most notorious instance was the introduction of a head tax. Scholars have written extensively about the Chinese Immigration Act of 1885, wherein Chinese workers came to work on railway construction (Nijboer 2010, 5). Designed to reduce the flow of Chinese immigration by imposing a head tax, the Act was only partially successful in achieving that objective. The tax was increased several times during the following years, but was often evaded by employers advancing the tax to prospective workers who would then pay it off while working cheaply for employers. But this was not an isolated example. Post-World War I legislation instituted the separation of preferred and non-preferred countries as well as a literacy test for all immigrants. Race was clearly the primary factor in constructing the list. Preferred countries comprised Britain, the United States, the Irish Free State, Newfoundland, Australia, New Zealand, and South Africa (Green and Green 2004, 108).

Within that racial context, immigration policy took into account a concept called absorptive capacity: "the ability of the economy to provide employment for new immigrants at the prevailing nominal wage" (Green and Green 2004, 109). The intention here was to fine-tune immigration volume with the state of the economy. The flow could increase in prosperous times and be reduced or cut off completely in hard times, as it was during parts of the 1930s Great Depression. This approach has not been used in recent recessions such as that of 2007–2008 when immigration levels were maintained, an indication that a broader conception of economic advantage had replaced the earlier and narrower one.

During and after World War II, Canada underwent a partial transformation from a resource-based economy towards a manufacturing one (Green and Green 1999, 430). Informed by Keynesian notions of national economic management and an economy based on strong domestic demand—though always moderated in the Canadian case by continued export dependency—immigration policy aimed to promote population growth as well as to enable certain economies of scale. However, the earlier concepts of absorptive capacity, along with a concern for preserving the racial composition of the population, remained in place until the 1960s. In this period, the "desired immigrant was essentially unskilled, needed to meet growing labour demand in sectors such as mining and forestry" (Ferrer, Picot, and Riddell 2012, 2). There were of course exceptions as with immigration of skilled workers from Europe after World War II.

Within immigration policy there was an ongoing tension between the "long-run benefits (i.e., population growth and economic development), [and] the government's commitment to matching short-run labour market conditions" (Green and Green 1999, 430). At the institutional level each priority found a bureaucratic champion. The Department of Labour advocated using immigration to fill occupational gaps, whereas the Department of Citizenship and Immigration tended to favour a long-run approach (1999, 430).

In formal terms, discrimination in immigration ended in the 1960s. With the introduction of a points system in 1967, selection was based on individual characteristics rather than on nationality. This was an innovation internationally and many countries regarded the system as a "best practice" worthy of emulation (Duncan 2012). The points system comprised an "objective scale based on education, age, [and] language" (Green and Green 1999, 431). Successful applicants were classified as independent applicants, nominated relatives and family class. Green and Green (2004, 120) argued that the introduction of the points system showed the relevance of the economic motive for immigration, since if "immigration policy were a tool exclusively of demographic policy, nation building or foreign policy [...] there would be no need to control the skill composition." More specifically, the points system bought into the short-term view of "immigration as an immediate labour market policy" (Green and Green 2004, 119) given that points allotted to occupations were continually reviewed in relation to the vacancies in the economy.

The Immigration Act of 1976 appeared to downgrade the importance of economic factors. Its expressed goals were "(i) to facilitate the reunion in Canada of Canadian residents with close family members from abroad; (ii) to fulfil Canada's legal obligations with respect to refugees and uphold its humanitarian traditions; add (iii) to foster the development of a strong and viable economy in all regions of Canada" (Green and Green 1999, 432). The order of priorities placed an emphasis on humanitarian goals and family reunification, which implied a shift away from economic needs (Challinor 2011, 2). However, economic factors continued to play a role, as the response to the recession of the early 1980s reduced inflow and included restricting intake of independent applicants to those who had job offers (Green and Green 1999, 432).

By the mid-1980s, declining birth rates and an aging population led to demographic factors taking on greater prominence. Given existing birth rates and levels of immigration, population decline was projected. In that context, "Immigration, as an economic policy, would be used primarily to bolster population growth and to readjust the age structure of the population so that there would be enough workers to pay for the baby boomers' pensions and healthcare" (Green and Green 1999, 434). Sheer numbers, rather than fit with skill shortages or occupational demand, assumed greater importance. In this period, the target for immigration "was dramatically raised from about 85,000 permanent arrivals in 1985 to 250,000 in 1992," indicating no less than a "new philosophy of immigration" (Hiebert 2006, 40).

In evaluating the long history of Canadian immigration policy, Green and Green (2004) draw attention to its mixed motives. In the early years, policy was designed to exclude "undesirable" ethnic, religious, and ideological immigrants. More recently other policy goals have influenced intake: the points system, meeting international obligations towards refugees, and family reunification initiatives undermined this aspect of immigration. As such, immigration policy became less discriminatory. Economic motives loomed large and continue to do so. Long-term goals of stimulating population growth (and consequently a growing domestic economy) contrasted with short-term objectives. These short-term objectives included adapting immigration to particular occupational shortages and cutting the flow of immigrants in times of high unemployment, while being able to increase it in more prosperous times. The former orientation—growing the population irrespective of the state of the business cycle—has been joined in recent years by demographic concerns about maintaining an adequate population in the face of declining fertility rates. Increasing the intake of immigrants in prosperous times may be positive for all sectors of the population, but it is worth noting that it also exerts a general downward pressure on wages. Maintaining high flows in times of recession or slow growth is arguably detrimental to labour and advantageous to business. The impact is particularly felt in the low-wage segment of the labour force, and among recent immigrants as well (see Barass and Shields forthcoming). For them, this adverse experience can have long-term or permanent effects, a phenomenon known as "scarring." Business interests have been privileged given that a continuous flow of new workers places downward pressure on wage costs. We can see this in the retreat from adjusting immigration levels to the "absorptive capacity" of the economy. This suspicion is reinforced by other elements of the immigration policy package: imposing user fees on immigrants for settlement services, restricting and stigmatizing immigrant access to social services in the name of cost control and fiscal austerity, and prioritizing flexible labour market attributes (such as good general level of education, in preference to specific in-demand skills that immigrants may bring). The general educational characteristics preferred in the profile of desirable immigrants fits a preference for human capital that is above all flexible and adaptable—a defining objective of neoliberal labour market policy.

By the 1990s, there were changes in the points system that allotted more significance to "general human capital characteristics, notably education" (Ferrer, Picot, and Riddell 2012, 4; Grady 2009). Ferrer, Picot, and Riddell (2012, 5–6) advance five reasons why occupational imbalances fell out of use in this period:

(1) There was considerable difficulty in obtaining reliable information on occupational imbalances, either in the short or long run; (2) Selecting the number of immigrants desired in each occupation proved to be difficult [...]; (3) It is difficult to adequately respond to regional or localized labour shortages. Many occupational imbalances are unique to a regional labour market [...]; (4) Points assigned to occupation were based on the immigrant's 'intended occupation.' However, there is no requirement that new arrivals work in their intended occupations [...]; (5) The immigration system had difficulty responding quickly. Even if short-term shortages could be identified, it was difficult to bring immigrants quickly to fill them.

Contemporary Classes of Immigrants

According to the Immigration and Refugee Protection Act (IRPA) 2002, permanent residents are defined as "persons who have been admitted to live in Canada on a permanent basis and who have the right to work and study in Canada, but have not become Canadian citizens" (CIC 2014, 11). There are four main classes through which permanent residents are admitted: economic, family, refugee, and "other."

The distribution between them is provided in Chart 7, below. The economic class, of primary interest here, includes "principal applicants" (the individual candidates whose skills are assessed) as well as their spouses/partners and dependents. In 2013, there were 64,765 principal applicants, and 83,416 spouses and dependents admitted through the economic class (CIC 2014, 12).

Chart 7: Canada – Permanent Residents by Category, 1989 to 2014

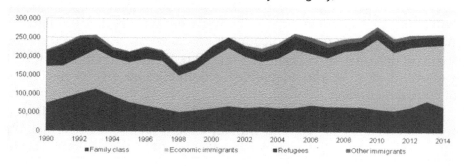

Source: cic.gc.ca/english/resources/statistics/facts2014/permanent/01.asp

Since 1994, the number of immigrants admitted under the economic category has exceeded the other categories combined. Since 2008, it has accounted for at least 60 percent of all immigrants admitted to the country, except in 2013, where it was at 57.2 percent.

Within the Economic Class there are a number of programs that target specific groups of immigrants. Notwithstanding the argument about shifting to general educational/human capital criteria, attention is still paid to the particular skills of immigrants within the economic category. According to Stan Kustec (2012, 14), the Federal Skilled Worker Program "addresses knowledge-based and longer term needs for skilled professionals." However, others have argued that the Provincial Nominee Programs (PNP) and Temporary Foreign Worker Programs (TFWP) represent a shorter-term emphasis on "labour market driven immigration" (Lowe, 2010, 26). The same may be true of the Federal Skilled Trades Program that targets "the kind of workers who are likely to apply as the selection criteria puts more emphasis on practical experience rather than formal education" (CIC 2013a, 10). The PNP is officially described as a program that provides "provinces and territories with a mechanism to respond to their particular economic needs by allowing them to nominate individuals who will meet specific local labour market demands, and to spread the benefits of immigration across Canada by promoting immigration to areas that are not traditional immigrant destinations" (CIC 2014, 13). PNPs are not subject to points systems and their selection criteria varies across provinces. In total, there are around 60 different streams for applicants in PNPs across Canada (CIC 2013a, 11). Many immigrants entering Canada under PNPs "have pre-arranged jobs, and hence the short-term needs of employers are embedded in the selection process" (Ferrer, Picot, and Riddell 2012, 14). Indeed, compared to FSWT, "PNP tends to focus on shorter-term, occupational and specific labour needs identified by a province" (Kustec 2012, 14). The use of PNPs expanded considerably in the 2000s, rising to 7.3 percent of all immigrants by 2013 (CIC 2013b, 7). This represents a certain "privatization" of the immigration process since under PNPs (and the Temporary Foreign Worker [TFW] programs), selection decisions reside increasingly with employers.

There is also the Canadian Experience Class that allows "some skilled categories of TFWs [Temporary Foreign Workers] with Canadian work experience and international students who have a Canadian degree and Canadian work experience" to become permanent residents (Ferrer, Picot, and Riddell 2012, 21). Other programs are directed at Business Immigrants and Live-in Caregivers. The latter is unusual among temporary migrant worker programs in providing a possible pathway to permanent residency for participants. Chart 8 below gives the distribution within the economic category.

Chart 8: Composition of Annual Economic Migration to Canada, by Program, 1996 to 2015

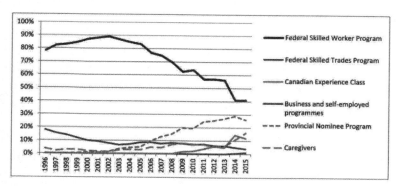

Source: **OECD. 2016 Recruiting for success. Challenges for Canada's Labour Migration System.** Available online.

With the exception of the TFWP—this will be considered in some detail later in the chapter—Canada's other immigration programs tend to emphasize humanitarian factors, such as Family Reunification and Refugees. (These programs do have an economic impact but, being less directly connected to the labour market and employment, are not addressed here. It must be said, though, that in the end most immigrants do enter the labour market—whether formal or informal—and thus contribute economically).

Immigrants in the Labour Market

Immigration policy in Canada has served distinct broad economic purposes over the years. These purposes shift over time, responding to changing circumstances and political imperatives. First, the total volume of immigration can be linked to political criteria. Such criteria include nation-building, particular economic strategies (such as the Keynesian paradigm, in which immigration contributes to aggregate demand), and interpretations of demographic factors (efforts for example to avert population decline for political, social, or economic reasons).

Second, there are two contending interpretations of labour market needs associated with immigration. These interpretations exist side-by-side; however, the emphasis between the two has shifted over time.

The first—and currently predominant—of these interpretations of immigration stresses *general* human capital. Here, the level of education held by a given immigrant is key. A well-educated immigrant will be adaptable and flexible, particularly in the face of a changing economy. Such immigrants will possess the human capital to do well and, in turn, to make valuable contributions to the economy and society. A different outlook contrasts to this human capital model: the specific skill or educational qualification held by economic immigrants should align with identified needs, or skill shortages, within the Canadian labour force. By filling such needs, employment and economic success is virtually guaranteed.

The education and skill levels of immigrants are quite high (Alboim and McIsaac 2007, 3), leading to the expectation that "new permanent residents are well positioned [...] to fill jobs in higher skilled occupations" (Kustec 2012, 12).

However, the economic performance outcomes of immigrants, in comparison to their Canadian-born counterparts, have deteriorated since the 1980s (Ferrer, Picot, and Riddell 2012, 7). The earnings of newly arrived immigrant men fell from 80 percent in 1980 to 60 percent in 1996, compared to Canadian born (Reitz 2005, 3). Employment rates also declined from 86 percent in 1980 for newly arrived immigrant men to 68.3 percent in 1996. (The comparable figures for Canadian-born men were 91 percent and 85.4 percent respectively.) The trends for newly arrived immigrant women were similar (Reitz 2001b, 590–95). Unemployment rates were higher for immigrants as were underemployment rates. According to a 2008 study,

> 42 percent of immigrants aged 25 to 54 were overqualified for their work, holding higher educational qualifications than their jobs required. In contrast, only 28 percent of native-born Canadians were similarly overqualified (Challinor 2011, 11).

It is no surprise that poverty is often the lot for these immigrants (Kustec 2012, 17; see also Shields 2004; and Shields et al 2011). The highest rates of poverty are seen among those from Africa and Asia; the result of this is "a growing disparity between rich and poor is emerging along ethnic and racial lines" (Grady 2009, 31). Immigrants are overrepresented in the precarious workforce (Lewchuk et al 2015) and, like other new entrants such as young people, find it difficult to find employment appropriate to their education and skills.

All this influences the impact of immigration on the labour market, although there is no consensus on what exactly that impact is. Aydemir and Borjas (2006, 2) point out that, in textbook terms, "immigration should lower the wage of competing workers." Their comparative study of Mexico, Canada, and the US found "a numerically sizeable and statistically significant inverse relation between labour supply shocks and wages in each of the countries under study [...] a 10 percent labor supply shift is associated with a 3 to 4 percent opposite-signed change in wages" (2007, 5). There were differences between the countries depending on the composition of immigrants (higher skilled in Canada) but the average effect was similar. However, there are contradictory studies in the literature. Tu (2010, 13) argues that: "substantial immigrant inflows after the policy change in late 1980s [the removal of absorptive capacity concept] did not adversely affect native wage growth rates in the following decade."

Immigrants the world over are often highly skilled and well-educated, so it is surprising to see low earnings, high unemployment and under-employment, and increased poverty among them. This outcome is contradictory to human capital theory, which "suggests that workers' earnings reflect the productive value of their skills [...]. Immigrants' skills have risen to unprecedented levels, yet their earnings have fallen in both relative and absolute terms" (Reitz 2005, 5). In practice many immigrants must take "survival jobs" and/or subsist in the shadow economy (see Gottfried et al 2016)

Why Do Immigrants in General Do Less Well than Human Capital Theory Would Suggest?

One explanation advanced is decreasing returns on education, especially among immigrants (Reitz 2001a). Reitz (2001, 13) finds that the "education premium" for immigrants is roughly half of what it is for the Canadian-born population (2001, 17), although this is challenged by others who detect "little or no evidence in either our male or female samples of declining returns to foreign education" in explaining the deterioration of immigrant earnings in early 1990s (Aydemir and Skuterud 2004, 3). There is disagreement too on how to measure the quality of education among immigrants, whose education levels are usually higher than their source country average. Hence RBC (2011, 4) comes to the conclusion that "without a more targeted measure of educational quality among immigrants, we do not know if this is an important piece of earnings gap." It is probable that lack of Canadian experience and non-recognition of skill or educational credentials attained outside Canada (or countries regarded by Canadian employers as equivalent, like the UK or US) reinforce each other. Job barriers tend to be multiple.

Indeed, the decline of relative immigrant earnings and conditions may be a function of an overall deterioration of labour market conditions for all workers (Kustec 2012, 18), particularly for new entrants to the labour market—foreign-born or not (Aydemir and Skuterud 2004, 1). In the context of the difficult labour market sketched in Chapter 1, any new entrant is going to be disadvantaged. Whether immigration volumes add to these difficulties or are generally beneficial depends largely on one's chosen economic perspective. Here two big economic policy paradigms may agree on the largely positive impact of immigration, though for different reasons. To oversimplify, a Keynesian view might argue that immigrants add aggregate demand to the economy. Alternatively, a neoliberal view suggests that immigrants—like free trade in goods—add competition. In this particular case, the competition is in the labour market, and enables the re-deployment of resources to occur in the most efficient way possible. This enhances productivity and competitiveness within the economy as a whole. As with free trade, there will be losers as adjustment takes place, but compensatory action can help. According to Milanovic (2016), "The first-order effects of free trade are positive, and we deal with the second-order negative effects by compensating the losers (paying unemployment benefits or retraining workers). The same principles should apply to migration." The assumption that free trade is necessarily beneficial is debatable (see McBride 2005, 72–78), but in any case, perceived inadequacy of the remedial measures may lead some to interpret immigration volumes negatively, such that they are seen as lowering wages or living standards. Inadequacy of social support is also detrimental to the immigrant experience. Looking at the general economic context, Hiebert (2006, 44) noted the transformation of the welfare state, leading to diminished social services that are potentially crucial for immigrants' success. While the exact content varies from province to province, arguably "the aggregate system falls well short of what would be needed to settle immigrants effectively," including crucial initiatives like language training (2006, 45).

Why do Immigrants with Skills and Qualifications Struggle to Find Appropriate Employment?

In the past, when physical labour was needed, immigrants could fit easily into the agricultural or industrial economy. The transition to a knowledge economy complicates adaptation and immigrant performance in the labour market. Previously, foreign credential assessment and recognition was less crucial. Today it is. But barriers in the credentialisation process serve "to convert immigrants into complementary labour, which is channeled into jobs that the Canadian-born shun," effectively wasting the skills of immigrants (Hiebert 2006, 44; Reitz, 2001, 7).

Non-recognition of credentials is a crucial problem facing immigrants. Hiebert (2006, 43) identifies a "disjuncture" between the state (which manages immigration policy) and professional associations (which regulate professions). He considers this one factor in the transition to a general human capital approach in immigrant selection. The transition constitutes "an admission of defeat: the State cannot control the credentialisation process so has decided to select Skilled Workers on their adaptability *in general*," instead of "specific fields of study" (2006, 43, emphasis in original). However, that does not solve the immigrants' problem which, in many cases, consists of underemployment when their credentials are not recognized.

Harald Bauder (2003, 699) develops a critical explanation of credential non-recognition, arguing that "professional associations and the state actively exclude immigrant labour from the most highly desired occupations in order to reserve these occupations for Canadian-born and Canadian-educated workers." This would indicate that while official policy became non-discriminatory decades ago, the same is not true of societal attitudes or employers' hiring practices. Compounding the problem is a jurisdictional issue with professional standards and credentials being regulated at the provincial level whilst admission of immigrants, and the human capital criteria used in that process are federal. Racial discrimination has been shown by a "resume-sending experiment," in which "job applicants with English-sounding names are about 40 percent more likely to receive a call back for an interview than applicants with ethnic-sounding names" (RBC 2011, 4). Within this context, Reitz (2005, 12) came to the conclusion that "racial discrimination definitely is one cause of skill under-utilization."

Another crucial element is employers' valuation of Canadian work experience. Lack of such experience "creates a vicious circle for new labour market entrants and leads many highly skilled immigrants to take survival jobs" (Alboim and McIsaac 2007, 4). Studies of immigrant labour market outcomes found similar results indicating that "immigrants receive a smaller earnings premium for work experience, compared to the native-born" (Reitz 2001, 13) and "foreign work experience is not as valued as domestic work experience" (Kustec 2012, 18). Digging deeper, we find that this "has occurred by far most strongly among immigrant men from non-traditional source countries" (Aydemir and Skuterud 2004, 3).

We can list the problems identified here as follows: "employer and regulatory requirements for Canadian work experience, credential recognition, licensing for regulated professionals, lack of labour market language training, lack of customized upgrading and support opportunities, and lack of information overseas and in Canada" (Albo-im and McIsaac 2007, 4), to which racial discrimination needs to be added (Lowe 2010, 25).

Given these problems, RBC (2011, 1) called for "more extensive language training, faster credential recognition, or other integration initiatives. More rigorous evaluation of existing programs would also be helpful in understanding why gaps persist and how we can best address them." In 2005, the federal government introduced the Internation-ally Trained Workers Initiative, part of which was to provide funding "to provinces, territories and stakeholders such as regulatory bodies, educational institutions and the private sector to promote the recogni-tion of foreign credentials for targeted occupations" (Auditor General 2009, 38). In addition, a Foreign Credentials Referral Office was cre-ated within CIC, and became operational in 2007 with the aim of pro-viding "internationally trained and educated individuals with access to integrated, authoritative information about the Canadian labour mar-ket and credential assessment, recognition and licensing processes" (2009, 38). In sum, the federal government launched initiatives by the late 2000s to address problems in credential recognition. However, problems persist; skilled immigrants continue to report major obstacles such as language barriers and requirements for Canadian experience. There remains the suspicion that Canadian experience requirements were "a coded way for employers to favour the Canadian-born" regard-less of credential recognition (Canadian Press 2014). Government's response may have alleviated some of the problems but probably not the core discriminatory factors at work.

Temporary Foreign Workers

For much of Canada's history there has been an assumption that im-migrants coming to work would settle permanently. That is, with some exceptions, migrant workers would become citizens. Essentially the message to those arriving was "come, work hard, and you can become citizens and be part of the nation-building project" (see Shields and Bauder 2015). However, a more recent trend has been to import labour temporarily with no expectation that workers would remain once their services were no longer required.

In post-World War II Europe there had been similar experimentation with so-called "guest-worker programs." Migrant workers were originally intended to provide only temporary labour, allowing "industrialized countries to fill job vacancies with reduced upward pressure on wages and profits" (OECD [cited in Castles 1986, 772]). Typically they were employed in "unskilled, dirty, hard jobs that nobody else wanted to do" (1986, 773). Although the individual workers themselves may have been temporary, they occupied a segment of the workforce that was permanent. Thus migrants rotated through the low-end of the labour market in Western European countries, which "did not integrate immigrants as equals, but as economically disadvantaged and racially discriminated minorities" (Castles 2006, 742–43). With the European economic crisis of 1970s, guest worker programs were terminated (Castles 1986). Later versions of temporary worker programs in the 1990s incorporated a number of restrictions that had been absent in the earlier years. These included labour market tests to ensure that imported labour matched real labour market needs (Ruhs 2006).

Whatever the trends in Europe, in the 2000s Canada steadily expanded its use of a rotating workforce to fill an apparently permanent, and growing segment of work performed in the Canadian economy. Numbers of temporary foreign workers increased especially after a Conservative government replaced the Liberals in 2006 (see Charts 11a and 11b). It has been argued that the Conservative government shifted immigration policy to a very short-term horizon with immediate benefits prioritized over economic benefits that might be realized over a period of years (Root et al 2014).

Origins of Temporary Foreign Worker Programs

Sector or occupation-specific migrant worker programs originated with the Commonwealth Caribbean Agreement in 1966, which allowed Caribbean males to enter Canada for seasonal agricultural work. Later, this program was expanded to include Mexican workers, eventually evolving into the Seasonal Agricultural Worker Program (SAWP). The Foreign Domestic Worker Program was established in 1981, enabling the temporary employment of women, often from Mexico and the Philippines, as domestic workers. This program was also expanded over time and evolved into the Live-In Caregiver Program in 1992; it became the only temporary foreign worker stream allowing caregivers to apply for permanent residency, provided that they worked for two years full-time within the first four years of their entry (CIC Website; Sweetman and Warman 2010, 20).

The TFWP was originally designed to fill short-term scarcity of executives, academics, engineers, and other highly skilled individuals and evolved out of Canada's first formalized migrant worker program, the 1973 Non-Immigrant Employment Authorization Program (NIEAP). It had established a new class of temporary residence tied specifically to non-permanent employment. Thus as early as the 1970s, generalised temporary migrant worker programs began to emerge (Fudge and MacPhail 2009). The NIEAP was "new" in that it provided an overarching frame in which to bring in people temporarily to fill certain, employer-identified "shortages" in the labour force (Sharma 2002).

Over time the NIEAP came to identify distinct streams for highly skilled and low-skilled migrants. Unlike lower skilled migrants, those assessed with high-level skills could bring their dependents to Canada; their partners were also eligible for work visas (Fudge and MacPhail 2009). The 2002 IRPA extended into different categories of migrant workers. A Low-Skilled Pilot Project was initiated in 2002 to facilitate the entry of greater numbers of low-wage temporary foreign workers. The rationale was "that the country was experiencing local shortages of labour that might slow down growth either because of a lack of availability of suitable workers or because of the ensuing rise in wages" (Gross 2010, 107). The great majority of entrants under this project remained temporary notwithstanding provisions under the Provincial Nominee Program (PNP), which allowed employers to nominate low-skill TFWs for permanent status. Relatively few received employer nominations (Elgersma 2007).

Immigration, Refugees and Citizenship Canada (IRCC), formerly Citizenship and Immigration Canada (CIC), and Human Resources and Social Development Canada (HRSDC) both have responsibilities in the functioning of TFWP. Employers need to "demonstrate that recruitment efforts among permanent residents were unsuccessful" (Foster 2012, 25). The HRSDC "investigates the availability of permanent residents to fill the position and whether hiring the foreign worker will be beneficial to permanent residents" (Sweetman and Warman,

2010, 19) and must approve the employer's request in the form of a Labour Market Impact Assessment (LMIA), formerly known as a Labour Market Opinions (LMO). After receiving approval, employers are authorized to recruit foreign workers; the CIC processes work permits.

Not all temporary workers require an LMIA. Workers with temporary immigration status or temporary work authorization can include students, refugee claimants, and those entering under the International Mobility Program (PBO 2015, 1). In fact, in 2012, almost 70 percent of foreign workers were exempt from LMIA requirements (PBO 2015). These workers are admitted to advance the general interest of Canada rather than fill particular jobs. One consequence is that there can be relatively little knowledge about the occupational skill levels of these workers.

Currently the TFWP is divided in to four sections: the TFWP (low-wage and high-wage); the Live-in Caregiver Program, recently changed to the Caregiver Program; and SAWP. Official statistics (see Charts 11a and 11b) show that the number of foreign workers in Canada increased steadily. By including both documented and undocumented workers, the number could be much higher, though estimates of how many may fit into the undocumented category vary considerably (Marsden 2012). In all regions, there was an increase in the share of total employment or work performed by TFWs, but particularly in the western provinces (Gross 2014).

Rationale and Criticisms of the TFW Programs

The basic rationale for the temporary worker programs is that they prevent wages from being driven up in occupations or sectors suffering from temporary labour shortages. Applying market principles would suggest that if the shortfall of workers is longer-term or permanent, then wages and other working conditions should be adjusted upward to attract more workers (PBO 2015, 2, 5). However, if the labour shortage is only short-term there will not be time for market adjustments to occur and an influx of temporary labour will be justified (Gross 2014, 4). Conditions are stipulated to temporary worker programs to ensure that existing workers' conditions are not undermined. These include provisions that there must be a definite job offer, with pay and conditions equivalent to those received by Canadians in the same occupation or sector, employers must show that they tried to recruit or train Canadians for the positions they want to fill, and so on. In addition, after 2002 there were requirements that employers pay return airfares, provide proof of medical insurance, pay into workers' compensation schemes, and provide or assist with accommodation (Gross 2014, 5). These conditions do not apply to all temporary workers. Those entering under trade agreement provisions and some provincial nominee programs, for example, are exempt (PBO 2015, 7). Recent adjustments to policy and programs have facilitated entry by shortening wait times for approval of LMO/LMIAs, and the number entering has increased sharply, suggesting that Canada has faced endemic labour shortages (Gross 2014, 7).

Given the unemployment rate in Canada in this period, it might be more accurate to depict labour shortages as existing at prevailing wage rates and conditions. This is true of the low-skilled sector in particular: "employers may have resisted increasing the compensation package offered to attract domestic workers" (PBO 2015, 15). In other words, in market terms, the jobs are undervalued and the only way they can be filled, short of allowing market pressures to operate, is to increase the pool of those willing to work at those wages and conditions. An additional advantage for employers is that turnover is typically high in such situations, but for workers under LMIAs, leaving their existing employment is not really an option. They are tied to employers for specific periods of up to two years. Some employers are heavily dependent on TFWs.

In 2013, TFWs made up 50 percent or more of the employees in the top 10 percent of all the businesses that hire TFWs (see Chart 9). Here again is evidence that it is not a temporary program for filling acute labour shortages, but rather a permanent source of cheap labour on which businesses are built.

Chart 9: Businesses Built on TFWs: Number of Employers Using TFWs and the Percentage of TFWS in their Workforce in 2013

TFW percent	Number of Employers	Percentage of Employers
All	12,162	100 percent
10percent	6,097	50 percent
30percent	2,578	21 percent
50percent	1,123	9 percent

Source: ESDC 2014/ https://www.canada.ca/en/employment-social-development/services/foreign-workers/reports/overhaul.html?=undefined&wbdisable=true

To the extent that labour shortages in particular occupations and sectors are permanent, TFWPs distort the market; these programs operate to the benefit of employers unwilling or—as a result of poor efficiency—unable to pay wages and provide conditions that would prevail if the market were freer (Foster 2012; Vosko 2014, 452). A House of Commons (2009) report on *Temporary Foreign Workers and Non-Status Workers* found that the "program has changed considerably from its roots as a focused program for rare instances of genuine labour market shortage. Instead, for many participants (employers and workers alike), the temporary foreign worker program has become the faster and preferred way to get immigrants to Canada to meet long-term labour shortages" (2009, 5). The fact that temporary worker migrants now outnumber permanent immigrants heightens the economic emphasis in Canadian immigration policy.

TFWs have a more exclusively economic rationale, whereas permanent immigration is also motivated by humanitarian, family and other social or nation building priorities, where economic implications are sometimes only ancillary consideration (Sweetman and Warman 2010, 21).

With the growth of TFW admissions, there is an "increasing emphasis on (im)migrants as economic units—not nation builders" (Lowe 2010, 26). The government has claimed that the massive influx of low-skilled migrant workers over the past decade or so is just a temporary solution to a booming economy in Western Canada (Foster and Barnetson 2014). However, the "temporary" foreign worker program seems to have become a permanent staple of the Canadian labour market (Foster 2012; Foster and Barnetson 2014, 362). Trends in general Canadian immigration policy reveal a sharp departure from permanent immigration (Goldring and Landolt 2011, 327). This leads to "a two-tier system, with settled residents and citizens and an array of presumably temporary 'others'" (Goldring 2010, 50). The latter have "no pathway leading to formal political participation and . . . they are not considered members of the nation where they live and work" (2010, 53). Within the literature, this phenomenon towards permanent temporary migration is described as the "managed" or "circular" migration of "unfree labour." This type of migration also results in increased numbers of undocumented migrants (see Hannan et al 2016).

There are two additional lines of criticism of these programs. The first considers the impact on the domestic workforce. The second looks at the treatment of TFWs.

The TFWP is said by its proponents to provide a steady supply of low-waged and lower-skilled workers to employers (especially those in agriculture, various restaurant trades, and baby-sitters, nannies and other care-givers employed in the home). The corollary to this argument is that local workers are deprived of employment opportunities at rates and under conditions that market forces indicate would be necessary to fill and retain these positions. Dominique Gross (2014) makes the case that there is little empirical evidence of labour shortages. Her research also suggests that the loosening of TFWP provisions—including allowing employers to pay 15 percent below the relevant median wage, and consequent expansion in the number of temporary workers—led to increasing unemployment rates in some provinces, notably Alberta and British Columbia. Similarly, she noted (18–19) that compared to the United States, fees for Canadian employers to hire temporary workers were set too low to provide any incentive to increase efforts at domestic worker recruitment. In short, there is little evidence that the temporary worker program really does fill bona fide short-term shortages. And a rather more specific argument—albeit a less well-articulated one—that such a program provides a supply of cheap labour to inefficient employers to the detriment of the existing labour force, looms large. To the extent that agricultural employment under the TFWP is genuinely seasonal, it may be an exception to this critique. Yet, as a detailed analysis of the program found,

The labour shortage in agriculture has been couched in terminology of "reliability" and "suitability." There is no shortage of low-skilled Canadian workers, but rather, the shortage is qualitative in that even unemployed Canadians refuse to work in agriculture because of low wages and difficult working conditions (Verma 2003, 6)

These programs also contribute to production of cheap food which historically has been important to controlling the reproduction costs of labour (Shields 1992).

It is true, of course, that TFWs derive benefits from their employment in Canada. Typically their pay is better than that they could obtain in their home countries, or they would not be in Canada in the first place. The remittances they are able to send home are an important source of support for the families they often leave behind. For countries like the Phillipines and Mexico the value of remittances from Canada far exceeds levels of foreign aid (http://cidpnsi.ca/canadas-foreign-aid-2012/). Countries of origin derive significant benefits in terms of contributing to balance of payments and, quite possibly to economic and social stability. But there are also offsetting factors, not least of which are the strains on families as a result of separation.

Here, though, the focus will be on the difficulties encountered by temporary foreign workers in Canada. The incidence of such difficulties casts a cloud on the whole program, or at least on its administration and implementation. In addition to the dubious benefits it confers on inefficient low-wage employers and associated reduction of opportunities for Canadian workers, it exposes many temporary foreign workers to actual or potential abuse and exploitation. Though not all temporary foreign workers are poorly treated, there are enough documented cases to raise major concerns about the program among trade unions, lawyers specializing in the area, and social movements representing migrants.

Most documented problems pertain to temporary migrant workers in the lower waged streams of the TFWP. In 2013 there were 124,216 entrants in the Seasonal Agricultural Worker program, the low-skills, and the temporary care-givers streams, compared to 76,324 in the high-skills streams (CIC 2013).

A list of problems encountered by agricultural workers is provided in Chart 10.

Chart 10: Top 10 Factors that Heighten Vulnerability for migrants in Canadian Agriculture

Top ten factors that heighten vulnerability workers who have entered Canada under the new Pilot Project for Occupations Requiring Lower Levels of Formal Training (referred to as the "NOC C and D Pilot").

1. Migration status and access to health care, which are tied to employers/employment contract

2. Concentration in occupations with high rates of accidents/injury

3. No *independent* reporting mechanism (for health violations/abuse) and appeals process

4. Inadequate rights and protections to enable fair labour representation

5. Inconsistent/inadequate housing guidelines and underregulated housing

6. Social exclusion, poor access to transportation, language barriers, illiteracy

7. No mechanism to assist workers in switching employers or sector-specific work permits

8. No direct path to permanent residency

9. LMO process has no consequences for employer infractions (e.g. health/safety violations)

10. Debts to third-party recruiters/intermediaries

Source: Hennebry 2010, 76.

The Seasonal Agricultural Worker Program is frequently cited as a "best-practice" among temporary foreign worker programs (Hennebry and Preibisch 2010, 8). Yet it has many shortcomings. The program allows employers to "specify the sex and nationality of their employees, a practice in conflict with human rights legislation at the provincial and federal level" (Preibisch 2010, 416). This permits "employers to segment production and divide the workforce on the basis of citizenship, language, gender and nationality," and "creates competition among labour supply countries" (Hennebry and Preibisch 2010, 10). Due to the competition between migrant sending countries, "consular representatives are under pressure to maintain good relations" with employers (Binford, 2009, 510). Given the imbalance of power between migrants and employers, the pressure is on the migrant worker to comply with employer requests and avoid protests or complaints.

More generally the TWFP presents employers with a means of making their workforces more flexible: "low-skilled TFWP represents an extreme version of labor flexibility; it provides employers with a pool of unfree workers who are disposable at will" (Fudge and MacPhail 2009, 43). One reason low-income migrant workers are attractive to employers is their disadvantaged legal status. Canadian citizens and permanent residents are entitled to geographic mobility (they can travel anywhere), access to welfare services, and employment rights (Goldring and Landolt 2011). Workers who arrive in Canada through the low-income workers stream of the TFWP are effectively indentured labourers. This is not an exaggeration. Low-income workers in this pro-

gram are permitted to work only with one employer; their geographic
mobility is limited; they are often forbidden to unionize; they can be let
go by an employer easily; they have very few routes to permanent settlement and enhanced rights; and, in certain situations, they may be paid
below the minimum wage (Barnetson and Foster 2014; Foster 2012,
40). Although covered by employment standards legislation, enforcing
employer compliance is very difficult due to language difficulties, lack
of knowledge of rights, and slow enforcement procedures, all which
mean that temporary workers will often have departed the country
before a resolution of complaints (Choudry and Thomas 2014). Leah
Vosko (2014, 456) observes that "although there is variation in policies
applicable to workers migrating under different entry categories, on
the whole temporary migrant workers lack security of the person and
full access to social benefits and statutory entitlements; many are also
ineligible for most settlement services and prevented from migrating
with their families." Predictably, precarious work and ES violations are
rampant within the TFWP. Jason Foster noted that in Alberta, during
a targeted inspection campaign, 74 percent of employers with TFWs
were found to have breached employment standards, with the most
frequent violations involving illegal deductions, unpaid statutory holiday pay, and inadequate record keeping (Foster 2012, 40). In addition,
the many low-income migrants working within the agricultural sector
are often exempt from employment standards.

Work by Kaity Cooper and Jodie Gauthier (2015), as well as work by
Fay Faraday (2014), document the grim experiences of many temporary foreign workers. Often extended families are dependent on their
remittances, and so by extension dependent on the foreign worker's
good behaviour. Moreover, recruiters will avoid family members and
even whole communities that get a reputation for sending "trouble
makers." Often foreign migrants will have paid big fees ($3000 to
$12,000 according to Faraday 2014, 33) to recruiters to get them the
job, even though such fees may be illegal. They may also have had to
pay airfares—even though employers should be responsible for these—
and they may well be in debt to the recruiter, another factor that en-
forces docile behaviour on the part of the foreign worker. Many lack
language skills and knowledge about the Canadian situation, which
renders them vulnerable to exploitation by both employers and recruiters. For example, lacking knowledge about how to apply for renewal of
permit, many foreign workers end up paying fees that are ten times
above the real cost (Faraday 2014, 41). Frequently they are isolated

from the broader community, either the result of remote locations (as with many agricultural workers) or of being live-in caregivers.

Foreign workers who complain or try to join unions may find themselves blacklisted, as proven in a BC Labour Relations Board involving Mexican workers. Here, the Mexican government and consulate was found to have colluded with employers to block unionists from returning to Canada (Faraday 2014, 44).

2014 Review and Overhaul of the TFWP

Following the 2006 election, the new Conservative government streamlined the process for hiring temporary and low-skilled foreign workers and made it easier for employers to obtain permission. An expedited three- to five-day LMO system was implemented and new job categories such as food workers were added. Requests for foreign workers increased from 150,000 in 2006 to 230,000 in 2007; 85 percent of requests were granted (Fudge and MacPhail 2009). Criticism of these TFWPs mounted, to the point where the federal government imposed a three-month moratorium on LMOs for food preparation workers in 2014 (Stevens 2014). In response to mounting criticism, the federal government set out to re-organize the TFWP in 2014.

In 2013 and 2014 a number of scandals focused on the displacement of domestic workers. Businesses such as McDonald's and the Royal Bank of Canada were accused of (and subsequently apologised for) replacing their domestic workers with foreign ones (Stevens 2014). In the RBC example, Canadian employees were essentially training their successors, who had been admitted to Canada under the TFWP. After training they would return to their home country and the work would be outsourced; this would effectively put the Canadian workers who had trained them out of work. In 2012, a Saskatchewan Tim Horton's franchise faced allegations of human rights violations when TFWs employed in the restaurant were allegedly forced to live in a basement (the basement belonged to the owner's friend), while the franchise owner made illegal payroll deductions. More than 200 cases of exploitation of foreign workers have been investigated by the Saskatchewan Ministry of the Economy (Stevens 2014). TFWs tied to one employer experience a power differential that can lead to exploitive working conditions. If TFWs are unable to leave an abusive position and find another job, or if they are afraid to report an abusive employer for fear of being dismissed, much lower working conditions become acceptable. In a case involving Chinese mining companies, it emerged that the group had advertised for Mandarin speakers—a condition that few Canadian miners would be able to meet. They planned to eventually hire between 1,600 and 2,000 Chinese nationals under the TFW program to work in four BC underground mines. Reporters investigating the case found that some 200 of these had arrived at the time the case broke. Mining union representatives stated that there were many unemployed miners in Canada who were being excluded from the employment opportunity.

Following the increased public and media criticism of the TFWP and the publicised abuses of the program, a major review and overhaul was initiated. The changes include the following: new names for programs and departments; increased LMO costs; a new labour market opinion system; new definitions of TFWs; caps on the percentage of TFWs employed in a single workplace; and a promise to expand inspection and enforcement regimes. HRSDC, now rebranded as Employment and Social Development Canada, and CIC, now Immigration, Refugees and Citizenship Canada (IRCC), had jointly run the TWFP. The TFWP has been split, with the creation of a new program called the International Mobility Program (IMP). The IMP will be run primarily by IRCC and include all TFWs in positions or groups that do not require an LMO. The new TFWP will be run primarily by ESDC and will include those workers requiring LMOs. LMOs have also been reworked into a new system called Labour Market Impact Assessments, here referred to as LMIAs (ESDC 2014).

Chart 11 gives the distribution of workers within the TWFP by program, and includes the numbers of those in the IMP.

Chart 11a TWP and IMP Permit Holders, 2006 to 2015

	2006	2007	2008	2009	2010	2011	2012	2013	2014	2015
Temporary Foreign Workers with LMIA										
Live-in Caregivers	27,368	35,423	39,968	41,707	39,632	36,422	28,373	23,846	23,174	20,466
Agricultural Workers	24,936	29,144	33,575	34,510	35,320	36,636	38,256	41,697	45,281	46,827
Other	57,790	76,438	104,478	115,516	109,783	94,997	99,199	111,788	109,847	87,978
Temporary Foreign Worker Program work permit holders										
Higher-skilled	51,590	61,660	73,355	77,208	73,623	67,205	69,784	76,278	69,929	54,831
Lower-skilled	5,844	14,523	31,543	39,363	38,098	29,875	31,813	38,655	41,002	32,026
Other occupations	624	674	765	780	733	907	956	987	891	2,298
Total unique persons	110,021	140,804	177,601	191,139	184,022	167,304	165,121	176,541	177,704	154,859

Note: "Other Occupations" includes permit holders who hold permits with a not stated occupation and permits with an IRCC synthetic occupation that is not included in ESDC's National Occupational Classification.

Chart 11b: International Mobility Program Work Permit Holders by Program, 2006 to 2015

International Mobility Program Participants	2006	2007	2008	2009	2010	2011	2012	2013	2014	2015
Agreements	26,175	29,532	33,912	36,686	43,516	52,578	59,932	64,079	63,453	62,817
Canadian Interests	119,180	131,880	152,221	177,377	209,175	236,282	268,904	299,863	330,898	334,586
Other International Mobility Program work permit holders	32	27	83	119	114	55	46	36	323	157
Total unique persons	144,621	160,289	184,913	212,935	251,117	286,142	325,323	359,109	390,273	393,372

Source: open.canada.ca/data/en/dataset/052642bb-3fd9-4828-b608-c81df-f7e539c]

LMIAs, it has been argued, act as a more rigorous test of labour market disruption than the previous LMO system. For instance, the vast majority (85 percent) of LMO requests, prior to these changes, provided either a favourable response or a neutral one, in which latter case a TFW could still be hired (Fudge and MacPhail 2009). Short periods for advertising were all that had been required to demonstrate that Canadians were unavailable to fill the position (Hennebry and McLaughlin 2011). The cost for employers to apply for an LMIA per employee was increased from $275 in 2013, to $1000 in 2014 (ATTET 2014). Employers were also required to provide new information when applying for an LMIA, such as the number of Canadians who applied for the job, the number of Canadian applicants the employer interviewed, and an explanation of why those Canadians could not be hired. Employers will also now have to confirm that they are aware of the rules that Canadians cannot be laid-off or have their hours reduced as the result of TFWs (ESDC 2014). New criteria divided TFWs into two categories, low-wage and high-wage, as opposed to previous categories associated with skill level criteria. Low-wage workers are simply defined as earning less than the provincial median wage; high-wage workers are defined as those earning over the provincial median wage (ATTET 2014).

The Conservative government's adjustments to the program following negative publicity may prove short-lived. There are already signs of considerable employer "push-back" from the Canadian Federation of Agriculture. Such push-back includes calls for the expansion of the Seasonal Agriculture Worker Program beyond the traditional areas of tobacco, fruit, and vegetables to include other commodities such as grain, oilseeds, and maple syrup. In addition, they also called for more foreign workers in their food processing operations (Cotter 2016). The Canadian Chamber of Commerce (2016) also launched a detailed critique of the implementation and effects of one of the components of the TFWP, Express Entry, that was aimed at highly skilled personnel. In response, the Liberal government has announced that a parliamentary committee will review the TFWP (Mas 2016). Notwithstanding these criticisms and the review, the Trudeau government moved quickly to simplify the process of recruiting certain types of high skilled worker.s Processing time for visas and work permits is to be cut to 2 weeks, rather than months as previously (Freeman 2016). Other announced or planned changes include further opening doors to permanent residency (pm.gc.ca/eng/minister-immigration-refugee

s-and-citizenship-mandate-letter) and abolition of the "four-in, four-
out" rule, which limited how long TFWs could stay in Canada. After
four years, the worker would have to leave Canada for four years (cbc
ca/news/politics/liberals-scrap-4-in-4-out-rule-for-temporary-foreign
workers-1.3895110).

The government's Advisory Council on Economic Growth (2016
6) has called for easing the restrictions on temporary immigration or
the grounds they were too onerous and time-consuming. Similarly, cit
ing both demographic factors and claimed skill shortages, the Counci
(2016) recommended a 50-percent increase in the number of perma
nent economic migrants (150,000) over the coming five years; this is
a goal that, if achieved, would increase permanent immigration from
300,000 to 450,000 (Advisory Council 2016). This reflects the de
mographic fact that without immigration, the size of the labour force
contracts. Conceding that not all skill gaps could be fixed through im
migration the Council mentioned, but with little detail, the need for
better domestic training and education programs.

Conclusions

From its inception, Canada has been a "settler" country in which newcomers soon came to outnumber the indigenous inhabitants. In addition to its demographic role, immigration, supplemented increasingly
by the use of temporary migrant workers, has and continues to play a
significant role in structuring the labour market. A number of issues
surround the area and contribute to uncertainties and difficulties in
the labour market.

First is a disagreement about the reasons for immigration that has
an impact on the numerical level at which immigration should be set
and the preferred profile of immigrants. Broadly the reasons can be
separated into economic, within which there is a division between
those who emphasize the long-term benefits from population and consequent economic growth. They are less inclined to worry about specific attributes that immigrants bring other than, perhaps, a preference
for adaptability, often seen as being conferred by general educational
rather than specific occupational skills. Others argue that the immigration flow should be turned on and off in response to short-term
economic conditions and should target those in possession of specific
skills needed by Canadian employers. Non-economic motives range

from "nation building," often with racial connotations in the early days, to concerns with humanitarian issues and family re-unification in more recent times.

Second, there are issues surrounding the treatment of immigrants, either at the point of selection, or subsequently once they have entered the country. A number of studies have pointed to non-recognition of overseas qualifications, and overt discrimination as explaining why immigrants' incomes and employment opportunities often fall short of what might be expected on the basis of objective educational criteria or human capital attributes. This situation is particularly acute for temporary migrant workers who are frequently used to boost the size of the pool in the low-wage sectors of the labour market, have few rights, often experience exploitative conditions, and generally do not have the right to apply for permanent status.

References

Advisory Council. 2016. "Attracting the Talent Canada Needs Through Immigration." budget.gc.ca/aceg-ccce/pdf/immigration-eng.pdf

Alboim, Naomi and Elizabeth McIsaac. 2007. Making the Connections: Ottawa's Role in Immigrant Employment. *IRPP Choices* 13(3): 1–24.

AMSSA. 2013. "Info Sheet: Temporary Foreign Workers Program." Affiliation of Multicultural Societies and Service Agencies of BC.

ATTET. 2014. "Changes to the TFWP." Association des travailleuses et travailleurs étrangers temporaires.

Auditor General of Canada. 2009. 2009 Fall Report. www.oag-bvg.gc.ca/internet/English/parl_oag_200911_02_e_33203.html.

Aydemir, Abdurrahman and George J. Borjas. 2007. "Cross Country Variation in the Impact of International Migration: Canada, Mexico, and the United States." *Journal of the European Economic Association* 5(4): 663–708.

Barass, Susan and John Shields. Forthcoming. "Immigration in an Age of Austerity: Morality, the Welfare State and the Shaping of the Ideal Migrant," in Bryan Evans and Stephen McBride, eds., Forthcoming. *Austerity: The Lived Experience.* Toronto: University of Toronto Press.

Basok, Tanya. 2003. "Human Rights and Citizenship: The Case of Mexican Migrants in Canada." Working Paper 72. La Jolla: Center for Comparative Immigration Studies.

Bauder, Harold. 2003. "'Brain Abuse,' or the Devaluation of Immigrant Labour in Canada." Antipode 35(4): 699–717.

Binford, Leigh. 2009. "From Fields of Power to Fields of Sweat: The Dual Process of Constructing Temporary Migrant Labour in Mexico and Canada." *Third World Quarterly* 30(3): 503–17.

Canadian Chamber of Commerce. 2016. *Immigration for a Competitive Canada: Why Highly Skilled International Talent is at Risk.* Ottawa: Chamber of Commerce.

Canadian Press. 2014. "Skilled immigrants face hurdles in finding jobs, government report says." *CBC News* (8 September). Available online.

Castles, Stephen. 1986. "The Guest-Worker in Western Europe: An Obituary." *International Migration Review* 20(4): 761–78.

Castles, Stephen. 2006. "Guestworkers in Europe: A Resurrection?" *International Migration Review* 40(4): 741–66.

Choudry, Aziz and Mark Thomas. 2012. "Organizing Migrant and Immigrant Workers in Canada," In Stephanie Ross and Larry Savage, eds., *Rethinking the Politics of Labour in Canada.* Halifax and Winnipeg: Fernwood.

Challinor, Ashley E. 2011. "Canada's Immigration Policy: A Focus on Human Capital." *Migrationpolicy.org.* Migration Policy Institute. migrationpolicy.org/article/canadas-immigration-policy-focus-human-capital.

CIC. 2012. "Canada Facts and Figures: Immigration Overview: Permanent and Temporary Residents." Ottawa: Citizenship and Immigration Canada.

CIC. 2013. "Canada Facts and Figures: Immigration Overview: Permanent and Temporary Residents." Ottawa: Citizenship and Immigration Canada.

CIC. 2014. "Review and Overhaul of the Temporary Foreign Worker Program. Citizenship and Immigration Canada." cic.gc.ca/english/work/apply-who-permit.asp

Cooper, Kaity and Jodie Gauther. 2015. "Bringing Up BC: The Negative Impacts of the Temporary Foreign Worker Program on Vulnerable Workers and Proposals for Regional Action. Paper presented at the Conference on Temporary Migrant Workers Morgan Centre for Labour Studies, Simon Fraser University, October 8–9, 2015.

Cotter, John. 2016. "Farmers want Ottawa to allow more producers to hire foreign seasonal workers." iPolitics (24 February). Available online.

Duncan, Natasha. 2012. *Immigration Policy Making in the Global Era: In Pursuit of Global Talents.* New York: Palgrave Macmillan.

Eden, Lorraine and Maureen A. Molot. 1993. "Canada's National Policies: Reflections on 125 Years." *Canadian Public Policy* 19(3): 232–51.

Elgersma, Sandra. 2007. "Temporary Foreign Workers." Parliamentary Information and Research Service. Ottawa: Library of Parliament.

ESDC. 2014. "Overhauling the Temporary Foreign Worker Program: Putting Canadians First." Employment and Social Development Canada. canada.ca/en/employment-social-development/services/foreign-workers/reports/overhaul.html?=undefined&wbdisable=true

Faraday, Fay. 2014. *Profiting from the Precarious: How Recruitment Practices Exploit Migrant Workers.* Toronto: Metcalfe Foundation.

Ferrer, Ana M., Garnett Picot and W. Craig Riddell. 2012. "New Directions in Immigration Policy: Canada's Evolving Approach to Immigration Selection."

Canadian Labour Market and Skills Researcher Network. Working Paper No. 107.

Foster Jason. 2012. "Making Temporary Permanent: The Silent Transformation of the Temporary Foreign Worker Program." *Just Labour: A Canadian Journal of Work and Society* 19 (autumn): 22–46.

Foster, Jason and Bob Barnetson. 2014. "The Political Justification of Migrant Workers in Alberta, Canada." *International Migration and Integration* 15(2): 349–70.

Freeman, Sunny. 2016. "Tech Sector celebrates simplified foreign-worker requirements." *The Star* (2 November). Available online.

Fudge, Judy and Fiona MacPhail. 2009. "The Temporary Foreign Worker Program in Canada: Low-Skilled Workers as an Extreme Form of Flexible Labour." *Comparative Labor Law and Policy Journal* 31(5): 101–139.

Grady, Patrick. 2009. "The Impact of Immigration on Canada's Labour Market." *Fraser Forum* 12: 28–32.

Goldring, Luin. 2010. "Temporary Worker Programs as Precarious Status: Implications for Citizenship, Inclusion and Nation Building in Canada." *Canadian Issues/Themes Canadiens*, Spring/printemps: 50–54

Goldring, Luin, and Patricia Landolt. 2011. "Caught in the Work-Citizenship Matrix: The Lasting Effects of Precarious Legal Status on Work for Toronto Immigrants." *Globalizations* 8(3): 325–41.

Gottfried, Keren, John Shields, Nasima Akter, Diane Dyson, Sevgul Topkara-Sarsu, Haweiya Egeh, and Sandra Guerra. 2016. "Paving Their Way and Earning Their Pay: Economic Survival Experiences of Immigrants in East Toronto", Precarious Work and the Struggle for Living Wages – Alternate Routes: A Journal of Critical Social Research 27: 137–161.

Grandea, Nona and Joanna Kerr. 1998. "'Frustrated and displaced': Filipina domestic workers in Canada." *Gender and Development* 6(1): 7–12.

Green, Alan G. and David A. Green. 1999. "The Economic Goals of Canada's Immigration Policy: Past and Present." *Canadian Public Policy/Analyse de Politiques* 25(4): 425–51.

Green, Alan G. and David A. Green. 2004. "The Goals of Canada's Immigration Policy: A Historical Perspective." *Canadian Journal of Urban Research* 13(1): 102–39.

Gross, Dominique. 2014. "Temporary Foreign Workers in Canada: Are They Really Filing Labour Shortages?" C.D. Howe Institute.

Hannan, Charity-Ann, Harald Bauder, and John Shields. 2016. "'Illegalized' Migrant Workers and the Struggle for a Living Wage." *Alternative Routes* 27: 109–136.

Hennebry, Jenna, and Janet McLaughlin. 2011. "Key Issues and Recommendations for Canada's Temporary Foreign Worker Program: Reducing Vulnerabilities and Protecting Rights." Waterloo, ON: International Migration Research Centre.

Hennebry, Jenna. 2010. "Not Just a Few Bad Apples: Vulnerability, Health and Temporary Migration in Canada." *Canadian Issues* 73–77.

Hennebry, Jenna L., and Kerry Preibisch. 2010. "A Model for Managed Migration? Re-Examining Best Practices in Canada's Seasonal Agricultural Worker Program." *International Migration* 50(s1): e19–e40.

Hiebert, Daniel. 2006. "Winning, Losing, and Still Playing the Game: The Political Economy of Immigration in Canada." Tijdschrift voor economische en sociale geografie, 97(1): 38–48.

House of Commons. 2009. *Temporary Foreign Workers and Non-Status Workers: Report of the Standing Committee on Citizenship and Immigration*, 40th Parliament, 2nd Session. Ottawa: Parliament of Canada.

Kustec, Stan. 2012. "The role of migrant labour supply in the Canadian labour market." Paper prepared for Citizenship and Immigration Canada. Research and Evaluation. Available online.

Lewchuk, Wayne, Michelynn Laflèche, Stephanie Procyk, Charlene Cook, Diane Dyson, Luin Goldring, Karen Lior, Alan Meisner, John Shields, Anthony Tambureno and Peter Viducis. 2015. *The Precarity Penalty. The Impact of Employment Precarity on Individuals, Households and Communities and What to Do About It.* Toronto: United Way.

Lowe, Sophia J. 2010. "Rearranging the Deck Chairs? A Critical Examination of Canada's Shifting (Im)Migration Policies." *Canadian Issues* (Spring): 25–28.

Mas, Susana. 2016. "Temporary Foreign Worker Program Review to be Launched by Liberals" cbc.ca/news/politics/temporary-foreign-worker-program-liberals-review-1.3453344

McBride, Stephen. 2001. *Paradigm Shift: Globalization and the Canadian State* Halifax: Fernwood.

McBride, Stephen. 2005. *Paradigm Shift: Globalization and the Canadian State*. Halifax: Fernwood, 2nd edn.

McLaughlin, Janet. 2009. *Trouble in our Fields: Health and Human Rights among Mexican and Caribbean Migrant Farm Workers in Canada.* PhD Diss. University of Toronto.

Marsden, Sarah. 2012. "The New Precariousness: Temporary Migrants and the Law in Canada"*Canadian Journal of Law and Society* 27(2): 209–29.

Milanovic, Branko. 2016. "Migration's Economic Positives and Negatives." *Social Europe* (29 January). Available online.

Nijboer, Harriet. 2010. *Federal-Provincial Relations on Immigration: Striking the Right Balance*. Faculty of Law. University of Toronto.

Preibisch, Kerry. 2010. "Pick-Your-Own Labor: Migrant Workers and Flexibility in Canadian Agriculture." *International Migration Review* 44(2): 404–41.

RBC. 2011. "Immigrant Labour Market Outcomes in Canada: The Benefits of Addressing Wage and Employment Gaps." RBC Economics: Current Analysis. December.

Reitz, Jeffrey. 2001a. "Immigrant Skill Utilization in the Canadian Labour Market: Implications of Human Capital Research." *Journal of International Migration and Integration* 2(3): 347–78.

Reitz, Jeffrey. 2001b. "Immigrant Success in the Knowledge Economy: Institutional Change and the Immigrant Experience in Canada, 1970-1995." *Journal of Social Issues* 57(3): 577–611.

Reitz, Jeffrey. 2005. "Tapping Immigrants' Skills." *IRPP Choices*, 11(1): 1–18.

Root, Jesse, Erika Gates-Gases, John Shields and Harald Bauder. 2014. "Discounting Immigrant Families: Neoliberalism and the Framing of Canadian Immigration Policy Change – A Literature Review." RCIS Working Paper. Ryerson Centre for Immigration and Settlement No. 7 (October).

Ruhs, Martin. 2006. "The Potential of Temporary Migration Programmes in Future International Migration Policy." *International Labour Review* 145 (1-2): 7–36.

Sharma, Nandita. 2001. On Being Not Canadian: The Social Organization of "Migrant Workers," in Canada. *Canadian Review of Sociology/Revue canadienne de sociologie* 38(4), 415–39.

Sharma, Nandita. 2002. "Immigrant and Migrant Workers in Canada: Labour Movements, Racism and the Expansion of Globalization." *Canadian Woman Studies* 21(4): 18–26.

Shields, John. 1992. "The Capitalist State and Farm Labour Policy," in David A. Hay and Gurcharn S. Basran, eds., *Rural Sociology in Canada*. Toronto: Oxford University Press, pp. 246–66.

Shields, John. 2004. "No Safe Haven: Markets, Welfare and Migrants," in Philip Kretsendemas and Ana Aparacio, eds., *Immigrants, Welfare Reform and the Poverty of Policy*. New York: Praeger, pp. 35–60.

Shields, John, Philip Kelley, Stella Park, Nathan Prier and Tony Fang. 2011. "Profiling Immigrant Poverty in Canada: A 2006 Census Statistical Portrait," *Canadian Review of Social Policy Revue canadienne de politique sociale*, (65–66): 92–111.

Shields, John, and Harald Bauder. 2015. "Introduction: Understanding Immigration Settlement and Integration in North America" in Harald Bauder and John Shields, eds., *Immigrant Experiences in North America: Understanding Settlement and Integration*. Toronto: Canadian Scholars Press.

Stanford, Jim. 2000. "Canadian Labour Market Developments in International Context: Flexibility, Regulation and Demand." *Canadian Public Policy* 26: S27–S58.

Statistics Canada. 2016. "150 years of immigration in Canada. Canadian Megatrends." statcan.gc.ca/pub/11-630-x/11-630-x2016006-eng.htm.

Stevens, Andrew. 2014. *Temporary Foreign Workers in Saskatchewan's "Booming" Economy*. Canadian Centre for Policy Alternatives. Saskatchewan Office.

Sweetman, Arthur and Casey Warman. 2010. Canada's Temporary Foreign Workers Programs. *Canadian Issues* (Spring): 19–24.

Tu, Jiong. 2010. *The Impact of Immigration on the Labour Market Outcomes of Native-Born Canadians*. IZA discussion Paper. No. 5129, Bonn.

Vosko, Leah. 2014. "Tenuously Unionized: Temporary Migrant Workers and the Limits of Formal Mechanisms Designed to Promote Collective Bargaining in British Columbia, Canada." *Industrial Law Journal* 43(4): 451–84.

Tilson, David. 2009. "Temporary Foreign Workers and Non-Status Workers: Report of the Standing Committee on Citizenship and Immigration." House of Commons Canada.

Tucker, Eric. 2003. "Diverging trends in worker health and safety protection and participation in Canada, 1985–2000." *Relations Industrielles/Industrial Relations* 395–426.

Valiani, Salimah. 2009. "The Shift in Canadian Immigration Policy and Unheeded Lessons of the Live-in Caregiver Program." ccsl.carleton.ca/~dana/TempPermLCPFINAL.pdf

Valiani, Salimah. 2010. "The Rise of Temporary Migration and Employer-Driven Immigration in Canada: Tracing Policy Shifts of the Late 20th and early 21st centuries." yorku.ca/raps1/events/pdf/Salimah_Valiani.pdf

Verma, Veena. 2003. *Canada's Seasonal Agricultural Workers Program as a Model of Best Practices in Migrant Worker Participation in the Benefits of Economic Globalization* Ottawa: North-South Institute.

6

Supplying the Labour Market by Adjusting Benefits

The supply of labour has an impact on its price. If labour is scarce, other things being equal, then wages will be high, and vice versa. Measures taken by the state, even if enacted for entirely unconnected reasons, can impact the size of the available labour force. For example, most states have enacted limits on child employment, as a means of protecting children from exploitation as well as ensuring that they enjoy a period in which education—rather than employment—is their primary activity. Compulsory schooling, supplemented by a legal framework that governs the ages at which (and conditions under which) children can be employed, tends to keep children out of the labour force. These limits include the minimum age at which children can be employed, or on the number of hours they may work if they are older than the minimum age. Either way, the exclusion of children reduces the size of the potential labour force. Similarly, provisions for mandatory retirement have reduced the number of older people who are working. Mandatory retirement provisions permitted companies to force workers of a certain age (normally 65) out of their labour force and into retirement. Typically, this was also the age of pension eligibility, both as far as state pensions such as the Canada Pension Plan (CPP) and private occupational pension plans were concerned. Individuals thus "retired" might be able to find other jobs, but in an era of a standard employment relationship (SER) (i.e. full-time, full-year employment) followed by pension income, this was uncommon. In recent years, there has been a trend toward the elimination of mandatory retirement (Gomez and Gunderson 2007). Often framed in terms of an individual's right not to suffer discrimination on the basis of age, this new legislation also has collective implications. To the extent that mandatory retirement has been abolished, or pension eligibility modified to apply at a higher age, the size of the potential work force has increased as workers who would formerly have retired retain their jobs, for economic or other reasons.

Some social programs offer the possibility of non-participation in the labour force by making income available through social assistance of various types; this process has often been referred to as the "de-commodification" (of labour). The effect is to reduce the size of the potential labour force and hence of the supply of labour. A variety of mostly provincial social welfare programs provide income and other support to some population groups who are not working—poor people, disabled people, and so on.

The trend in recent years, however, has been for government policy to promote participation in the labour force: in some provinces restrictions on child labour have been eased; in many jurisdictions, mandatory retirement has been abolished; de-commodification opportunities have been reduced (by attaching, for example, stringent job search conditions to some social benefits). Federally, diminished unemployment insurance benefits and coverage are in alignment with these provincial measures.

A constitutional amendment passed in 1940 made unemployment insurance an exclusive responsibility of the federal government. The Employment Insurance (EI) system (first named Unemployment Insurance; below I will use the acronym EI to refer to the system as a whole) was originally based on contributions from employers, employees, and the government in the ratio 40:40:20. From 1990 the government ceased to make a financial contribution. At the beginning of the program in 1940 just over 42 percent of the workforce was covered by the legislation.[1] However, in a process that until 1971 could be characterized as "almost unbroken expansion and liberalization" (Pal 1988, 35), coverage and benefits improved. Workforce coverage expanded to 90 percent following the passage of the 1971 Unemployment Insurance Act; benefit payments increased to 66 2/3 percent of insurable earnings from 40 percent. Average weekly benefit payments were 41 percent of average weekly wages/salaries, compared to 29 percent immediately prior to 1971 (Grubel et al 1975a, 176). Eligibility requirements were relaxed and for the first time, the new program recognized illness, injury, quarantine, pregnancy, and retirement as qualifying reasons for receiving benefits (Unemployment Insurance Commission 1977, A12–A20).

In a reversal of the trend toward expanding EI coverage, since 1971 amendments and changes have generally restricted and tightened the scheme's provisions. In 1995, a federal budget was passed

1 See Pal (1988, 38–41) for a summary.

that set about a fundamental restructuring of the EI system. Some of the retrenchment was the result of the cost of employment insurance. From the mid-1970s, governments became preoccupied with fiscal constraints and anti-inflationary measures in preference to maintaining employment levels. Many social programs suffered from reduced funding as a result. The changes were part of a gradual but broader shift of paradigms, away from the post-war Keynesian approach towards neoliberalism. We can see this process taking place in some of the debates around employment insurance and in changes to the EI system over time.

A Shift in Thinking

The shift in EI from a generous social program in 1971 to a more stringent system that directs the unemployed towards rapid re-integration in the labour market, is a powerful shift towards neoliberalism in political and economic thinking. In the post-war era, there had been a political consensus in Canada that the state had an important role to play in ensuring the well-being of its citizens. This meant providing them with opportunities and protecting them with a social security net, especially in times of hardship. The welfare state at that time was arguably influenced by an ethos of communal social obligation. Following the 1971 Unemployment Insurance Act, the EI system reflected this political ethos most impressively (Lin 1998; Nichols 2012; Osberg 2009). This Act established very high coverage of the labour force and set a relatively high maximum replacement rate of 67 percent for individuals and up to 75 percent for those with dependents (Lin 1998). Moreover, it expanded the definitional scope of employment insurance to include compassionate care, maternity, and sickness benefits (Prince 2009).

Following its highpoint in 1971, the EI system was incrementally reformed and diminished in ways that reflected the growing influence of neoliberalism (Bernhardt 2015; Nichols 2012). In the neoliberal view, each individual became responsible for commodifying his or her labour effectively through investment in human capital. A given person's position within society and the labour market, whatever it may be, then becomes nothing more than the natural result of individual productivity, work ethic and investment in the "right" kind of human capital (McBride 2000). By this definition, most of the people on welfare or EI are seen as deficient in some way. Addressing the deficiencies in their human capital (or reforming their "attitude") becomes a policy priority.

Within this neoliberal context, EI became much less of a social program (Courchene and Allan 2009). It was redesigned not as a universal program for all to fall back on in times of hardship, but as private insurance, available exclusively to those individuals who had paid into the program sufficiently and *earned* the right to draw from it (Courchene and Allan 2009).

The neoliberal turn in politics in Canada included attacks on EI and on other social programs. Such programs were seen as having a negative impact on the labour market. Beginning in the 1970s, EI was increasingly portrayed as overly generous and as incentivizing moral hazard on the part of the recently unemployed (Corak 1993; Nichols 2012; Osberg 2009, 13–14). In this context, moral hazard refers to an individual (i.e., an unemployed person) who—being given some protection from risk—will act differently. That is, EI encourages people to remain unemployed longer than they otherwise would have done without that protection.

Regarding unemployment benefits, Robinson (1986, 119–319) summarized the orthodox position: unemployed workers receiving unemployment benefits can afford to reject jobs and wage rates they might otherwise be forced to accept, thereby inflating the unemployment rate. Paradoxically, it was also argued that a generous EI system increased labour force participation because some individuals would be motivated to get a job given the prospect of qualifying for benefits. Reductions in benefit levels would ease pressure on wage levels, in addition to providing the added bonus of reducing public expenditure. Reduced benefits would lead to falling unemployment, as lower wage levels triggered an increase in employment opportunities. Alternatively—or in addition—such proposals could be presented in moral terms: those on EI were "scroungers" who were "work shy" (cf. Robinson, 447).

Politicians have argued, based on these economic models, that if benefits are too generous, individuals will abuse the system, either by seeking employment purposefully in order to qualify for EI, or by delaying their search for a new job to the final weeks before their claims expired (Corak 1993; Osberg 2009). From this, a new kind of scholarship that we can call the "work disincentive" literature arose, arguing that benefits permitted unemployed workers to turn down what they considered to be unsuitable jobs, waiting instead for better options. This literature provided the theoretical perspective to undermine the system with the claim that it encouraged voluntary unemployment and thus actually increased the unemployment rate.

Does EI Increase Unemployment?

Empirical efforts to demonstrate such an effect were far from conclusive. Rae and Jump (1975) noted that once the impact of the EI program on aggregate demand (and therefore the creation of jobs) was considered, the unemployment-inducing tendency was largely off-set, leaving at most half a percentage point increase. But while the work disincentive arguments may have been inaccurate, they remained politically influential, allowing the state to cut back on benefits. Later evidence (Burtless 1987; Atkinson and Micklewright 1991; Blank 1994; Card and Freeman 1994) confirmed both the influence of the theory and the lack of empirical substantiation. Reviewing the evidence in the context of this literature Altman (2004, 538) noted that conventional economic theory predicted

> that unemployment insurance negatively impacts the economy through its positive effect on market wages and thereby upon average costs and unemployment; through its positive affect upon search unemployment; and through making unemployment more affordable to individuals with a strong leisure preference amongst potential labor force participants and the currently employed. These predictions have not obtained strong, if any, support in the empirical literature. Yet, the theoretical predictions of the conventional wisdom still profoundly influence public policy in part for lack of a viable theoretical alternative.

Leaving aside the question of whether a viable theoretical alternative exists, it is clear that the work disincentive arguments meshed well with the general ideological turn toward a definition of unemployment as an individual rather than a systemic problem. Once the federal government had ended its own contributions to the system, from 1989, it began to draw from surpluses in the EI account for other purposes. These other purposes included the provision of "active" labour market measures, rather than "passive" income support. Especially from the mid-1990s these measures contributed to the federal government's objectives of fiscal restraint and balanced budgets (see Campeau 2005, Chapters 8 and 9 for a detailed account).

EI benefits and services were also criticized for discouraging labour mobility from regions of chronic high unemployment to regions with lower unemployment. Once again, the system was depicted as being too rigid, preventing the proper functioning of the labour market.

The effect of all of these factors led to a redesign of the EI system, restricting access to those applicants who are seen as the most "deserving." It also became less generous, ensuring that those who did qualify would be sufficiently motivated to re-enter the labour market as quickly as possible (Osberg 2009). In essence, the contemporary system is one that is committed to this neoliberal understanding of human behaviour and consequently eschews "public handouts," seeking to re-attach workers to the labour market with all possible haste.

Despite the length of time that EI has been operational in Canada, and the many changes it has undergone, most of the arguments associated with it are familiar and recycled over time. Contemporary debates also reflect older discussions. The essence of classical economics—and, more recently, neoliberal opposition to EI—rests on its interference with the free operation of markets. Giving benefits, or any other program that makes individuals less dependent on the vagaries of the market, improves the bargaining power of labour vis-à-vis capital (Pal 1988, 20), an undesirable result from this perspective. This accounts for business' original caution not only about EI but, indeed, about full-employment per se (Kalecki 1943; Sawyer 1985, Chapter 7).

In ideational terms, all this can be represented (admittedly in oversimplified form) as a conflict between advocates of neoliberalism and supporters of Keynesianism. Business and labour, along with various allies, were the main protagonists in this drama. In the classic Keynesian world, unemployment was the main economic evil to be avoided and monetary and particularly fiscal policies were deployed in the quest for full-employment. Given the probability of fluctuations in economic performance, however, spending on unemployment benefits could play a useful supplementary role as an "automatic stabilizer." To the extent that macroeconomic policies were successful in achieving full-employment, very little money was required for unemployment benefits. If a recession did occur, however, the payment of such benefits could play a significant role in sustaining aggregate demand and assisting an economic recovery (Sherman 1976, 190–91). In later variants of Keynesianism, as it became clear that demand management was failing to ensure full employment, EI could play a useful role by providing financial support while workers adapted to structural changes in the economy. Even during the Keynesian period there were procedures in place to "activate" the unemployed. Claimants were required to undergo counselling interviews and, in some cases, to enroll in training courses. Gonick (1978, 26) reported that the benefit control system set in place by the Commission in the mid-70s established a quota for disqualifications and disentitlements aiming to cut off around 40 percent of potential recipients.

The purpose and functionality of EI changed dramatically in Canada as Keynesianism gave way to neoliberalism as the guiding paradigm. During the 1970s, and early 1980s in particular, EI was aimed at economic stabilization in ways that protected citizens; at some level, it was informed by a sense of social obligation. That said, it was also true that the system was highly gendered in its design, supporting a male-dominated labour force defined by nuclear families with male bread-earners in full-time employment (Macdonald 2009; Nichols 2012). EI provided unemployed workers with the flexibility to find a suitable replacement job closely matched to their expertise and skills by offering near universal coverage, low qualification standards, generous replacement rates and relatively long duration of coverage. Today, qualification is much more stringent, the replacement value is lower, coverage duration is shorter and the process is governed by other requirements that pressure recipients to re-enter the workforce quickly and with much less emphasis placed on their area of expertise, their skills or their preferences for work (Léonard 2013; Mowat Task Force 2011).

The Employment and Immigration Reorganization Act 1977 was an important milestone in the shift from what is often termed "passive" income support to "activation" as a condition for benefits. The Act further integrated EI with labour market policy by authorizing the "developmental" use of EI funds. This involved training allowances for claimants enrolled in approved training courses, participating in special job creation projects, or participating in approved work-sharing arrangements.

The unemployment crisis of the early 1980s made it politically difficult to deny benefits, or to further tighten eligibility or reduce benefit levels. Arguments that all or most unemployment was voluntary felt unconvincing. However, following the easing of the recession and the re-election of the Conservative government in 1988, pressure on the unemployment insurance system intensified. In 1989 Employment Minister Barbara McDougall announced that the government intended to save money by making benefits harder to acquire and harder to keep. Qualifying periods were to be increased, benefit periods reduced, and penalties for those who quit their jobs voluntarily increased. Savings with these measures were estimated to amount to 12 percent of the total unemployment budget; these funds were redirected to training and work experience programs. Public reaction was sharply divided. Businesses were in favour of the changes, while labour, anti-poverty, and women's groups were opposed. Then in June 1989 Finance Minister Michael Wilson announced the government's intention to cease contributing to the unemployment insurance fund at all. This severed the link to general revenues.

Subsequently, in 1993, the Mulroney government introduced Bill C-113; this made EI requirements even more stringent, eliminating anyone who quit his or her job without just cause, was fired for misconduct, or refused to accept suitable employment. Moreover, the Bills introduced between 1993 and 1994 (C-113 and C-17) reduced the maximum replacement rate of EI from further from 60 percent to 55 percent. In 1996, the federal government, now under the Liberals, introduced Bill C-12, the Employment Insurance Act, that replaced the 1971 Unemployment Insurance Act. Part of the new architecture of C-12 was designed to adopt a new "hours-system" that fundamentally altered entry requirements, duration, and level of benefits. The premise of switching from a "weeks worked" to an "hours worked" system was to allow EI to better match up with the changing nature of work in the labour market, which—even in 1996—was increasingly temporary, contingent, and part-time. As a result, a system was designed to count every hour of work, given that many in the labour market would not meet the minimum threshold of 15 hours a week required for a week to be counted within the old "weeks worked" qualifying system. However, the threshold of hours of work required, which varied between 420 and 700 for regular claimants, and 910 hours of work for new workers and re-claimants, was set so high that fewer people qualified for coverage than under the previous "weeks worked" system (Vosko 2011, 7).

The fiscal impact of the cumulative changes in the program can be seen in Chart 12 below.

Chart 12: Public expenditure on EI as % of GDP

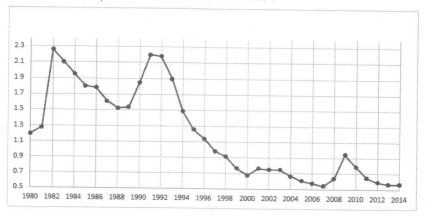

OECD (2017), Public unemployment spending (indicator). doi: 10.1787/55557fd4-en (Accessed on 24 March 2017)

The decline in coverage was dramatic. A study based on Statistics Canada data showed that in 1997 coverage was less than half of what it had been in 1989; that is, it was 36 percent, down from 74 percent (Canadian Labour Congress 1999). Women, whose coverage had declined from 70 percent in 1987 to 31 percent in 1997,[2] and young people—55 percent to 15 percent—were particularly hard hit. An updated version of the study (Canadian Labour Congress 2003) showed slight increases in the ratio of EI beneficiaries to the unemployed but the situation was not dramatically different overall. More recent StatsCan data shows a beneficiaries to unemployment ratio of around 45 percent in 2004, rising to just over 50 percent in 2009, and falling again to just under 40 percent by 2014 (Employment and Social Development Canada 2015).

The capacity of the EI system to act as an automatic stabilizer in times of recession has been diminished. Mendelsohn and Medow (2010, 6) tracked the average percentage of the unemployed receiving benefits in the first 18 months of the recessions of 1981–82 (71 percent); 1990–91 (76 percent); and 2008–2009 (46 percent). Clearly the system functioned differently, and much less effectively by the time of the most recent crisis.

The steps that have brought us to this situation are summarized in Chart 13.

2 The CLC's figures refer only to women on lay-off and do not include those on maternity leave.

Chart 13: Snapshot of Major Reforms to Employment Insurance in Canada, 1971 to 2015

Year and Major Changes to EI	1971	1976–1979	1990	1993–1996	2009–2015
Maximum replacement rate of salary[1]	67 percent	60 percent (1979)	60 percent	55 percent (1994)	55 percent
Minimum number of weeks worked required to qualify for EI	8	10–20	10–20	System changed to count number of hours rather than weeks worked. 420–700 hours or 10.5–18 weeks[2] for new claimants and re-applicants[3]	420–700 hours or 10.5–18 weeks[4] for new claimants. 910 hours or 23.5 weeks[5] for new labour market participants and re-applicants
Maximum duration of EI coverage in weeks	51	50	50	45	45
Percentage of unemployed receiving EI benefits[6]	88 percent	70 percent (1979)	80 percent	48 percent (1996)	38 percent
Number of weeks of EI coverage forfeited based on various penalized actions[7]	3	6	7–12	Ineligible for EI[8]	Ineligible for EI

Notes: 1. For claimants without dependants. 2. Based on a 40-hour work week. The variation in weeks required is the result of regional unemployment levels and number of hours worked in the previous 52 week cycle. 3. Changes enacted in May 1996 became effective 1 January 1997. 4. Ibid. 5. Based on a 40-hour work week. 6. Figures refer to those receiving regular benefits and do not include those on special benefits. 7. For quitting without just cause, dismissal for misconduct or refusal to accept suitable employment, failure to attend a placement interview, or refusal to follow instructions from personnel handling their claims. 8. Zhengxi Lin, 1998. "Employment Insurance in Canada: Recent Trends and Policy Changes," Analytical Studies Research Paper Series: Statistics Canada No. 125: 5.

Sources: David Gray 2006, "Recent Changes to the Employment Insurance Regime: Encouraging Work On-Claim and Off-Claim," Canadian Public Policy 32(1); Service Canada 2015, "Employment Insurance and Regular Benefits" (available online); Mowat Task Force 2011, "Making it Work: Final Recommendations of the Mowat Centre Employment Insurance Task Force" (available online); Scott Cameron and Helen Lao 2014, "Response on the Financing of Employment Insurance and Recent Measures" (Ottawa: Office of the Parliamentary Budget Officer); Zhengxi Lin 1998, "Employment Insurance in Canada: Recent Trends and Policy Changes" (Analytical Studies Research Paper Series: Statistics Canada No. 125). Thanks to Jacob Muirhead for compiling this chart, which is intended to summarize the impact of numerous adjustments, major and minor, to the EI program.

Chart 13 illustrates the trends in EI reform over the years, recording its evolution from a widely available social assistance program in 1971, to a system that currently serves a much-reduced percentage of unemployed Canadians.

Further tightening of the system included Bill C-38, which was introduced in 2012/2013 by the Harper government. This explicitly stipulated that EI applicants must meet an extensive set of job-search criteria in order to be eligible for and maintain EI. Examples of the qualifying requirements include the following (Léonard 2013): recipients must be willing to commute up to an hour for a job offer if it pays anywhere between 70–90 percent of their previous salary; the longer that claimants draw on EI, the more they are expected to accept lower-paying jobs that are not necessarily tied to their original field and may come in as low as 70 percent of the claimant's previous salary (Fitzpatrick 2012); recipients must also demonstrate a sustained effort to secure a job through networking such as by attending job fairs, assessing employment opportunities, developing a resume, submitting job applications, and so forth (Fekete, 2015; Léonard, 2013).

It was estimated that the more stringent requirements of Bill C-38 excluded 8,000 previously funded EI recipients in 2013 and saved the government $32 million (Léonard 2013). This was all taking place as the EI system accrued a $3.6 billion surplus in 2013 (Goar 2013). The provisions of Bill C-38 put downward pressure on wages and pressured skilled workers to take the first job they could find, with very little regard either for that individual's talents and the suitability of a new job (Jackson 2012; Léonard 2013).

As a result of changes to EI over the years, total expenditure on EI has significantly decreased in real terms, even though the population of Canada has increased (Finnie and Irvine 2011; Statistics Canada 2014a). In terms of compensatory generosity of EI over time, Koning and Banting (2013, 590) point out that the average EI recipient received (in constant dollars) around $7,000 in the early 1990s, but only $5,000 in 2007. In addition, far fewer people, both relatively and absolutely, actually qualify for EI today than did in 1991 (Statistics Canada 2014b; Lin 1998).

What has Been the Effect of These Changes to EI?

A recurring criticism in scholarship on this topic is as follows: the current architecture of EI in Canada requires a drastic overhaul to better reflect the Canadian labour market in the twenty-first century (Bernhardt 2015; Mowat Task Force 2011; Osberg 2009; Vosko 2011; Vosko and Clark 2009). Effectively, such an overhaul means reducing the number of hours needed to qualify for benefits.

In particular, even after changes in EI eligibility and qualification rules to reflect hours worked, the numbers seem to be based on an outdated SERs, from the 1960s and 1970s, a time when work was largely full-time and permanent. Certainly, most part-time and contingent workers fail to accumulate enough hours to qualify. We have seen how the SER model of work is increasingly rare as evidenced by a multitude of studies highlighting the growth of precarious employment (Lewchuk et al 2013, 2015; Koning and Banting 2013; Mowat Task Force 2011; Vosko 2011), and this is reflected in the exceptionally low coverage rate of EI in today's Canada.

There is also much criticism of the discriminatory nature of EI, particularly against disadvantaged and/or marginalized populations in Canada. A number of studies, for example, discuss how the EI system discriminates based on gender (Bernhardt 2015; Mowat Task Force 2011; Nichols 2012; Vosko 2011; Vosko, Macdonald and Campbell 2009). Women are over-represented in part-time and temporary work outside of SERs. Despite paying into the EI system, therefore, women find it harder to actually qualify for a claim based on their positions within the labour market. Finally, new entrants and re-claimants need 910 hours of work in the past 52 weeks in order to qualify for EI. Again, given the fact that women are more likely to be working temporarily or part time, it is less likely that they will be able to meet this requirement. Vosko estimated that it would require a part-time new labour market entrant (most likely a woman) 52.3 weeks to qualify for EI based on the 910 hours worked requirement (2011, 7). Moreover, in order to qualify for maternity benefits, an applicant must have worked a flat rate of 600 hours, a difficult threshold for anything other than full-time employment.

Similar points are made with respect to Aboriginal workers, youth, and migrant populations, all groups that are statistically more likely to be working precariously in non-standard employment situations (Koning and Banting 2013; Mowat Task Force 2011). Migrants by definition suffer discrimination based on the number of hours of work required to qualify for EI, given that they are new to the Canadian labour market and unlikely to have completed what is roughly equivalent to 6 months of full-time work (Koning and Banting 2013, 589). This discrimination is a growing issue in Canada, as the number of economic immigrants and TFWs has skyrocketed over the past two decades to close to 600,000 people yearly from barely 100,000 in the 1990s (Rai 2013).

Despite paying into the EI system, migrant workers often do not qualify for EI:

> about 50 percent of temporary workers and almost all international students have a closed permit, which means that they are not allowed to work for more than one employer. They therefore cannot meet the 'available for work' test for unemployment benefits, despite their monthly contributions to the program (Koning and Banting 2013, 591).

In addition, migrants disproportionately end up in urban settings, where unemployment rates are traditionally lower than they are in rural areas. The problem here is that minimum requirements to qualify for EI vary by region and are based partly on regional unemployment rates. The lower the unemployment rate in a region, the higher the threshold for "minimum hours worked" for EI eligibility. As well, in regions where unemployment is low, claimants also receive EI for shorter durations of time (Vosko 2011).

A final criticism relates to the regressive nature of EI (Koning and Banting 2013; Mowat Task Force 2011; Zon 2014). In 2015, EI only covered earnings up to $47,600. Earnings over this set amount are not insured. This means that lower-income workers pay more as a share of their earnings than higher income workers, who do not contribute to EI on any of their income above $47,600. In addition, all part-time and temporary workers are required to pay into EI, despite the fact that many—and particularly marginalized populations—never meet the threshold requirements needed to make a successful claim. The end result is a system in which precarious workers contribute a larger share of their earnings than any other group, but may never qualify to draw from it.

Conclusions

A variety of social programs have an impact on labour-market participation. These programs can either provide opportunities for individuals to subsist outside the labour market, or they can encourage (or coerce) them to participate in it in the absence of alternatives. Where social assistance is more generous (enabling some individuals to be "de-commodified" as far as sale of their labour power is concerned), the size of the potential labour force is decreased, and by extension so is the supply of labour. Other things being equal, this is likely to enable labour-force participants to extract higher wages and better conditions because of the relative scarcity of the labour that they are supplying. However, for many years both provincial social policies and federal employment insurance have emphasized attachment to the labour force and thus have reduced the extent of decommodification possible under the social policy system.

EI in Canada facilitates a labour market in which only a minority of unemployed Canadians can receive unemployment benefits; the system then pressures even these Canadians to take the first job available. For those outside the system entirely, the lack of access often results in membership in a reserve army of cheap labour with few options outside of precarious work. For those still covered by EI, the system has been transformed. In the 1970s, it had been a relatively generous social program that provided opportunities for workers to wait for suitable employment that matched their skill set and previous earnings levels. More recently, it defines unemployment as an individual rather than systemic problem and seeks to push individuals back into the labour market as quickly as possible, with much less attention to suitability of employment. Thus activation and reattachment of the individual to the labour market, whatever its condition, became a priority. The idea of expanding the opportunities available in the labour market (demand-side policies based on the recognition that unemployment was a systemic problem) faded from view.

References

Altman, Morris. 2004. "Why Unemployment Insurance Might Be Good Not Only for the Soul, It Might Also Be Good For the Economy." *Review of Social Economy* 62(4): 517–41

Atkinson, Anthony B. and John Micklewright. 1991. "Unemployment Compensation and Labor Market Transitions." *Journal of Economic Literature* 29: 1679–1727.

Bank of Canada. 2015. Inflation Calculator. Available online.

Bernhardt, Nicole S. 2015. "Racialized Precarious Employment and the Inadequacies of the Canadian Welfare State." *SAGE Open* 5(2): 1–3.

Blank, Rebecca. 1994. "Does a Larger Social Safety Net Mean Less Economic Flexibility?," in Richard B. Freeman (ed.), *Working Under Different Rules*. New York: Russell Sage Foundation: 157–87.

Burtless, Gary. 1987. "Jobless Pay and High European Unemployment," in R.Z. Lawrence and C.L. Schultze, eds., *Barriers to European Growth: A Transatlantic View*. Washington, DC: Brookings Institute, pp. 105–62.

Campeau, Georges. 2005. *From UI to EI: Waging War on the Welfare State.* Vancouver: UBC Press.

Cameron, Scott and Helen Lao. 2014. "Response on the Financing of Employment Insurance and Recent Measures." Ottawa: Office of the Parliamentary Budget Officer.

Canadian Centre for Policy Alternatives. 2014. "EI is Not Actually Helping the Poor." Available online.

Canadian Labour Congress. 1999. *Left Out in the Cold: The End of UI for Canadian Workers.* Ottawa: Canadian Labour Congress.

Canadian Labour Congress. 2003. *Falling Unemployment Insurance Protection for Canada's Unemployed.* Ottawa: Canadian Labour Congress.

Card, David and Richard B. Freeman, eds., 1994. "Small Differences that Matter: Canada vs. the United States," in David Card and Richard B. Freeman, eds., *Working Under Different Rules: Labor Markets and Income Maintenance in Canada and the United States.* New York: Russell Sage: 189–222.

Corak, Miles. 1993. "Is Unemployment Insurance Addictive? Evidence from the Benefit Durations of Repeat Users." *Industrial and Labor Relations Review* 47(1): 62–72.

Courchene, Thomas J., and John R. Allan. 2009. "A Short History of EI, and a Look at the Road Ahead." *Policy Options* 30(8): 19–29.

Employment and Social Development Canada. 2015. Employment Insurance Monitoring and Assessment Report 2014/2015. "Chapter 2. Assisting Canadians during unemployment: Employment Insurance Regular Benefits." Available online.

Fekete, Jason. 2015. "PMO flooded with angry emails over employment insurance changes and OAS." Ottawa Citizen. February 23. Available online.

Finnie, Ross and Ian Irvine. 2011. "The Redistributional Impact of Canada's Employment Insurance Program, 1992–2002." *Canadian Public Policy* 37(2): 201–218.

Fitzpatrick, Meagan. 2012. "Worker's EI History to Affect Claims Under New Rules." *CBC News* (24 May). Available online.

Gomez, Rafael and Morley Gunderson. 2007. "Mandatory Retirement: Myths, Myths and More Damn Myths." Paper presented at the John Deutsch Institute Conference, "Retirement Policy Issues in Canada." October 26–27, 2007 at Queen's University.

Gonick, Cy. 1978. *Out of Work.* Toronto: James Lorimer and Co.

Goar, Carol. 2013. "Jim Flaherty's EI Dilemma." *The Toronto Star* (18 September). Available online.

Gray, David M. 2006. "Recent Changes to the Employment Insurance Regime: Encouraging Work On-Claim and Off-Claim." *Canadian Public Policy* 32(1): 99–110.

Jackson, Andrew. 2012. "The Economics of EI Reform." Behind the Numbers, Ottawa: Canadian Centre for Policy Alternatives. Retrieved from behindthenumbers.ca/2012/05/24/the-economics-of-ei-reform/

Kalecki, Michael. 1943. "Political Aspects of Full-Employment." *Political Quarterly* 14: 322–41.

Koning, Edward A., and Keith G. Banting. 2013. "Inequality Below the Surface: Reviewing Immigrant's Access to and Utilization of Five Canadian Welfare Programs." *Canadian Public Policy* 39(4): 581–601.

Léonard, André. 2013. "Employment Insurance: Ten Changes in 2012-2013." Publication No. 2013-03-E. Ottawa: Library of Parliament.

Lewchuk, Wayne, et al. "It's More than Poverty: Precarious Employment and Household Wellbeing." Reports of the Poverty and Employment Precarity in Southern Ontario Research Group.

Lin, Zhengxi. 1998. "Employment Insurance in Canada: Recent Trends and Changes." *Canadian Tax Journal* 46(1): 58–76.

MacDonald, Martha. 2009. "Income Security for Women: What about Employment Insurance?" In Marjorie Griffin Cohen and Jane Pulkingham, eds., *Public Policy for Women: The State, Income Security, and Labour Market Issues*. Toronto: University of Toronto Press.

MacDonald, Martha. 2009. "Women and EI in Canada: The first decade," in Alexandra Dobrowolsky, ed., *Women & Public Policy in Canada*. Don Mills, ON: Oxford University Press.

McBride, Stephen. 2000. "Policy from What? Neoliberal and Human Capital Theoretical Foundations of Recent Canadian Labour Market Policy," in Mike Burke, Colin Mooers, and John Shields, eds., *Restructuring and Resistance: Canadian Public Policy in an Age of Global Capitalism*. Halifax: Fernwood.

Mendelsohn, Mathew and John Medow. 2010. *Help Wanted: How Well did the EI Program Respond During Recent Recessions?* Toronto: Mowat Centre.

Mowat Task Force. 2011. "Making it Work: Final Recommendations of the Mowat Centre Employment Insurance Task Force." ww.mowateitaskforce.ca

Nichols, Leslie. 2012. "Orloff versus Misra et al: Assessing Feminish Approaches to Gender, the State, and the Transition to Employment Insurance in Canada." *MP: An Online Feminist Journal* 3(6): 172–207.

Osberg, Lars. 2009. "Canada's Declining Social Safety Net: The Case for EI Reform." Toronto: Canadian Centre for Policy Alternatives.

Pal, Leslie. 1988. *State, Class, and Bureaucracy: Canadian Unemployment Insurance and Public Policy*. Kingston/Montreal: McGill-Queen's UP.

Prince, Michael J. 2009. "Supporting Working Canadian Families: The Role of Employment Insurance Special Benefits." Ottawa: Caledon Institute of Social Policy. Retrieved from www.caledoninst.org/Publications/PDF/1047ENG.pdf

Rai, Vikram. 2013. "Labour Market Information for Employers and Economic Immigrants in Canada: A Country Study." Research Report 2013-01. Ottawa: Centre for the Study of Living Standards.

Rea, Samuel and Gregory Jump. 1975. *The Impact of the 1971 Unemployment Insurance Act on Work Incentives and the Aggregate Labour Market*. Ottawa: Unemployment Insurance Commission.

Robinson, Derek. 1986. Monetarism and the Labour Market. Oxford: Clarendon.

Sawyer, M.C. 1985. *The Economics of Michael Kalecki*. London: Macmillan.

Sherman, Howard J. 1976. *Stagflation: A Radical Theory of Unemployment and Inflation*. New York: Harper and Row.

Statistics Canada. 1997. "1996 Census of Canada: Population and Dwelling Counts." Retrieved from statcan.gc.ca/daily-quotidien/970415/dq970415-eng.htm

Statistics Canada. 2014a. "Canada's Population Estimates, Third Quarter, 2014." Retrieved from statcan.gc.ca/daily-quotidien/141217/dq141217d-eng.htm

Statistics Canada. 2014b. "Employment Insurance, December 2014." Retrieved from statcan.gc.ca/daily-quotidien/150219/dq150219a-eng.htm

Townson, Monica and Kevin Hayes. 2007. "Women and the Employment Insurance Program." Ottawa: Canadian Centre for Policy Alternatives.

Unemployment Insurance Commission. 1977. Report on the Comprehensive Review of the Unemployment Insurance Programme in Canada. Ottawa: The Commission.

Vosko, Leah, Martha Macdonald and Iain Campbell, eds. 2009. *Gender and the Contours of Precarious Employment*. London: Routledge

Vosko, Leah. 2011. "The Challenge of Expanding EI Coverage: Charting Exclusions and Partial Exclusions on the Bases of Gender, Immigration Status, Age, and Place of Residence and Exploring Avenues for Inclusive Policy Redesign." Toronto: Mowat Centre for Policy Innovation.

Vosko, Leah and Lisa F. Clark. 2009. "Canada: Gendered Precariousness and Social Reproduction," in Leah Vosko, Martha MacDonald, and Iain Campbell, eds., *Gender and the Contours of Precarious Employment*. New York: Routledge.

Zon, Noah. 2014. "That Federal Budget Surplus? Its Coming from your EI Premiums." Mowat Centre. Available online.

Lin, Zhengxi. 1998. "Employment Insurance in Canada: Recent Trends and Changes." Analytical Studies Branch Research Paper Series No. 125. Ottawa: Statistics Canada.

7

Regulating Employment: Work, Employment, and Basic Income Security

Introduction

For many workers, employment conditions (pay, hours, vacations, benefits) are regulated by union-negotiated collective agreements. Most public-sector workers are covered by such agreements, but public-sector workers are a minority of the total workforce. Of those employed in the private sector, only a small minority—less than 20 percent—are unionized. Conditions for unorganized workers, the majority of the labour force, are governed either by individual contracts or by company policies. Underpinning these arrangements, however, are regulations that establish certain minima (for example, minimum wage and employment standards legislation) or provide for norms and enforcement, as with health and safety legislation. This legislation has a significant impact on life inside the labour market. It provides a degree of work security, through protections governing practices at the workplace, employment security by regulating employer conduct in hiring and firing, and income security, primarily by establishing minimum wage rates.

Two general points can be made at the outset. First, unionized workers, reflecting some degree of collective power, are expected to have higher employment standards than those who are unorganized. Second, employment standards are cast in universalist terms but widespread exemptions and modifications mean that actual minima vary greatly between categories of workers. And even when standards are improving and expanding, governments have always proven sensitive to the wishes of employers, and will avoid expanding such standards too much.

In contrast to the incremental erosion of the unemployment insurance system after 1971, the broad trend in such standards was towards incremental increases in protection through the 1980s and early 1990s. Such legislative and regulatory enhancement rested on concepts of establishing social minima, "a legislative floor below which conditions of employment are not to fall," universal application (though with certain specified exemptions), and notions of fairness. This meant that both workers and employers should be protected – the former from undue exploitation, the latter from unfair competition caused by a race to the bottom on standards and conditions (Vosko et al 2011).

Thereafter, the neoliberal "flexible labour markets" approach eroded employment standards, not to mention undermining the enforcement of those on the books (Lewchuk 2013; Baker et al 2004; Agocs 2002; Cohen and Klein 2008; Fairey 2005; Fudge and Vosko 2001; Lynk 2009; Tucker 2003). Providing a comprehensive account of this process is difficult because the Canadian employment standards regulatory regime consists of multiple sub-regimes divided by subject and jurisdiction. We saw in Chapter 2 that provinces have the bulk of jurisdiction over labour issues; the federal government sets standards only for a narrow range of industries covering roughly 10 percent of the Canadian working population (Bernstein et al 2006). In the discussion that follows, I will provide examples of the general trends that have been drawn from several of the larger provinces as well as from the federal jurisdiction.

In terms of categories used in comparative public policy analysis, Canada typically falls in the "liberal" category. That is, it is a liberal market economy (LME) in the "varieties of capitalism" literature (Hall and Soskice 2003), and a liberal welfare state in social policy (Esping-Andersen 1990). The OECD has created indices for measuring and comparing the degree of protection provided by labour standards, both for standard and for temporary workers (the closest proxy to precarious employment available in their data set). The indices use a variable constructed out of 21 indicators of employment protection, including such items as severance pay, notice of termination, circumstances allowing termination, etc. (OECD 2014). In terms of employment protections for individuals with regular contracts, Canada is far below the OECD average and second only to the USA for being the least protective. For workers with temporary contracts, Canada holds the dubious distinction of being the least protective country in the OECD.

Minimum Wages

Minimum wages in Canada were first introduced to ensure "fair wages" for people employed on public works projects or through government contracts. The *Fair Wages Policy* created a minimum wage for this group in 1900. Later, minimum wage policies of broader applicability were enacted by the provinces, though initially these focused on women workers. Trade unions, to which women were less likely to belong, were considered in a better position to ensure fair wages for men. Gradually, the minimum wage system was extended to cover male workers as well—in Manitoba (1934), Saskatchewan (1934), Alberta (1936), Quebec (1936), and Ontario (1936). PEI was the last province to do so in 1960. Gender and youth differentials existed, though they ended in 1974 and 1995 respectively (Statistics Canada 2013). However, functional equivalents have been implemented in recent years as with BC's so-called "training wage" for new entrants to the labour market in the early 2000s.

Reviewing minimum wage trends across Canada, Ken Battle (2015, 8) concluded that the trend from 1965 to the mid-1970s was for minimum wages to increase in real terms; from then until 1995 to 2005 (varying by province) a long term decline followed, after 2005, by a gradual restoration of its value. In the case of Ontario, the value of the minimum wage was eroded during the 1990s as the Harris government froze the wage for eight years. Expressed in 2015 dollars it fell from $9.95 in 1995 to $8.48 in 2003, before resuming an upward path to $11.06 in 2015, an increase of 30.4 percent since 2003. Yet, even after those increases it stood at only 45.5 percent of average earnings. Comparing the minimum wage to average earnings is one way of benchmarking its adequacy. On this measure, the provinces ranged from a high of 52.5 percent in PEI to a low of 34.9 percent in Alberta. Minimum wages in BC have fluctuated between 43.7 percent of average earnings (1965) through 53.7 percent (1975) to 45.8 percent (2014) (Battle 2015, 23).

Another way of benchmarking Canada's level of minimum wages is through international comparisons with broadly similar countries. Battle (2015, 28) helpfully summarizes the results:

> Canada ranks in the upper one-third internationally in terms of minimum wage rates but in the bottom third when comparing minimum wages to average wages. .... Canada ranks low inter-

nationally when its minimum wage is compared to average earnings. Canada's average minimum wage amounted to 44 percent of the wages of full-year full-time workers in 2013.

There has been much criticism of minimum wages in general on the grounds that they fail to provide an adequate income. New movements calling for a "living wage" have emerged (see McBride and Muirhead 2015) as well as more traditional demands for an enhanced minimum wage of $15 per hour (see Green 2015). These demands are a response to the continued and expanding presence of low-wage sectors, even in jurisdictions that have statutory minimum wages. Typically, minimum wage rates are at levels that consign their recipients to lives around or below the poverty level. Opponents of raising minimum wages often argue that to do so would cause job losses as employers would no longer be able to afford so many workers. David Green's (2015) careful review of the evidence on the minimum wage concluded that the benefits of raising it outweigh the costs. Job losses for (young) adult and adult workers range from insignificant to non-existent, and increased minimum wages could play a useful role in reducing poverty and inequality. The resistance to doing this must flow from low-wage employers who benefit from access to very cheap labour.

The realisation that lower wage rates within the labour market are insufficient to remove people from poverty, even if relatively stable employment can be achieved, has stimulated interest in various forms of guaranteed annual income or universal basic income proposals, designed to provide individuals with a decent income whether they are inside the labour market or not (see Macdonald 2016). The increased public discussion of such options, on both political right and left, and often linked to fears about the future employment impact of automation and computerization, is itself a sign that the labour market is failing to deliver acceptable income outcomes (Yakabuski 2016). In many ways the minimum income proposals, whether emanating from the political left or right, evade the fundamental problem – that under neoliberal capitalism not enough jobs are being generated to offer people full and fulfilling work. This point has been trenchantly expressed by Laura Pennachini (2017):

> the right to a job is primary, superior even to the right to property, and that a worker's relation to his job affects not only what he [sic] has, but his being . . . . So, rather than seeking to construct a "welfare for non-full-employment," absolute priority should be

given to creating jobs by getting rid of the ostracism around the aim of "full and good employment."

Defining Non-Wage Employment Standards

On the basis of the normative principles that informed the policy area until the 1990s, employment standards could be construed as promoting "decent work" that provided adequate income and security for workers. In practice, however, standards fell short of that threshold (Vosko et al 2011).

Employment standards covering hours of work, working time, overtime, overtime pay, split-shifts, meal breaks, and rest periods between shifts are conceptualized as providing a platform to protect workers from exploitation as well as guarantee some semblance of a work-life balance. Designated paid holidays, vacations, maternity, and compassionate care leave can provide workers with time to address family or personal issues while protecting employment (Willow and Schetagne 2011). Other employment standards apply to job security, unfair termination, severance pay, and resignation notice.

Some examples and definitions can be provided that illustrate the scope and limits of employment standards. The 40-hour week and 8-hour day were once considered a "normal" working week, though it did not achieve that status in employment standards legislation. Provinces like Ontario permitted a 48-hour week before overtime had to be paid. The idea of a normal work week has become further diluted as the result of averaging provisions that allow employers the flexibility to impose longer hours in some weeks as long as the average over a specified period remains within the legislated limit. This has been widely depicted as the return of the 60-hour week.

Occupational health and safety standards (OHS) are designed to guarantee safe and healthy working environments for workers. While significant differences between the provinces remain, the overall trend has been towards more "flexible" standards (Tucker 2003; Vosko 2013). What this usually means is a move from a system that is government regulated and monitored to one of self-regulation and individual responsibility for the employer and/or employee to identify and reject unsafe work (Lewchuk 2013).

Workers' compensation covers health care, income replacement, and rehabilitation for workers injured on the job and is funded through insurance premiums paid for by employers and employees (Willow and Schetagne 2011). This system has a long history. In 1910, the Progressive Conservative government appointed Sir William Meredith to conduct a royal commission mandated to evaluate the various compensation systems and make recommendations for Ontario (Storey 2009a, 79). Meredith drafted a "no-fault" act that compensated workers for their injuries, but which prevented workers from suing employers (Storey 2009a, 79–80). Meredith proposed the following five principles: no-fault compensation, collective liability, security of payment/benefits, exclusive jurisdiction, and independent board/administration (King 2014, 37). The Ontario government adopted the act in 1915, known as the Workmen's Compensation Act (WCA). Meredith's report and the five principles he outlined are the foundation upon which the workers' compensation system developed throughout Canada.

Precipitated by social movements of injured workers in Ontario in the late 1960s, major changes to the WCA and increased attention to OHS regulations occurred in the mid-1970s (Storey 2005). To confine our discussion here to the Ontario case, King (2014) identified a number of distinct periods since the 1970s. In the first period—and this came about as a result of the Weiler report—the calculation of benefits for workers was transformed in 1990. This involved a change to how permanently disabled workers received benefits based on a dual award system instead of a fixed monthly pension (King 2014, 55; Storey 2006a, 78). The dual award system meant that the disabled worker would receive a lump sum payment based on a level of impairment, the Non-Economic Loss award (King 2014, 57). The second award, the Future Economic Loss would pay 90% of the difference based on how much workers were earning before and what they could have been capable of earning (King 2014, 57–58).

Later, between 1994 and 1997, King (2014) identified a shift in priorities for the WCA in which it became more amenable toward employers and received greater government oversight (King 2014: 51). The Conservative government of Mike Harris introduced a number of neoliberal, or "recommodifying" reforms, such as the Early and Safe Return to Work and Labour Market Re-entry programs, often forcing workers to return to work before being fully healed (Storey 2006, 87). From 1997 to 2004, the articulated concern with the compensation system focused on the following: unfunded liability threatening the system in the long term; rising costs that were a result of benefits payments and rehabilitation services; and the highly bureaucratized character of the WCA, which fundamentally ignored the actual needs of employers, workers, or the economy (King 2014, 71).

The period from 2005 to 2009 highlighted the failures of the programs introduced in the 1990s (King 2014, 53). The now-renamed Workplace Safety and Insurance Board (WSIB) has continued to draw criticism for failing to meet the needs of injured workers (ibid). The criticisms include the WSIB cutting benefits for injured workers after ignoring advice from the doctors who treated them in favour of its own doctors (who an injured worker may never have met). The result is often penury for those who were injured at work and unable to return (Mojtehedzadeh 2016). There have been allegations that doctors who refused to change their opinions to enable the WSIB to disqualify claimants faced pressures, including termination by consultants employed by WSIB to review claims (Gallant 2016).

Within the employment standards regime, some groups of workers are singled out for *special protection on the grounds of vulnerability*. Thus child labour protections prevent children from being exposed to exploitive and dangerous working conditions and instead encourage them to stay in school. However, in Alberta and BC the policies regulating the employment of children were significantly rolled back in the early 2000s, to the point of being some of the most permissive in the developed world. These are considered by some to be in violation of ILO conventions (Barnetson 2009, 2010; Breslin et al 2008; Luke and Moore 2004; McBride and Irwin 2010).

Other groups of workers are excluded from the protections provided by employment standards legislation. This can either be through occupational exclusions (such as taxi drivers exempted from certain work hours stipulations) or through employment status exclusions (such as newspaper deliverers being classified as self-employed contractors) (Willow and Schetagne 2011). These exclusions vary by province as well as the specific stipulations in employment standards. To identify the specifics quickly becomes complex.

Compliance with employment standards by employers and the enforcement of them by governments vary significantly between jurisdictions and over time. Generally, proactive measures such as routine or random workplace inspections have given way to a "reactive" complaint-driven model in which the onus is on individual workers to enforce employment standards. The model has been criticised because the workers in question are often the least empowered within the labour force. Such a model serves to reduce the protection they receive from nominal rights and standards (Vosko 2013). Workers are unlikely to initiate proceedings against their employers for fear of dismissal. Furthermore, workers frequently are unaware of the rights provided by legislation, allowing for unscrupulous employers to violate standards more easily. This indicates a need for—but also the failure of—a third mode of enforcement which depends on education or supply of information to induce voluntary compliance. Compounding the issue of enforcement, when violations are brought to the level of proceedings and workers win, often the penalties for employers are light, further encouraging workplace standards violations (Thomas 2009; Vosko 2013).

Trends in Quality of Employment Standards in Canadian Jurisdictions

Ontario

In the post-1970s context of falling union density, statutory employment standards were intended to establish a legislative floor below which conditions of employment might not fall (Vosko et al 2011, 2–3). In that context they had the potential to be a primary tool in ensuring some degree of equality between employees and employers in order to protect workers' conditions. The Ontario Employment Standards Act (ESA) governs a variety of employer-employee relations, including pay, documentation and payroll records for employers, and anti-reprisal and anti-discrimination rights for workers. The Act outlines a process for conflict resolution and punitive action, and specifies the roles of affected actors throughout this process.

The Act had become more comprehensive over the several decades preceding 1995. In that year—1995—a Progressive Conservative (PC) government was elected and the area became targeted for greater flexibility for employers. Whatever criticisms might be levelled as to their adequacy, minimum standards initially were set in a normative framework of legislative protection for workers from employer exploitation. After 1995, promotion of "flexibility" in the labour market and for employers became the new norm (LCO 2012). The collateral damage to the worker was greater insecurity. The latter developments were ideologically and interest driven, as the Progressive Conservatives under Premier Mike Harris sought to retrench standards made under the NDP government of 1991–95 and its Liberal and Progressive Conservative predecessors (Thomas 2009). Business interests promoted the same agenda. The reforms generally followed the neoliberal flexibility hypothesis through weakened regulation. The Liberal government of post-2004 partially shifted back to the principles that had informed the earlier regime, but did not fundamentally depart from policies encouraging flexibility (LCO 2012; Haddow and Klassen 2006; Thomas 2009).

A few examples illustrate the trend. In 1991 the NDP government had passed the Wage Protection Act to extend back-wage protection to employees of bankrupt businesses. This was reversed in 1996 under the PC government's Bill 49, which reduced the amount of back-pay workers could seek from two years to six months. Bill 49 also limited the sum payable to $10,000. Furthermore, employees were barred from seeking back-pay through the courts if a complaint was filed through the ESA or if the employee was unionized (Haddow and Klassen 2006).

Working hour limits before 1995 were set to 8 hours per day and 48 hours per week. Overtime pay of time-and-a-half was set for working hours over 48, and the right to refuse overtime was established. In 2000 the PC government amended the ESA by raising permissible working hour limits from 48 to 60 hours per week. If the hours could be averaged to less than 176 over a four-week period no over-time pay would apply (LCO 2012). The effect of the return of the 60 hour week and averaging provisions was a significant reduction in employers' overtime costs and, as a corollary, potential overtime income for employees was reduced (see Thomas 2009, 121–24). The 2000 changes also revoked the need for employers to apply to the Ministry of Labour for permits to exceed working-hour limits. Instead employers could persuade employees to waive several of their working-hour rights through a signed declaration. Given the power imbalance in the workplace, workers could fear dismissal, a reduction in hours, or other negative outcomes from refusing their consent. Other changes to the Act "allowed" employees to waive their rights to blocks of vacation time; permitted 12-hour work days (though 11 hours of off-time per day cointued to be required); 30-minute eating breaks; and time off with pay on public holidays. Earlier 1996 changes also excluded unionized employees from ESA protections. Thus contracts could establish lower standards than those available under the Act.

The Toronto Worker's Action Centre estimated that over one million Ontario employees worked overtime in 2014 and 59 percent of these did not receive overtime pay. Moreover, less than a third of low-income employees (29 percent) were fully covered by the Act's overtime pay provisions, compared to 69 percent of middle-income and 71 percent of higher-income employees. Low-income workers such as residential care workers, farm workers, swimming pool installers, and landscapers are just some of the workers fully excluded from overtime premium pay (WAC 2015, 24). While the term 'employment standards' might imply generally applicable standards, in practice its applicability is highly stratified.

The Liberal government, which came into office in 2003, amended the ESA in some respects. From 2004, for example, Ministry approvals were required to permit workers to work in excess of 48 hours per week, and averaging provisions were changed. In 2009 employment standards provisions were amended to include some basic regulations for temporary workers. These included a requirement that workers be provided the name of the company, the pay, hours, and the nature of the work. Basic holiday pay, severance and termination stipulations were also extended to temporary workers. Certain fees which dissuaded employers from hiring temporary workers permanently were also prohibited under the legislation. However, agencies could still charge employers if the temporary worker was hired permanently within the first six months of a placement (Vosko et al 2011; LCO 2012).

The impact on workers of deficiencies and weaknesses in the ESA is significant. For part-timers, for example, no provision in the legislation guarantees notice of hours, minimum or guaranteed hours, or equal wages and benefits equivalent to full-time workers. This is left to the discretion of employers. The growth of low-wage, part-time, insecure work is the consequence. Employers can discriminate against workers who may do the same work but for fewer hours, creating huge wage gaps between full-timers and other workers (WAC 2015, 28). This leads to enormous stress among workers who find themselves in these types of jobs, many of whom need to take up several of them just to make a living, a task made much more difficult given the unpredictability of scheduling. Similarly, employers maintain excessive rolls of part-timers to keep them "hungry"—not a recipe for efficiency in any meaningful sense (see Unifor 2015). Employers can save money if individuals can be classified as self-employed and working under contract. In particular, employers are not required to pay EI payments, CPP contributions, or WSIB dues under these types of arrangements. Consequently, this type of misclassification is increasingly common, and exceptionally difficult for an underfunded Ministry of Labour to discover (WAC 2015, 29).

Where they have been conducted, proactive investigations in Ontario have uncovered a high incidence of violations of the Ontario ESA. In 2012 the Ministry of Labour conducted a proactive investigation of 105 temporary employment agencies and found 78 (or roughly 74 percent) in violation of the ESA (Ministry of Labour 2013). In 2013 "vulnerable workers" proactive investigations revealed that of the 306 employers investigated, nearly 80 percent were in violation of the Act. The violations included $240,000 of mandated employee pay which was recovered (Ministry of Labour 2014). In the low-wage precarious sector in the GTA a 2011 study found that:

Twenty percent of workers earned less than the minimum wage; 39 percent failed to receive earned overtime pay; 36 percent were fired or laid off without termination pay or notice; 34 percent did not receive vacation pay; 33 percent were owed wages and, of those, only 23 percent were paid after the investigation (LCO 2012).

Similar trends could be observed in the early 1990s with respect to the Occupational Health and Safety regime in Ontario. Initially it became more protective and influenced by labour. Expenditures on workplace health and safety training rose from $42 million in 1990 to $62 million in 1994. With the 1995 election the trend was reversed and the Workplace Health and Safety Agency was disbanded and the responsibility was given to the Workplace Safety and Insurance Board (WSIB). There was little consultation with labour. "Lighter touch" OHS regulations were introduced. These including shortened mandatory OHS training, and OHS funding ebbed considerably. The post-2004 Liberal government did hire more inspectors and initiated some proactive inspections. On balance, however, these measures did not significantly depart from the PC policies (Haddow and Klassen 2006).

Quebec

Quebec is anomalous among Canadian jurisdictions for being more resistant to the flexibility discourse as it applies to employment standards. The province appears to have made progress in strengthening some employment standards. In addition, it sought to do so with an explicit acknowledgement that such a move is necessary to help protect workers and to offset the increasingly rapid growth of precarity within labour markets (Bernstein 2006).

There were some efforts under the jurisdiction of the Quebec Labour Standards Act (LSA) to broaden the definition of the term employee to include some precarious workers (Bernstein 2006, 223–25). Second, the Act adopted anti-discrimination laws relating to employment type. That means it is illegal to pay an employee a lower rate than that paid to a full-time employee for the sole reason that they work fewer hours per week (Bernstein 2006, 225). Third, most exemptions found in other provinces do not apply in Quebec. For example, agricultural workers are not exempt from labour standards in Quebec, as they are in other provinces like Ontario or BC (Bernstein 2006, 227). Indeed, as Bernstein notes, Quebec has continuously sought to expand the scope of the legislation and as of 2002, the LSA provides "no exemptions for firm size and very few for sector of activity or type of employment." Finally, Quebec sought to strengthen, rather than weaken the connections between non-unionized and unionized workers in Quebec. In this respect, Quebec modified the LSA in 1999 to include provisions making it illegal for employers to negotiate individual or collective agreements that fall below the LSA. Thus, the Act represents the legally determined minimum labour standards to which a worker is entitled without exception (Bernstein 2006, 227). Furthermore, the Ministry in Quebec allows complaints from third parties, including unions, to be made on behalf of employees, and does not require employees to confront their employers directly with a complaint before bringing up their claim with the Ministry.

There are still problems with the LSA. Improvements in the minimum labour standards was coincidental with weakening the collective agreement decree system that provided a number of low-wage industries with a form of collective agreement coverage, indicating an attempt to address employers' demands (see Grant 2004). Also, employers can evade the Act by demanding that employees under contract incorporate themselves in such a way as to solidify their status as independent contractors. This status relieves employers of many responsibilities outlined in the LSA. Moreover, temporary employment agencies are not heavily regulated and, as a result, employers are able to take advantage of an employment triangle between employer, temporary agency and employee. Finally, although the Ministry does conduct proactive inspections, these inspections cover only a small percentage of employers and employees in Quebec. Consequently, Quebec's system is more individualized, reactive, and complaints-driven than it perhaps appears to be on paper (Bernstein 2006, 233–39).

British Columbia

When the NDP won office in 1991 employment standards legislation had not been altered in a decade. Between 1995–2001 workers in BC came to enjoy some of the most employee-friendly and progressive employment standards in Canada. The changes followed the recommendations of a yearlong independent review and consultation process conducted in 1994 by a well-known and respected UBC business professor Mark Thompson (Thompson 1994).

Thompson was familiar with debates around precarious work and the dissolution of the standard employment relationship and his recommendations were based on an explicit acknowledgement of the reality behind these debates. His report acknowledged the potential dangers of maintaining a model of employment standards that allowed for a number of exemptions to be made depending on the sector of employment and employment status of the individual. Indeed, the ESA adopted in 1995 established a relatively universal system that eliminated many exemptions for things like the minimum wage, hours of work, overtime averaging, severance or termination, vacation time and holiday pay. There was an effort to ensure that the same standards applied to all workers, whether they were employed full-time, part-time or temporarily, and regardless of sector. These changes were recommended by Thompson with the clear acknowledgment that employment standards should have very few loopholes, given the fact that they were becoming the main source of protection for an increasingly large share of BC's labour force. The legislation extended the employment standards floor to unionized workers (collective bargaining agreements had now to "meet or beat" the ESA), and strengthened the enforcement of regulations. The minimum wage was increased from $5 in 1990 to $7 by 1995, and the youth differential wage was abolished, though the government reneged on a commitment to index the minimum wage to inflation.

These changes to the ESA were quickly and decisively reversed with the election of the Liberal government in May 2001 and with the implementation of flexible labour policies (Haddow and Klassen 2006). The Liberals had run on an exceptionally neoliberal platform (Cohen and Klein 2011, 60; Fairey 2007). During the campaign, the Liberal party relied heavily on a discourse of flexibility with respect to labour market reform and made this discourse one of the central components of its platform. The Liberals promised to enact significant changes to labour regulation in BC that would make worker-employer relations more flexible in the belief that it would make the province more globally competitive (McBride and McNutt 2007).

The language of flexibility attempted to put a positive spin on changes in the labour market. For other observers these were the very changes that had placed many workers in precarious and insecure conditions of employment where work is temporary, low-paying, unpredictable, without benefits, and where employees have had to come to terms with fewer legislative protections against employer mistreatment (Thomas 2009, 13–16).

The idea that employment standards in BC lacked flexibility prior to the Liberals' electoral victory is debatable. Mark Thompson (June 15, 1998, C3) was a vocal critic of that position and argued that the ESA he helped to create in 1995 was among the most competitive in North America regarding flexibility to negotiate hours of work, working on statutory holidays, as well as banking and averaging overtime hours. Marjorie Griffin Cohen (2013) noted that despite arguments advanced by the Liberal Party connecting reform of employment standards to BC's global competitiveness, many of the changes made between 2002–2004 affected sectors of the economy that did not face global competition.

In total, between 2002 and 2005, 42 changes were made to the ESA, with 34 being assessed as damaging to worker protections and only seven assessed as positive. Dismantling enforcement and monitoring of employment standards can be seen in the 2003–2004 statistics which showed a 46 percent year-over-year reduction in the number of employment standard complaints (Fairey 2005). The current ESA states that if collective agreements make reference to stipulations outlined within the Act they are excluded from those provisions, and the contents of the collective agreement take precedence. David Fairey (2009, 112–13) notes that this:

> enables parties to a collective agreement to "opt out" of the law, and misleads unionized workers into thinking that they have all the rights that the Act provides, when in fact they may not, because their union failed to ensure that all provisions of the Act are minimally contained in their collective agreement.

The legislation has the potential to open up a "race to the bottom" with respect to employment standards found in collective agreements by opening the door for corrupt arrangements between employers and "pseudo unions." Fairey argues that this is precisely what has happened in BC, where pseudo-unions, or employer-friendly unions (Fairey uses both terms) have commonly conceded to employers' substandard provisions relative to core parts of the ESA (Fairey 2009, 128). In addition, freezing the minimum wage at $8 for a decade allowed it to be eroded by inflation, moving BC's minimum wage from the highest in the country to the lowest. The $6 "training" wage remained in place for 10 years before it was finally abolished in 2011 (Fairey and Cohen 2013).

In BC, then, government policy and budget changes in the early 2000s drastically rolled back employment standards and the government's ability to proactively monitor remaining standards. Beginning in 2003, in order to reduce "red-tape" and roll-back involvement of government in labour market regulation, the Liberal government in BC cut the employment standards branch staffing by 33 percent, enforcement officer staff by 47 percent and closed nearly 50 percent of Employment Standards Branch offices, reducing their number from 17 to 9 (Fairey and Cohen 2013).

The "training wage" for inexperienced workers—a $6 minimum "training" wage for the first 500 hours of employment—was not explicitly age-based but was in fact a veiled return of the youth differential, and the exclusion of unionized workers from the provisions of the ESA (repealing "meet or beat" provisions), exemplify the significantly weakened labour standards in BC (Fairey 2005; Haddow and Klassen 2006). Other significant changes included allowing the minimum wage to atrophy; or, making it the lowest in the country, the reduction in the working age to 12 (possibly contravening the ILO convention on child labour), and the reduction in the length of a minimum shift to two hours (Cohen and Klein 2012; Fairey 2005). Furthermore the regulations on the work children could undertake were relaxed, including prohibitions on some types of dangerous work (e.g. using power tools) (Luke and Moore 2004; McBride and Irwin 2010). Collective bargaining rights were also reduced by making both unionization and collective bargaining a more difficult process (Tucker 2003; Lynk 2009).

The changes had real impact on the conditions of working life. For example, overtime averaging allowed employers to schedule employees for 12-hour days for up to one week or 10-hour days for up to 16 days without ever having to pay employees overtime (Fairey and Cohen 2013). In the previous iteration of the Act, 12-hour days exceeding three consecutive days or 10-hour days for five consecutive days would trigger overtime pay. Marjorie Griffin Cohen (2013) argues that changes to the Act created some of the most exploitative and weakest employment standards regulating youth employment among all OECD countries. BC has normalized the regulation of the youngest work start age in North America and has some of the most lax youth employment laws in the industrialized world (Cohen and Klein 2011, 69).

Declining employment standards have been linked to increased labour market precarity and poverty in BC. Although BC experienced steady economic growth and low unemployment between 2000 and 2008, it simultaneously suffered from growing economic insecurity and inequality, rising homelessness, declining real wages and increasing precarity in the workplace (Cohen and Klein, 60–61). MacPhail and Bowles (2008) examined the impact of policies designed to increase labour market "flexibility" by analysing government changes to employment standards, the Labour Relations Code, education and training, child-care policy and social assistance over a period between 1997–2004 (Macphail and Bowles 2008, 550). Their statistical analysis revealed that after controlling for a set of supply and demand side factors, the odds of being a temporary worker in BC after 2001, when the Liberal Party took power, were substantially higher for both men and women (14.0 and 17.4 percent respectively). Furthermore, the odds of being a temporary worker after 2000 increased more in BC, compared to Canada as whole and more than for each province separately. They found strong evidence of a "BC effect" induced by policy changes, including modifications to employment standards that directly impacted the level of precarity of workers in BC.

Similarly, Andrew Longhurst (2014) noted that temporary employment, which includes contract, seasonal, casual, and agency work, and is closely related to precarious employment, is on the rise in BC. Longhurst attributes a great deal of this growth in temporary employment to the massive expansion of the temporary employment agency sector, which grew by nearly 125 percent over the previous decade, and became a multi-billion dollar industry. Longhurst's account of the explosion of temporary agency employment in BC is related to a total lack of regulatory presence on the part of employment standard enforcement officers, as well as an exceptionally weak ESA (Longhurst 2014, 26–28). He contends that employers and temporary employment agencies frequently evade the Act's provisions on minimum wages, hours worked, payment for transportation for workers and even the requirement for all temporary employment agencies in the province to register for a license from the Employment Standards Branch (27). By using temporary labour agencies, employers are able to violate the Act with impunity. Precarious and often highly indebted temporary agency employees are unwilling to lodge complaints for fear of reprisal. And there is a near-complete lack of proactive monitoring or enforcement of the Act by the underfunded Employment Standards Branch (Longhurst 2014, 35).

Alberta

Alberta probably has the weakest and least enforced labour standards out of all the large Canadian provinces. Shelby (2001) describes the Albertan employment standards as "loose codes of employer conduct rather than inherent rights." These standards have been relatively stable, owing to factors such as the political dominance of the Alberta PCs and a political culture friendly to neoliberalism (Haddow and Klassen 2006). In the 2000s, OHS regulations and child labour laws underwent substantive changes in the direction of neoliberal flexibility. For example, in 2005, the province deregulated employment standards for youth in a manner that closely mirrored legislative changes made in BC in 2003. The reforms included decreasing the minimum legal working age from 15 to 12 years old, and also transferring responsibility for assessment and supervision of employers who hired these youth from employment standards officers onto parents (Shultz and Taylor 2006, 432).

OHS protections in Alberta have ebbed and flowed. Before the election of the neoliberal Klein government in 1993 Albertan workers had seen some success in strengthening health and safety protection. In 1980, OHS inspectors' powers had been expanded, and in 1988 penalties were increased tenfold with a maximum fine for employers who violated OHS of up to $150,000 for the first offence and $300,000 for second offences However, after 1993 these gains were reversed with the implementation of the 'Partnership' self-regulatory/voluntary OHS approach. This moved the Department of Labour from a proactive regulatory role to a passive consultation role focusing on voluntary compliance. Consistent with this approach government OHS expenditures (adjusted for inflation) fell over the 1990s. Prosecutions fell from 42 in 1988 to just two in 1998. In 2002, Bill 37 brought some progress with maximum penalties being raised, a degree of worker representation was implemented, and inspections rose fivefold, though recent gains must be viewed in the context of the massive retrenchment undertaken in the 1990s (Tucker 2003). Alberta is the only jurisdiction in Canada without joint health and safety committees (AFL 2011). In 2015 Alberta elected its first NDP government. Since the election some increases in minimum wages have been implemented and the wage is projected to rise to $15 per hour by 2018. In addition, legislation was enacted to provide mandatory insurance and compensation for paid agricultural workers as well as the application of health and safety standards while workers are on site.

Federal Jurisdiction

The 1965 *Canada Labour Code* (Part III) regulated working hours, minimum wages, statutory holidays, parental leave, and employment termination for workers in the federal jurisdiction. Roughly 12,000 enterprises with approximately 840,000 employees fell under the federal jurisdiction (Arthurs 2006). Employees of the federal jurisdiction are divided between: the postal and pipelines (14 percent); airlines (12 percent); broadcasting and telecommunications (18 percent); transportation (12 percent); and banking (30 percent) sectors (Chaykowski and Slotsve 2007).

Part III of the Canada Labour Code was amended in the 1990s and in 2012. Generally the federal jurisdictional labour standards have been weaker than Canada's provincial standards (Arthurs 2006). This was especially true after the 1990s when the federal Liberal government weakened employment standards to promote labour market "flexibility" in an effort to stimulate the private sector according to neoliberal economic ideology (Agocs 2002). In 2012 several changes were made to Part III, including a complaint based mechanism and six month time limits on unpaid wages.

Enforcement

Enforcement of employment standards has generally deteriorated over the past 20 years. Enforcement has become individualized in the sense that individual complainants are now responsible for taking the initiative and confronting employers about alleged violations before they approach government agencies about their complaints.

Government enforcement agencies have also experienced deep budget and staff cuts that undermine their capacity to investigate and address abuses.

Ontario

In Ontario, between 1997 and 2007 the number of workers covered by the ESA rose 24 percent while funding for programs decreased by 33 percent (LCO 2012). The enforcement branch of the Ministry of Labour had its resources cut by one quarter and its staff by one eighth from 1997 to 2001 (Haddow and Klassen 2006).

The Liberals in 2010 introduced the Open for Business Act (OBA) which streamlined the ESA enforcement procedures to move quickly through the 14,000 case backlog. This act focused on making enforcement more "efficient" and was criticized as a departure from principles underpinning the ESA (LCO 2012).

The OBA requires employees to try to remedy violations with their employer before the Ministry of Labour initiates a violation claim. Employees are responsible for collecting the information relevant to their complaints to reduce the investigatory demands on the Ministry. The Act also focuses on voluntary mediation of violations (Vosko et al 2011). It is easy to imagine a low-paid worker, isolated and precariously employed, being afraid or unwilling to risk his or her position or future employment reference to initiate a lengthy and doubtfully successful legal mediation. Thus, the resolution of employment standards issues is institutionalized in an intimidating and unequal system for employees. They are expected to represent themselves, distill fairly complex legislation around employment standards, and challenge their employers head on at the risk of losing their job. The prohibition on third party complaints is damaging to these workers since it deprives them of assistance that could help them realise minimum employment standards. More generally, workers who belong to unions have been excluded entirely from making complaints under the Act. Notwithstanding the assumption that unionized workers are better protected, the United Steelworkers of America (USWA 2015) noted that the vast majority of collective agreements did not contain language on termination and severance pay in the event of lay-offs and plant closure. This legal separation of workers into unionized and non-unionized not only serves to prevent the achievement of good working conditions for the majority of workers in Ontario who are not members of unions or included in collective agreements, but also fails to reflect the reality of those collective agreements that are in effect. Secondly, the ability to impose penalties was certainly limited. Employment standards officers can require the employer to pay the wages owed to the worker, but without any additional consequences. Some of the collection activities have been privatized. And, even if employers are caught abusing the ESA, they will only have to pay what was due legally in the first place (Vosko et al 2011, 61–62). There is little chance that a violation will trigger a wider audit of the company in question. Moreover, a substantial amount of moneys owed workers are from bankrupt employers compounding the difficulties of collection.

Quebec

The Quebec enforcement system seems more robust. Beginning in 2000, the Labour Standards Commission decided to emphasize compliance through general inspections of workplaces and gave enforcement standards officers the ability to inspect employers' books if they discovered individual complaints violations (Bernstein 2006, 239). Furthermore, complaints from third parties, including unions, are allowed and there is no requirement that employees confront their employers directly with a complaint before bringing up their claim with the Ministry.

Alberta

In 2005 changes to the Alberta *Employment Standards Code* moved the child labour protection system from a proactive monitoring of child labour to one where in restaurants and food services, for example, parents became effectively responsible for determining whether such work is permissible and safe (Barnetson, 2009a; Shultz and Taylor, 2006). "During the summer of 2005, regulations regarding the minimum working age were quietly, and without discussion or debate, changed to lessen restrictions on the employment of 12 to 14 year olds in Alberta. The regulations now allow these young adolescents to be employed without a permit as delivery persons, and as clerks in offices, retail stores, video stores, grocery stores, department stores, convenience stores and in restaurants and food service outlets"(Shultz and Taylor, 2006, 431).

More generally, and linked with the drive to decrease expenditures during the mid-1990s, there was a shift in emphasis in the enforcement of employment standards towards voluntary approaches to regulation, self-regulation, and diminished proactive investigatory programs. Enforcement was weak to begin with, starting in the mid-1990s the staff of the employment standards unit (with only 30 employees) were instructed to only answer specific questions and not provide additional information which could assist those with ESC complaints (Haddow and Klassen 2006). A labour leader in Alberta quoted in Haddow and Klassen (2006, 194) described "the enforcement of employment standards [in Alberta as] a joke, a joke."

British Columbia

Similar to Alberta, 2003 changes to the BC ESA shifted enforcement from a proactive system of permits and monitoring of child labour to a complaint-driven reactive system (Barnetson 2009, 2010; Shultz and Taylor 2006). The Employment Standards Branch can reject worker complaints unless workers have first confronted their employer directly with the complaint, using a 9-page "self-help kit" documenting their claim. In any case, the Branch only has the obligation to review complaints, rather than to investigate every one. If a worker does launch a complaint but no settlement is reached, the role of the standards branch is to help the parties involved arrive at a settlement. It is only after this lengthy process that an employment standards officer is allowed to arrive at a written decision in favour of one party or the other (Fairey 2007, 103).

Similarly, the Employment Standards Branch has lost the ability to force employer compliance with its determinations. Consequently, if employers refuse to pay, workers must file a separate claim in civil court (Fairey 2007, 104). The system leaves ample room for employers to take advantage of this situation and to settle with workers for an amount below what the worker is legislatively and legally entitled.

As a result of budget and staff cuts, the ability of the employment standards system in BC to undertake routine workplace inspections, or otherwise be proactive, has been seriously undermined (Cohen, May 22, 2008, A17). Complaints by workers dropped by 46 percent in the first year, and 61 percent in the following three years after a round of budget reductions began to take effect in 2003/2004 (Cohen, May 22,

2008, A17). For context, in 1990/91 the Employment Standard Branch received about 11,000 complaints of employer violations of the Act. In 2004/05, they received about 3400 (Fairey 2005 [cited in MacPhail and Bowles 2008, 551]).

The Situation in the Rest of Canada

By and large, trends in the rest of the provinces corroborate the neoliberal alterations to employment standards found in Ontario and BC that have served to increase precarity in labour markets.[3] Nowhere in Canada does a relatively balanced and proactive system of investigations exist. Instead, all of the provinces rely extensively on reactive complaints-based investigations. In fact, Newfoundland, PEI, New Brunswick, and Nova Scotia currently rely exclusively on a two-pronged approach for regulating employment standards that includes workplace education and reactive investigation. These provinces do not have proactive inspection programs at all. Quebec, Ontario, Alberta, BC, Manitoba, and Saskatchewan perform slightly better by carrying out a limited number of proactive inspections per year (Tucker-Simmons 2013, 17–18). Bob Barnetson (2010, 10) notes that complaint-driven enforcement in Canada has been the subject of some criticism. It tends to address mainly violations affecting former employees and reveals only a minority of actual violations. There is substantial evidence of widespread violations of employment standards in Canada. Ontario's Provincial Auditor noted that between 40 percent and 90 percent of proactive inspections (varying by sector) found violations of minimum standards. Similar rates of non-compliance were found federally, with 25 percent of federal employers not in compliance with most obligations under Part III of the federal act and 75 percent not in compliance with at least one provision. Complaints-driven systems, however, typically suggest that only about 1–2 percent of employers violate employment standards (Tucker Simmons 2013, 17).

However, even those provinces that do engage in proactive inspections, inspect a very small portion of the workforce. In the case of Quebec for example, the province conducted targeted inspections of 25,052 employees out of 1,729,000 workers protected under Quebec's Labour

3 With perhaps the exception of Quebec.

Standards Act in 2002–2003 (Bernstein 2006, 239). This means that only 0.02 percent of all employers in Quebec were subject to inspection. A similar proportion of employees and employers are inspected in the other provinces that engage in proactive inspections as well.

On the whole then, there appears to be a number of similarities between trends and shifts in employment standards regulation across the country. Considered as a "system" it has become highly individualized and reactive and unions have been excluded from coverage under the ESA. Actual legislative changes and executive orders have led to less protection for workers in a variety of different ways, and funding has been cut to the Ministry of Labour and Employment Standards Branches leading to a reduction in enforcement and monitoring capabilities.

On a brighter note in Ontario, the Minister of Labour has asked for an independent review of employment standards and the Liberal Kathleen Wynne government is said to be contemplating concessions and modifications to the ESA in favour of employees.[4] In addition, in 2014/2015 the Ministry of Labour started conducting proactive industry "blitzes" into high-risk areas where it believes standards are being violated (Mojtehedzadeh 2015). However, currently the system is not working in balancing worker rights and protecting employees from precarity. Indeed, a 2011 report undertaken by the Workers Action Centre found substantial violations of core standards: 22 percent of workers earned less than the minimum wage; 33 percent were owed unpaid wages; 39 percent did not receive overtime pay and 36 percent lost their jobs without termination pay (WAC 2011). These types of surveys are not uncommon and indicate a long-standing problem (Foster and Barnetson 2014, 358). In the late 1990s, a federal government Labour Standards Evaluation surveyed employers and found that 25 percent of employers were in widespread violation of the Canada Labour Code and 50 percent were in partial violation (Vosko et al 2011). Clearly, more steps need to be taken.

---

4 In May 2017 the Ontario government released its Changing Workplaces Review report (https://files.ontario.ca/changing_workplace_review_english_summary.pdf). The report appeared to presage significant changes to the Employment Standards and Labour Relations Acts and other measures, including a phased increase in the minimum wage to $15 per hour, were announced.

Conclusion

The majority of workers rely on employment standards for basic regulatory protection. In recent years the standards, arguably never generous, have been eroded. In addition, a significant "enforcement gap" exists at both the federal and the provincial levels. In Ontario, this enforcement gap was exacerbated after 1995 due to deregulation through inadequate funding, legislative reforms that place too much emphasis on individualized complaints processes and voluntary compliance rather than severe and strict punitive measures. It has also been amplified by the separation of unions from employment standards enforcement such that unionized employees are prevented from filing employment standards complaints with the Ministry of Labour (MOL), and sympathetic third parties find it difficult to represent the unorganized. As Weil (2012, 632) notes, "the implications of these developments are that, increasingly, those in precarious jobs, many of whom lack union representation, are left with insufficient regulatory protection from employer non-compliance, further heightening their insecurity." While employers may argue that strengthening employment standards would lead to unemployment, there is little evidence to back up such a position (Sarkar 2013, 1346).The shift towards more flexible and weaker employment standards protections beginning in the 1980s and early 1990s has led to greater self-regulation following the prescriptions of the neoliberal "flexibility hypothesis" (Lewchuk 2013; Baker et al 2004). Similarly in BC in the 2000s these flexibility regulations have contributed to the erosion of worker economic security, dualism in the labour market, increased incidence of non-standard employment arrangements, and growing precarity amongst workers (Agocs 2002; Cohen and Klein 2008; Fairey 2005; Fudge and Vosko 2001; Lynk 2009; Tucker 2003).

References

AFL. 2011. Policy Paper on Health and Safety. Alberta Federation of Labour, 8th Biennial Convention, 47th Constitutional Convention. https://d3n8a8pro7vhmx.cloudfront.net/afl/pages/2419/attachments/original/1317654113/2011%20Convention%20H&S%20Policy%20Paper.pdf?1317654113

Agocs, Carol. 2002. "Canada's Employment Equity Legislation and Policy,

1987–2000: The Gap between Policy and Practice." *International Journal of Manpower* 23(3): 256–76.

Arthurs, Harry. 2006. "Fairness at Work: Federal Labour Standards for the Twenty-First Century." labour.gc.ca/eng/standards_equity/st/pubs_st/fls/page00.shtml

Baker, Dean, Andrew Glyn, David Howell and John Schmitt. 2004. *Unemployment and Labor Market Institutions: The Failure of the Empirical Case for Deregulation*. Policy Integration Department Statistical Development and Analysis Unit. International Labour Office: Geneva.

Barnetson, Bob. 2009. 'Regulation of Child and Adolescent Employment in Alberta.' *Just Labour: A Canadian Journal of Work and Society* 13 (Spring): 29–47.

Barnetson, Bob. 2010. "Effectiveness of Complaint-Driven Regulation of Child Labour in Alberta." *Just Labour: A Canadian Journal of Work and Society* 16(1): 9–24.

Barnetson, Bob. 2011. "Children Working Along in Alberta: How Child Labour and Working-Alone Regulations Interact." *Just Labour* 17(18): 34–48.

Battle, Ken. 2015. *Canada Social Report: Minimum Wages in Canada 1965–2015*. Toronto: Caledon Institute.

Bernstein, Stephanie. 2006. "Mitigating Precarious Employment in Quebec: The Role of Minimum Employment Standards Legislation," in Leah F. Vosko, ed., *Precarious Employment: Understanding Labour Market Insecurity in Canada*. McGill-Queen's University Press.

Breslin, F. Curtis, Mieke Koehoorn and Donald C. Cole. 2008. "Employment Patterns and Work Injury Experience Among Canadian 12 to 14 Year Olds." *Can J Public Health* 99(3): 201–5.

Chaykowski, R.P. and G.A. Slotsve. 2007. The Extent of Economic Vulnerability in the Canadian Labour Market and Federal: Is there a Role for Labour Standards? *Social Indicators Research* 88(1): 75–96.

Cranford Cynthia J., Leah F. Vosko and Nancy Zukewich. 2003. "Precarious Employment in the Canadian Labour Market: A Statistical Portrait." *Just labour* 3(6): 6–22.

Cohen, Marjorie Griffin. 2008. "Labour Policies Have Dramatic Influence on Wage Gap." *The Vancouver Sun* (22 May). Available online.

Cohen, Marjorie Griffin. 2013. "Teenage Work: Its Precarious and Gendered Nature." *Revue Interventions économiques. Papers in Political Economy*, 47.

Cohen, Marjorie Griffin and Seth Klein. 2011. "Poverty Reduction in British Columbia?: How 'The Best Place on Earth' Keeps People Poorest." *Canadian Review of Social Policy*: 65–66, 58–73.

Esping-Andersen, Gosta. 1990. *Three Worlds of Welfare Capitalism*. Princeton: Princeton University Press.

Fairey, David. 2005. "Eroding Worker Protections: BC's New 'Flexible' Employment Standards." Canadian Centre Policy Alternatives. policyalternatives.ca/sites/default/files/uploads/publications/BC_Office_Pubs/bc_2005/employment_standards.pdf

Fairey, David. 2005. *Eroding Worker Protections: BC's New "Flexible" Employment Standards*. Canadian Centre Policy Alternatives.

Fairey, David. 2007. "New Flexible Employment Standards Regulation in British Columbia." *Journal Law and Social Policy* 21, 91–113.

Fairey, David. 2009. "Exclusion of Unionized Workers from Employment Standards Law." *Relations Industrielles/Industrial Relations* 64(1): 112–33.

Fairey, David and Marjorie Griffin Cohen. 2013. "Why BC's Lower-wage Workers Are Struggling." *The Tyee* (24 April). Available online.

Foster, Jason and Bob Barnetson. 2014. "The Political Justification of Migrant Workers in Alberta, Canada." *Journal of International Migration and Integration* 15(2): 349–70.

Fudge, Judge and Leah F. Vosko. 2001. "By Whose Standards? Reregulating the Canadian Labour Market." *Economic and Industrial Democracy* 22(3): 327–56.

Gallant, Jacques. 2016. "WSIB Denies it Pressured Physician." *Toronto Star* (27 August). Available online.

Grant, Michel. 2004. "Deregulating Industrial Relations in the Apparel Sector: The Decree System in Quebec" in Jim Stanford and Leah F. Vosko, eds., *Challenging the Market: The Struggle to Regulate Work and Income* Montreal: McGill Queen's University Press, pp. 136–50.

Green, David. 2015. "The Case for Increasing the Minimum Wage: What Does the Academic Literature Tell Us?" Vancouver: Canadian Centre for Policy Alternatives.

Haddow, Rodney and Thomas Klassen. 2006. *Partisanship, Globalization, and Canadian Labour Market Policy: Four Provinces in Comparative Perspective*. University of Toronto Press.

Hall, Peter A. and Soskice, David. 2003. *Varieties of Capitalism: The Institutional Foundations of Comparative Advantage*. Oxford: Oxford University Press.

Law Commission of Ontario. 2012. "Vulnerable Workers and Precarious Work: Final Report." www.lco-cdo.org.

Law Commission of Ontario (LCO). 2012. Vulnerable Workers and Precarious Work: Final Report. December, Toronto.

King, Andrew G. 2014. "Making Sense of Law Reform: A Case Study of Workers' Compensation Law Reform in Ontario 1980 to 2012." PhD diss., Université d'Ottawa/University of Ottawa.

Lewchuk, Wayne. 2013. "The Limits of Voice: Are Workers Afraid to Express Their Health and Safety Rights?" *Osgoode Hall Law Journal* 50(4): 789–812.

Longhurst, Andrew. 2014. "Precarious: Temporary agency Work in British Columbia." *Canadian Centre for Policy Alternatives*. Retrieved from policyalternatives.ca/sites/default/files/uploads/publications/BC%20Office/2014/07/ccpa-bc_precariousTempWork_fullReport.pdf

Luke, Helesia and Moore, Graeme. 2004. "Who's Looking Out for Our Kids?: Deregulating Child Labour Law in British Columbia." Vancouver: Canadian Centre for Policy Alternatives.

Lynk, Michael. 2009. "Labour Law and the New Inequality." *Just Labour: A Canadian Journal of Work and Society* 15, 125–39.

Macdonald, David. 2016. "A Policy-Maker's Guide to Basic Income." Ottawa: Canadian Centre for Policy Alternatives.

MacPhail, Fiona and Paul Bowles. 2008. "Temporary Work and Neoliberal Government policy: Evidence from British Columbia, Canada," *International Review of Applied Economics* 22(5): 545–63

McBride, Stephen and John Irwin. 2010. "Deregulating Child Labour in British Columbia," in Mona Gleason, Tamara Myers, Leslie Paris, and Veronica Strong-Boaq, eds., *Lost Kids: Vulnerable Children and Youth in Canada, the United States and Australia*. Vancouver: UBC Press, pp. 230–43

McBride, Stephen and Kathleen McNutt. 2007. "Devolution and Neoliberalism in the Canadian Welfare State: Ideology, National and International Conditioning Frameworks, and Policy Change in British Columbia," *Global Social Policy* 7(2): 177–201.

McBride, Stephen and Jacob Muirhead. 2015. "Challenging the Low Wage Economy: Living and Other Wages." *Alternate Routes* 27: 55–86.

Ministry of Labour, Ontario. 2013. Temporary Agency Blitz Results. February 14. Available Online.

Mojtehedzadeh, Sara. 2015. Ontario Employers Get Slap on Wrist for Mistreating Employees. *Toronto Star* (24 May). Available online.

Mojtehedzadak, Sara. 2016. "Ontario Watchdog Urged to Investigate WSIB." *Toronto Star* (29 January). Available online.

OECD. 2014. Strictness of Employment Protection Legislation: Regular Employment. OECD Stat (datasets EPL_R).

Pennachini, Laura. 2017. "Citizens Work or Citizens Income." *Social Europe*. March 14. Available Online.

Sarkar, Prabirjit. 2013. "Does an Employment Protection Law Lead to Unemployment? A Panel Data Analysis of OECD Countries, 1990–2008." *Cambridge Journal of Economic* 37(4): 1335–48.

Shultz, Lynette and Alison Taylor. 2006. "Children at Work in Alberta." *Canadian Public Policy* 32(4): 431–441.

Shelby, Jim. 2001. "Losing Ground: The Slow Decline of Workers' Rights and Privileges in Alberta 1975-2000." Alberta Federation of Labour.

Statistics Canada. 2013. Minimum Wage Database Introduction. Statistics Canada.

Storey, Robert. 2009b. "'They Have All Been Faithful Workers': Injured Workers, Truth, and Workers' Compensation in Ontario, 1970–2008." *Journal of Canadian Studies/Revue d'études canadiennes* 43(1): 154–185.

Storey, Robert. 2005. "Activism and the Making of Occupational Health and Safety Law in Ontario, 1960s–1980." *Policy and Practice in Health and Safety* 3(1): 41–68.

Storey, Robert. 2006a. "Social Assistance or a Worker's Right: Workmen's Compensation and the Struggle of Injured Workers in Ontario, 1970–1985." *Studies in Political Economy* 78(1): 67–91.

Thomas, Mark. 2009. *Regulating Flexibility: The Political Economy of Employment Standards*. McGill-Queen's University Press.

Thompson, Mark. 1994. *Rights and Responsibilities in a Changing Workplace: A Review of Employment Standards in British Columbia*. Ministry of Skills, Training and Labour. qp.gov.bc.ca/govtinfo/thompson.pdf

Thompson, Mark. 1998. "ESA Reflects Realities, Requests: Coalition Must Recognize Intent, Development before it Demands Restructuring." *The Vancouver Sun* (15 June). Available online.

Tucker, Eric. 2003. "Diverging Trends in Worker Health and Safety Protection and Participation in Canada, 1985–2000." *Relations industrielles/Industrial Relations* 58(3): 395–426.

Tucker-Simmons, Daniel. 2013. "Open for Business, Closed for Workers: Employment Standards, the Enforcement Deficit, and Vulnerable Workers in Canada." *Broadbent Institute.* Retrieved from broadbentinstitute.ca/en/blog/open-business-closed-workers-employment-standards-enforcement-deficit-and-vulnerable-workers

Unifor. 2015. *Building Balance, Fairness and Opportunity in Ontario's Labour Market:* Submission of Unifor to the Ontario Changing Workplaces Consultation. Tooronto: Unifor.

USWA. 2015. *Submission to the Ontario Changing Workplaces Consultation.* Toronto: USWA.

Vosko, Leah, Eric Tucker, Mary Gellatly and Mark Thomas. 2011. "New Approaches to Enforcement and Compliance with Labour Regulatory Standards: The Case of Ontario, Canada." *Comparative Research in Law and Political Economy. Research Paper No. 31/2011.*

Vosko, Leah. 2013. "Rights Without Remedies: Enforcing Employment Standards in Ontario by Maximizing Voice Among Workers in Precarious Jobs." *Osgoode Hall Law Journal* 50(4): 845–873.

Weil, David. 2014. *The Fissured Workplace: Why Work Became So Bad for So Many and What Can Be Done to Improve It.* Cambridge: Harvard University Press.

Willow, Johanna, and Sylvain Schetagne. 2011. "Mapping Basic Working Conditions in Employment Standards Laws Across Canada — 2011/2012." Canadian Labour Congress.

Worker's Action Centre. 2015. Still Working on the Edge: Building Decent Jobs from the Ground Up. Retrieved from workersactioncentre.org/wp-content/uploads/dlm_uploads/2015/03/StillWorkingOnTheEdge-WorkersActionCentre.pdf.

Workers Action Centre. 2015. Still Working on the Edge. Toronto: WAC.

Yakabuski, Konrad. 2016. "Thinking BIG about employment: the basic-income guarantee excites left-leaning activists, but also attracts those on the right" *Globe and Mail* (7 March). Available online.

8

Addressing Inequities

Introduction

We have observed above that the labour market has become an increasingly insecure and precarious place. Social policies and programs were designed in part to support people who are having trouble navigating the labour market. But in the period that the labour market has become more "flexible"—that is, more insecure—we can see a different general trend. This trend has been to make individuals participants in and dependent on the labour market. Such a trend might be achieved by encouragement, or coercively by making social benefits difficult to obtain or conditional on behavioural changes designed to promote labour market attachment. In elite discourse, social programs are seen as a "trampoline" to get people back into the labour force, rather than as a "safety net" providing a place of refuge from it. As the saying goes, "the best social policy is a job."

Apart from the general difficulties experienced by many (if not most) in today's labour market, that market is also a location of division and hierarchy. There are people who are automatically disadvantaged (at least in relative terms), while others are less so. Certain groups, including the disabled, women, Aboriginal peoples, some immigrants, racial minorities, and the young have been particularly disadvantaged. Legislation and programs have been devised to remedy the disadvantage faced by these groups and also to better integrate them into the labour market. This probably reflects a belief that work is so central to well-being that as high a proportion as possible of the total population should take up employment. Barriers to work participation must be removed. Of course, such a desire is compatible with a desire to increase competition amongst job seekers hence exerting downward pressure on wages, to reduce public spending on social benefits, as well as with the normative neoliberal position that people should not be dependent on the state. This chapter looks at the overall success of these policies.

In the Canadian labour market, the traditionally dominant white male working population is a shrinking component of the labour force

(Agocs and Burr 1996). The new majority in the workplace are the relatively disadvantaged groups in society, which include women, persons with disabilities, Aboriginal peoples, and immigrants, and racialized groups (ibid). Many have argued that inequality and disadvantage on the basis of race, gender, and disability result from systemic discrimination—attitudes that are deeply embedded within the culture and structures of the workplace (ibid). The difficulties facing young people seeking secure and acceptable positions in the labour market have been widely noted. In response, some policy and legislative efforts have been made to ameliorate this situation. This chapter considers, in turn, the situation of these groups of workers.

Women

Legislative and programmatic efforts to ameliorate these conditions may be either direct or indirect (see Chang 2000). The former would include anti-discrimination and employment equity legislation; the latter could feature state provision of affordable child care, a service that would enable women in particular to participate more fully in the labour market. In Canada, the absence of adequate social provision such as a national child care system detracts from whatever impact more direct initiatives have had. Even the direct measures do little to affect the occupational and sectoral distribution of employment, a factor which has an impact on pay differentials.

Charts 14 and 15 provide data on the industrial composition of the labour force by gender.

We can see that a higher percentage of the male workforce is found in the goods producing sector than is the case for the female workforce (31.8 percent versus 9.58). The reverse is true for services (90.42 of the female workforce compared to 68.2 of the male one). Gender differences are also to be found in the incidence of part-time as opposed to full-time work (see Chart 16).

The female part-time to full-time ratio barely shifted over the 1986 to 2016 period, but the ratio of males in full-time work declined significantly, though still remained higher than that for females.

Neither gender did well in real wage terms though amongst full-time workers women did somewhat better than men (see Chart 17).

Chart 14: Male Labour Force, Industrial Composition, 1986 to 2016

Industry	% of Total Employment			
	1986	1996	2006	2016
Goods-producing sector	**39.86**	**36.40**	**35.17**	**31.80**
Agriculture	4.81	3.96	2.75	2.14
Forestry, fishing, mining, quarrying, oil and gas	3.71	3.39	3.14	2.78
Utilities	1.31	1.26	1.06	1.07
Construction	8.69	8.74	10.86	12.93
Manufacturing	21.33	19.05	17.36	12.89
Services-producing sector	**60.14**	**63.60**	**64.83**	**68.20**
Wholesale and retail trade	15.69	15.09	15.38	15.10
Transportation and warehousing	7.17	7.05	7.06	7.36
Finance, insurance, real estate, rental and leasing	4.35	4.71	5.05	5.43
Professional, scientific and technical services	3.71	5.54	7.06	8.44
Business, building and other support services	2.25	3.14	4.16	4.57
Educational services	4.68	4.85	4.71	4.41
Health care and social assistance	3.36	3.62	3.59	4.32
Information, culture and recreation	3.67	4.20	4.49	4.53
Accommodation and food services	4.24	4.91	4.65	5.42
Other services (except public administration)	4.16	4.44	3.76	3.84
Public administration	6.85	6.04	4.92	4.79

Chart 15: Female Labour Force, Industrial Composition, 1986 to 2016

Industry	% of Total Employment			
	1986	1996	2006	2016
Goods-producing sector	**16.20**	**13.22**	**11.88**	**9.58**
Agriculture	2.64	2.10	1.39	1.01
Forestry, fishing, mining, quarrying, oil and gas	0.75	0.73	0.81	0.74
Utilities	0.44	0.52	0.38	0.42
Construction	1.31	1.19	1.60	1.88
Manufacturing	11.05	8.69	7.71	5.52
Services-producing sector	**83.80**	**86.78**	**88.12**	**90.42**
Wholesale and retail trade	17.29	16.24	16.71	15.28
Transportation and warehousing	2.60	2.58	2.39	2.46
Finance, insurance, real estate, rental and leasing	8.27	8.46	7.66	7.12
Professional, scientific and technical services	3.92	4.97	5.99	6.91
Business, building and other support services	2.42	3.14	4.14	3.88
Educational services	8.43	9.14	9.67	9.89
Health care and social assistance	16.95	18.48	18.99	22.39
Information, culture and recreation	4.11	4.44	4.50	4.10
Accommodation and food services	7.58	7.98	7.97	8.11
Other services (except public administration)	6.19	5.37	4.80	4.77
Public administration	6.06	5.97	5.28	5.50

Source for all above charts: Statistics Canada. Table 282-0008 - Labour force survey estimates (LFS), by North American Industry Classification System (NAICS), sex and age group, annual (persons unless otherwise noted), CANSIM (database).

Chart 16: Labour Force Participation by Gender

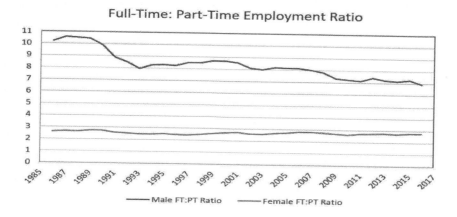

Full-Time: Part-Time Employment Ratio

——— Male FT:PT Ratio ——— Female FT:PT Ratio

Source: Statistics Canada. Table 282-0002 - Labour force survey estimates (LFS), by sex and detailed age group, annual (persons unless otherwise noted), CANSIM (database).

Chart 17: Wage Increases and Inflation by Gender and Employment Status, 1997 to 2016

Inflation*	42.04
Full-time Median Wage Increases	
Male	35
Female	39.3
Part-time Median Wage Increases	
Male	39.1
Female	35.5

*Bank of Canada Inflation Calculator bankofcanada.ca/rates/related/inflation-calculator/

Source: Statistics Canada. Table 282-0151 - Labour force survey estimates (LFS), wages of employees by type of work, National Occupational Classification (NOC), sex, and age group, unadjusted for seasonality, annual (current dollars unless otherwise noted), CANSIM (database).

Chart 18 records the pay gender gap in 1997 and 2016 respectively.

Chart 18: Gender Pay Gap 1997 and 2016

	1997	2016
Full Time Employees	.773	.864
All Employees (including part-time)	.73	.815

Source: Statistics Canada. Table 282-0151 - Labour force survey estimates (LFS), wages of employees by type of work, National Occupational Classification (NOC), sex, and age group, unadjusted for seasonality, annual (current dollars unless otherwise noted), CANSIM (database).

Various explanations have been advanced to explain the gender pay gap. Kaufman (2002) identifies human capital/skills deficits, worker preferences for particular occupations, and economic structures of industrial and occupational segregation, and stereotyping or discimination. Most Canadian discussions of the gender pay gap have drawn on one or more of these factors.

Nicole Fortin et al (2012) argue that due to the increasing importance of education and credentials in the modern "knowledge-based economy," women have been able to attain a growing share of labour market participation (Fortin et al 2012, 133) and, to some extent women's wages have been protected relative to those of men as the result of better representation of women in the public sector, where pay equity provisions apply and which has not experienced private-sector deunionization to the same extent as the traditionally male-dominated goods producing sectors. So part of the *relative* gain comes from an overall polarization where male earnings performed more poorly than those of females (Fortin et al 2012, 134).

A number of factors narrow the pay gap between men and women. In cities with large-sized public sectors, the pay gap is smaller. This seems related to the presence of unions, equity/discrimination regulations, and transparency in promotion in the public sector (McInturff 2015, 7). The presence of gender-sensitive policies such as subsidized childcare, extended parental leave, and paternity leave diminishes the gender gap between women and men. Subsidized childcare, particularly for single mothers, is crucial to increasing women's economic equality and access to the labour market (Neysmith et al 2009). In Canada, Quebec stands out for provision of these programs and its gender gap is lower than elsewhere (McInturff, 2015, 6). Unionization plays an important role in reducing the pay gap between women and men (Feminist Alliance for International Action [FAFIA] 2008). According to the Canadian Labour Congress, the most important benefit of unionization for any worker is a formal contract embedded in a collective agreement, which specifies wages in a formal system of pay-by-position. Such contracts also usually provide for promotion and job security, as well as for non-wage benefits such as pensions, holidays, and health plans (FAFIA 2008). These union contracts work to dismantle systemic gender discriminatory systems and processes which have both resulted in a wage gap and have marginalized women in the labour market. It is important to note that in the private sector, unionization does not close the gender wage gap as much as it does in the public sector (FAFIA 2008). The public policy implications are that a growing public sector, major priority to child care provisions and subsidization, and promotion of unionization are all beneficial to the achievement of gender equality. However, the actual direction of public policy has been one of public sector austerity and hostility towards unionization (see Chapter 9).

Newman and White (2006) found that career disruption continues to be more common for women than men. This has both structural and cultural roots: women are seen as "natural caregivers" and are therefore expected to take unpaid leave to care for children and/or aging parents in lieu of services not covered by the state. This is what feminist economists call "provisioning labour": "the daily work performed to acquire material and intangible resources for meeting the responsibilities that ensure the survival and well-being of people" (Neysmith et al 2009, 95). Stasiulis and Bakan (2005) point out that "Women's increased and unpaid work operates as shock absorber to promote the apparent 'efficiency' of market-oriented mechanisms" (41). However, Chart 19 seems to indicate that at least as far as child rearing is concerned this factor is significantly less important than formerly.

Chart 19: Employment Rate of Women with Children by Age of Youngest Child: Selected years

	Less than 3 y	3 to 5 y	Less than 6	6 to 15	Less than 16	Spouse less than 55 but with children at home
1976	27.6	36.8	31.4	46.4	39.1	60.9
1986	49.4	54.5	51.4	61.9	56.7	69.3
1996	57.8	60.5	58.9	69.8	64.5	72.4
2010	65.4	69.1	66.8	78.8	73.1	80.2
2016	67.2	72.3	69.3	78.7	74.1	81.3

Sources: Ferrao, Vincent. 2010. Paid Work in 'Women in Canada: A Gender-based Statistical Report.' Component of Statistics Canada Catalogue no. 89-503-X. and statcan.gc.ca/pub/89-503-x/2010001/article/11387-eng.pdf. Statistics Canada. Table 282-0211 - Labour force survey estimates (LFS), by family type and family age composition, annual (persons unless otherwise noted), CANSIM (database).

Women continue to be socialized in their educational careers differently than men. Women are more likely to be encouraged to pursue female-dominated occupations like teaching and nursing, while men may look toward engineering, science, and business (Neysmith et al 2009). While teaching and nursing have historically been well paid and unionized as part of the public sector, engineering, science, and business are more commonly found in the private sector. This has led to perpetual "'occupational segregation'" and a corresponding gendered wage gap, as well as a lack of women in corporate and political leadership (ibid; see also McInturff, 2015).

In 2001 the federal government established a Pay Equity Task Force to address inequities in pay structures. Pay equity provisions contained in section 11 of the Canadian Human Rights Act also serves as responses to women's disadvantaged position in the labour market (FAFIA 2008). However, the process of investigation can be both long and costly. In September 2006, the Government of Canada refused to improve the federal pay equity law, despite strong and repeated recommendations from the government's own Pay Equity Task Force and from the Parliamentary Committee on the Status of Women (FAFIA 2008). The Employment Insurance Act has often failed to reflect the needs of women (Porter 2003). Two out of every three working women who pay into EI do not receive any benefits if they lose their jobs. Those least likely to qualify for EI are more likely to fall into the age group 25 to 44, and to have young children (FAFIA 2008). Because Aboriginal women, women of colour, and immigrant women undertake more non-standard work, the failure of the Employment Insurance scheme to adequately take into account the effect of non-standard employment patterns on access to benefits also affects them disproportionately (FAFIA 2008). This compounds the lack of access to opportunities and income equality that these groups face: "Human rights laws have not, so far, been effective at addressing and eliminating systemic racism, which results in under-representation of women of colour in political office, academia, senior management positions, and media" (FAFIA 2008). Canadian efforts to counteract issues of racism often seem minimal perhaps because of an unwillingness to admit that there is a problem of racism (FAFIA 2008).

While legislation has been enacted to address the permanence of the gender-pay gap in Canada, most of the policy implementations apply only to public-sector employees. Aside from the federal level, six provinces (Manitoba, Ontario, New Brunswick, Nova Scotia, PEI, and Quebec) have enacted pay equity legislation, and three provinces (Saskatchewan, Newfoundland, and BC) have "policy frameworks" established for negotiating public-sector pay equity. Only Alberta lacked specific pay equity legislation or negotiating frameworks (Schirle 2015, 309). But only two provinces have addressed pay equity in the private sector.

While broad analyses focus on the gender wage gap as a whole, Schirle (2015) attempts greater specificity by focusing on full-time employees in the private sector across provinces over the 1997–2014 period (310). The author finds considerable variation in the gender wage gap across provinces, both in its quantitative outcomes and in its qualitative composition. Much of the literature on the gender wage gap finds that occupation and industry variables are associated with the gap between male and female earnings. However, there are significant "unexplained" differences, which Shirle identifies primarily as the "portion of the wage gap ... thought to capture both wage discrimination against female employees as well as any gender differences in productive characteristics that have not been accounted for by the explanatory variables" (314). These may account for the majority of the differences in sex-specific private sector wages.

Schirle concludes that provincial differences in the size of the gender pay gap shrink substantially when controlled for industry and occupational differences. Still, since the gap cannot be fully explained by measurable differences, there is a heightened importance on continued occupational desegregation. Education and skills training are equalizing rapidly, so at least quantitatively (highest educational level, years of training, etc.), policy interventions concerning employment equity and affirmative action could prove effective. However, as Schirle rightly points out, the qualitative differences in the types of training and education given to men and women—these the result of socialization bias or human capital decisions—can provide a "pre-labour market gender [imbalance]" (317) that would limit the successes of these policies.

Aboriginal Peoples

"Aboriginal" refers to Canada's First Nations, Inuit, and Métis populations. The Aboriginal population in Canada has experienced higher unemployment rates, as well as lower-than-average earnings, when they are employed (CSLS 2012). In 2011, the population of people who identified as Aboriginal of working age, living off reserves and outside the territories, was 670,500. This represented 2.4 percent of the total working age population in Canada (CSLS 2012).

According to the Report on Equality Rights of Aboriginal People in 2013, Aboriginal people in Canada face persistent conditions of disadvantage and barriers to equality of opportunity, especially in regard to employment opportunity. Pendakur and Pendakur (2011) found that Aboriginal people face substantial earnings gaps in comparison with Canadian born majority-group workers with similar characteristics (such as age and education). Minimal progress has been made to address these gaps in labour market performance. Drost and Richards (2003) argue that although Aboriginal concerns are receiving more attention in public policy debates, most public attention is devoted to on-reserve communities. They argue that this approach is inadequate, given that today growing numbers of Canada's Aboriginal population live off-reserve and in cities. First Nations peoples both on and off reserves face barriers to equality that are entrenched in cultural, structural, and even legislative histories. Wilson and MacDonald (2010) examined three censuses: 1996, 2001, and 2006. They found that in 2006, Aboriginal peoples' incomes were 30 percent lower than the rest of Canadians ($18,962 and $27,097 respectively). Over the ten years between 1996 and 2006, the income gap had decreased only slightly. Little change can be detected in more recent data as Chart 20 below indicates.

Chart 20: Indigenous Pay Inequity

Aboriginal group	Characteristic	2010	2016
Aboriginal population	Average hourly wage rate (current dollars)	20.06	23.3
Aboriginal population	Average weekly wage rate (current dollars)	743.41	854.92
Non-Aboriginal population	Average hourly wage rate (current dollars)	22.49	25.79
Non-Aboriginal population	Average weekly wage rate (current dollars)	818.56	942.6

Source: Statistics Canada. Table 282-0233 - Labour force survey estimates (LFS), average hourly and weekly wages and average usual weekly hours by Aboriginal group and age group, Canada, selected provinces and regions, annual (number unless otherwise noted), CANSIM (database).

One explanation for long-standing wage and income differentials, advanced by Richards and Vining (2004), concluded that poor education levels condemn many Aboriginals to poverty. Indeed, only 8 percent of Aboriginals hold a bachelor's degree, compared with 22 percent of the rest of Canadians (Wilson and MacDonald 2010). However, Shauna MacKinnon (2015) is highly critical of supply-side and human-capital explanations as well as policy interventions for improving the labour market outcomes of the indigenous population. She points to the recent polarizing trends in labour markets. Here, the growth of very high-skill, and low-skill/low-wage jobs, and the hollowing out of the middle, in conjunction with degree inflation, has demonstrated that human capital advancements are not sufficient to ensure secure employment and earnings. She claims that the level of unemployment and poverty among indigenous Canadians highlights the inadequacy of Canadian labour market policy. MacKinnon argues that it also demonstrates the persistent prevalence of racialized poverty and inequality. As a result, neoliberal and individualistic human capital responses are insufficient responses to the marginalized position of indigenous peoples in Canada. To counter these trends, MacKinnon suggests that a holistic, anti-colonial educational approach that provides short-term training programs to adults and youth alike should be established to "address all the barriers to work and raise aspiration and confidence" (168).

Only minimal progress has been made to address the gaps in labour market performance for Aboriginal people. Mendelson (2004) found that "on average the Aboriginal population suffers from higher unemployment, lower levels of education, below average incomes and many other indicators of limited socio-economic circumstances."

The Federal government has supported employment services targeting both the on and off reserve workforce, through the Aboriginal Human Resource Development Agreements (AHRDAs). In addition, there are several special arrangements (such as the Urban Aboriginal Programs) that are being undertaken in a few provincial settings, working alongside indigenous organizations (Mendelson 2004). The Aboriginal Human Resource Development Agreements were part of the national Aboriginal Human Resources Strategy. These five-year agreements allowed Aboriginal organizations or groups to implement and control their human resource programs and services in their own communities (Caverly 2006).

The government also responded to the inequities experienced by the Aboriginal population in regards to gaps between available labour and employability by developing specific job- and training-related programs for Aboriginal people in Canada. An example is the Aboriginal Skills and Employment Training Strategy, designed to link training need to labour market demands by helping Aboriginal people prepare for and find employment, as well as to retain them in the long-term: "All Aboriginal people, regardless of status or location, may access its programs and services, which include: skills development; training for high-demand jobs; job finding; programs for youth; programs for urban and Aboriginal people with disabilities; and access to child care" (Aboriginal Skills and Employment Training Strategy). The Aboriginal labour force suffered from Canada's economic downturn and did not recover nearly as rapidly as the non-Aboriginal population in 2010 (Aboriginal Skills and Employment Training Strategy).

The over-representation of Aboriginal people among Canada's poor under a neoliberal framework helps to demonstrate that Canadian policies have failed to adequately address the persistent economic gaps. However, these issues also existed long before neoliberalism, and therefore it seems reasonable, following MacKinnon (2015), for policy-makers and practitioners alike to look into the history of colonial practices in Canada, with specific attention to the treatment of Aboriginal people. Until Canadian policy-makers recognize the impact of measures such as the Indian Act, and until programs are established to deal with their long-term effects, operations to secure equal access to the labour market will likely have minimal impact (MacKinnon 2011). The level of unemployment and poverty among Aboriginal people in Canada is an important indicator of the inadequacy of Canadian labour market policy and the prevalence of racialized poverty and inequality.

Persons with Disabilities

Persons with disabilities face barriers to participation in the labour force despite the fact that the *Canadian Charter of Rights and Freedoms* and the *Canadian Human Rights Act* protect and ensure access to the labour market for persons with activity limitations by guaranteeing equality and by prohibiting discrimination based on physical or mental disability (Human Resources and Social Development Canada 2006).

In 2011, the employment rate for persons aged 25 to 64 with a disability was 49 percent, while persons without a disability in the same age group had a 79 percent employment rate (Turcotte, 2014 December 3). This gap tends to narrow with education: 77 percent of persons with a moderate disability and a university degree were employed, compared with 83 percent of persons without a disability (ibid). However, employment retention and job quality continue to be problems, along with career advancement and limited opportunities in management (ibid). And while many advocates believe that a significant portion of the disabled population can, with minor accommodation, be incorporated into mainstream labour markets through employment equity (Hum and Simpson 1996), some 12 percent of persons with disabilities report being denied employment because of their disability (Turcotte 2015).

Both men and women with severe disabilities tend to be employed in the lower paid and more precarious parts of the service sector (ibid). Chouinard (2010) explores the experience of women with disabilities in terms of government employment assistance in Canada. She explains that although women and men with disabilities face many of the same barriers to employment, these barriers are often multiplied in the case of women. Women with disabilities occupy marginalized places within the labour market and are more likely to be unemployed, live in poverty, and have part-time and precarious work (Fawcett 2000). Women who are affected by disabilities, be they mental and/or physical, are often the "'last hired and first fired'" (ibid).

There is a common belief that the best defence against poverty for persons with disabilities is employment (see Fawcett 2000). Yet many cannot find adequate work and must rely on public assistance. However, the Canada/Quebec Pension Plan includes several disability programs (Campolieti 2001). For example, the Canada Pension Plan (CPP) "provides disability benefits to people who have made enough contributions to the CPP and who are disabled and cannot work at any job on a regular basis. Benefits may also be available to their dependent children." To qualify their disability must be both "'severe'" and "'prolonged'" (www.esdc.gc.ca/en/cpp/disability/index.page)

> "*Severe* means that you have a mental or physical disability that regularly stops you from doing any type of substantially gainful work.

> *Prolonged* means that your disability is long-term and of indefinite duration or is likely to result in death."

These programs are important. They provide "'eligible claimants'" with income replacement benefits and rehabilitation services. Other benefits apply at the provincial level. Programs and eligibility for services and supports vary across provinces and territories. This variation in disability programs, services, and supports has been accelerated since 1996, when the federal government withdrew from an active role in social policy in favour of largely condition-free block funding for social programs to provincial and territorial governments under the Canada Health and Social Transfer (Chouinard 2010). Eligibility for benefits is determined by the incapacity to work, which is measured in Canadian provinces on a scale of incapacity and/or as an absolute measure of medically defined conditions of disability (Cohen et al 2008, 17).

Persons with disabilities (PWD)who receive income support are regularly reviewed for financial eligibility and disability status (ibid, 18). This creates a regime of constant monitoring and pressure to "get off" benefits and into the labour force. This process is reinforced by disqualifications and, sometimes, reinstatements. In BC, persons were required to complete a complicated 32-page Persons with Disabilities Benefits form to receive $906.42/month; this number is $554 lower than Canada's Low Income Cut off Rate (Cohen et al 2008, 11).[5] Furthermore, while Alberta permits PWD to hold up to $100,000 in assets and still be eligible for assistance, applicants in BC were ineligible if they held more than $3,000 (ibid). The Ontario Disability Support Program (ODSP) has come under repeated scrutiny from advocacy groups like the ODSP Action Coalition, which maintains that the program is plagued by "the complex application and disability adjudication process, the inconsistent and unfair provision of benefits like medical transportation and special diet, the lack of clear information given to clients, unfair treatment of clients by their local office, the rules related to earnings, and improving the employment supports program" (ODSP Action Coalition n.d.). Indeed, despite modest increases in rates between 2005 and 2008, benefits have not kept up with the rate of inflation: ODSP rates would have to be increased by 24.4 percent for PWD to have the same buying power as they did in 1993 (ODSP, 2015 March). And in 2014, another $36 million was cut in the Ontario budget for PWD who were *working*, making disability benefits seem more like a punishment than a support (ibid). Life on benefits for the disabled is hardly an easy option.

If benefits are subject to greater conditionality and discipline, the alternative of leaving the benefit system and obtaining employment rarely poses an easy solution. Labour policy developments for Canadians with disabilities have been criticized on two grounds. First, programs designed to move disabled persons into paid employment have focused principally on the individual, employing experts and specialists to improve her/his human capital (Wilton and Schuer 2006). And, at the hiring end, programs emphasize voluntary compliance by business and incentives over government regulation that would reduce barriers to employment and in the workplace environment. As it stands, workplaces and labour policies in contemporary capitalist economies re-

5 This data is current as of 2008. As of 2012, the limit had been increased to $5000 for single persons and $10,000 for families (see BC Reg. 197/2012).

main largely geared toward an able-body/mind norm (ibid). Secondly, programs focusing on transitioning the disabled into jobs assume that employers are willing to accommodate disabled persons and provide them with living wages and secure employment. Of course, this is true of some employers. However, the continued disadvantage experienced by the disabled reveals that it is very far from being the norm.

Recent (Racialized) Immigrants

I argued in Chapter 5 that Canada is a country of immigrants (see also Challinor 2011). Economic category applicants for immigration to Canada are selected according to a point system, which favours highly educated, younger, skilled workers who are fluent in one of Canada's official languages (Owen 2003). These people, therefore, are well-endowed with human capital. Canada has increasingly set in place certain education and skills provisions that should work to advantage potential migrants (Challinor 2011). However, there are systemic barriers that foster a mismatch between the skills and education levels of economic-class migrants and labour-market performance in Canada (see also Chapter 5). This highlights both integration challenges in the post-industrial economy and a sharp division between the stated intent of immigration policy and the actual outcomes (Challinor 2011). A 2015 report by the Canadian Department of Justice recognized the barriers to equitable labour market outcomes by the racialized and immigrant population. The report acknowledges the numerous studies that have identified "barriers to employment and social mobility for non-white Canadians, especially those who are immigrants" (Department of Justice 2015). The factors that the report identifies include refusal to recognize the credentials of non-white immigrants and employment discrimination against racial minorities with identifiable linguistic characteristics and racial features. While there may be a "skills-gap" argument pertaining to racialized and indeed immigrant Canadians, this is partially dismissed when controlling for education and age. When education and age are taken into account, first-generation racialized men still earn only 68.7 percent that of non-racialized men in Canada. Clearly there is a very real "colour code" (Block and Galabuzzi 2011, 4).

This is at odds with human capital theory, particularly given that newcomers to Canada are increasingly well-educated. In 2008, close to

45 percent of new immigrants held a university degree, almost double that of 14 years earlier (Houle and Yssaad 2010). According to Houle and Yssaad (2010) employment-education mismatch is high among newcomers; some two-thirds of immigrants are working in jobs below their credentials, as compared with 40 percent of Canadian-born workers. Some reasons for this include the limited recognition of foreign credentials and work experience (due to few standardized assessments); the inability of newcomers to communicate in English or French; and home country discriminatory behaviours based on country of origin (ibid). Indeed, French, American, and British immigrants experienced higher rates of employment that matched their credentials than immigrants from South Korea and the Philippines (ibid). Thus, racialized immigrant workers are often excluded from the upper segments of the labour market (Bauder 2003; see also Houle and Yssaad 2010). Moreover, prolonged under- or unemployment can lead to deskilling, thereby seriously affecting newcomers' prospects of re-entering their profession. The earnings gap between visible minorities and non-visible minorities is substantial and does not seem to have narrowed significantly (Block and Galabuzzi 2011).

For immigrant women of colour there are greater economic hardships. Too often, the foreign training and education that earns women access to Canada under the immigration point system are not recognized by Canadian employers, forcing educated women into the service or manufacturing industry. Such work is characterized by poor working conditions or abusive treatment (Houle and Yssaad 2010). The lack of funding, targeting and coordination in the planning, development, and delivery of labour market services and programs for immigrants has a direct impact on the experience of the immigrant as well as on our ability to maximize available human capital (Alboim and McIsaac 2007). Given that immigration is expected to play an increasingly important role within the labour supply equation, difficulties related to immigrant labour-market integration (foreign credential recognition, and language training) are key factors for improving economic performance of newcomers to Canada (Kustec 2012).

Young People

For many years the Canadian youth unemployment rate has consistently been several percentage points above average unemployment rates. It fluctuates significantly, and tends to be sensitive to changes in the business cycle. See Chart 21.

Chart 21: Canadian Unemployment Rate by Gender and Age Group

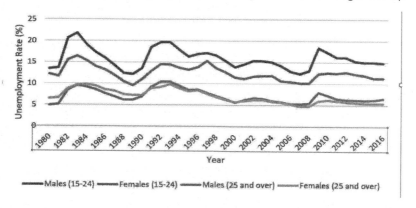

Source: Statistics Canada. CANSIM Table 282-0002 - Labour force survey estimates (LFS), by sex and detailed age group, annual (persons unless otherwise noted)

Bernard (2015) points out that the youth unemployment rate and the labour-force participation rate tend to fluctuate in an inverse manner. These fluctuations are heavily influenced by varying educational enrollment rates, especially among 20 to 24-year-olds. In effect the education system serves as a refuge in depressed labour market conditions.

Chart 22 tracks the relationship. Despite the fluctuations there is little sign of any real progress in youth unemployment and participation rates since the mid-1970s, suggesting that the issues faced by youth are endemic to the existing economic model and policy paradigm. Despite this, there is little sign of a change in policy stance.

Other aspects of young people's experience of working life over the past two decades also show little progress (see Chart 23).

Chart 22: Participation Rate and Unemployment Rate, Population Aged 15 to 24, 1976 to 2014

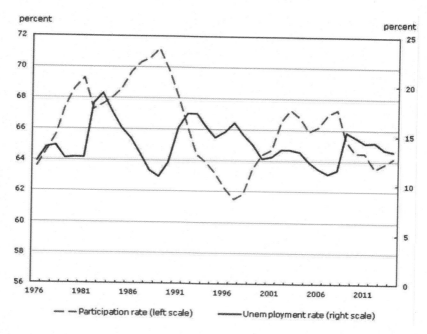

Graph taken directly from Bernard, A. 2015. "Youth Labour Force Participation: 2008 to 2014," Statistics Canada. Source: statcan.gc.ca/pub/11-626-x/11-626-x2015052-eng. htm.

Chart 23: Not Much Progress in Select Employment Conditions for Young People Over Time.

	Men			Women		
	15 to 24 years	25 to 34 years	35 to 54 years	15 to 24 years	25 to 34 years	35 to 54 years
	non-student employees (percentage)					
Union coverage						
1997	16.0	29.6	44.8	13.3	28.8	40.4
2007	17.1	28.4	36.9	14.6	31.8	37.2
2012	17.7	28.0	34.3	16.7	32.6	37.1
Temporary work						
1997	24.1	9.7	6.5	23.1	10.1	8.5
2007	24.6	9.9	7.2	25.8	11.9	8.6
2012	27.6	10.7	7.6	28.4	13.8	9.1
Involuntary part-time						
1997	10.8	3.4	2.0	18.8	8.4	8.1
2007	6.4	2.1	1.6	11.7	5.0	5.1
2012	9.4	2.7	1.9	16.0	6.6	6.1
Overqualified academics[1]						
1997	...	17.9	11.1	...	18.3	12.6
2007	...	18.8	16.4	...	20.5	18.9
2012	...	18.5	16.9	...	21.8	20.3

... not applicable
1. Percentage of university graduates in a profession requiring skills at a high school level or less.
Source: Statistics Canada, Labour Force Survey, 1997, 2007 and 2012.

Source: Taken from Galarneau et al 2013.

The condition of the youth labour force has implications for educational-skills attainment, debt, home-ownership, and the stratification of the overall labour force based on age. Regarding stratification it can be noted that whereas 27 percent of females were employed *part-time* in the overall labour force in 2009, for females in the youth labour force this figure stood at 55 percent (Ferrao 2010; Statistics Canada 2017). The proportion of females and males in the youth labour force working *full-time* has declined drastically since the 1980s in Canada. While in 1980, 80 percent and 72 percent of the male and female youth labour force worked full-time respectively, these figures had fallen to 59 percent and 44 percent in 2016 (see Chart 24 below).

Chart 24: Youth Labour Force by Employment Type and Gender

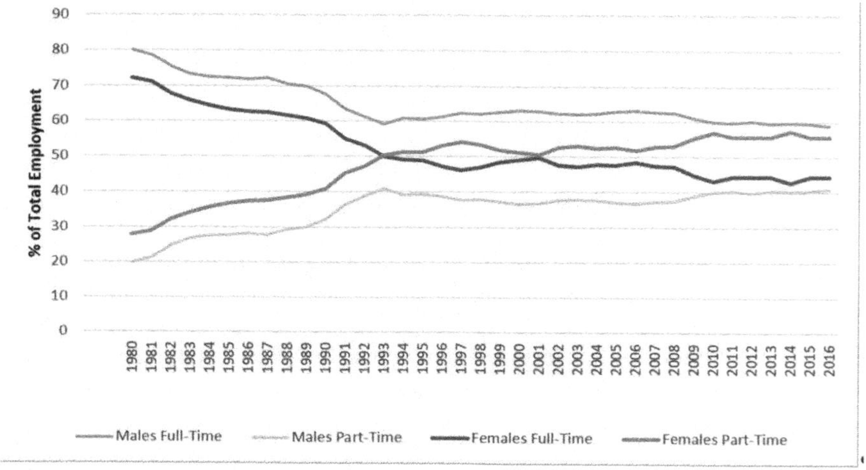

Source: Statistics Canada. CANSIM Table 282-0002: Labour force survey estimates (LFS), by sex and detailed age group, annual (persons unless otherwise noted).

In Canada, youth labour force wages fall well below the age cohorts of those 25–54 years old and those 55 years old and over. While this is not necessarily surprising given arguments surrounding seniority, experience, and human capital acquisition more generally, the magnitude of the differences can be viewed as an area of concern. Being unable to enter the labour force and set out on a career path as planned, desired, or dreamed may set a negative tone for the rest of one's career. Contrasting experience with that of the past cohorts might lead to discontent, pessimism, and distrust. Many works on youth employment issues begin with the consequences of unemployment, resorting to terms such as "scarring effects" and "lost generations" (Lee et al 2012).

The real wages of young workers have remained essentially unchanged in the last 40 years. Entering the job market in periods of low demand leads to initial lower wages, a disadvantage that may affect the individual for years to come. Alternatively, experiencing periods of unemployment, especially when prolonged, leads to a significant "wage penalty." Experiencing unemployment increases health problems, and the likelihood of further unemployment, whether it is due to the lack, loss, or underdevelopment of skills, or a stigma attached to past unemployment. Various life-transitions have been extended to later ages. Thus in 2011, 25 percent of young people aged 25 to 29 still lived with their parents, compared with 11 percent in 1981. Among those aged 20 to 24, 59 percent lived with their parents in 2011 compared with 42 percent in 1981. In addition, a greater number of young people are starting their careers later. The fulltime employment rate peaked at age 25 in 1976, compared to age 31 in 2012 (Galarneau. 2013).

On top of the relatively flat real wages and poor employment opportunities, young people have also faced increasing costs of education, housing, food, clothing, transportation, recreation, and so on.

The term 'education' would include post-secondary tuition as well as other costs such as text books, school supplies, etc. The result is a world of uncertainty, precarity, and debt.

To address the problems associated with youth labour market dysfunction, both levels of governments have implemented youth labour market initiatives. In 2000, an analysis of federal and provincial initiatives towards youth unemployment and school-to-work transitions explored these issues (McBride and Stoyko 2000, 220). Surveying today's policy profiles reveals that little has changed in the basic approaches, which consist of three broad categories. First, there are and were programs focused on career counselling and provision of information to help young people better navigate the labour market. Second, some programs offer direct employment creation through internships, summer jobs, grants, subsidies or tax credits to encourage businesses and non-profits to create jobs for youth, along with money or loan guarantees to enable youth to start their own businesses. Third, various work experience programs—such as internships, mentorships, and work study arrangements exist to expose young people to the world of work. General support for education and skills development might have been added to the list. Most of the measures, except those directly creating jobs, operate on the supply-side. Those participating might improve their chances, relative to others, of obtaining work, but except for the job creation programs, the volume of available work would be unaffected.

Today's approaches in addressing these issues across Canada are similar: provide financial support for employers to hire young people into full-time positions, make available job market information and guidance on career choices, and support education and skills development, seen as vital to individual career success.

The Government of Canada's Youth Employment Strategy (YES) launched in 1997, is the federal government's program to "help young people, particularly those facing barriers to employment, get the information and gain the skills, work experience and abilities they need to make a successful transition into the labour market" (Service Canada 2016). The focus is on individual responsibility with provision of some assistance to designated groups. Directed by Employment and Social Development Canada (ESDC), its national strategy contains three specific programs targetting areas of youth labour market entrants between 15 and 30 years old: *Skills Link*, *Career Focus*, and *Canada Summer Jobs*. According to an ESDC news release, since 2005, YES has helped over 772,000 young Canadians "get the training and work experience they need to enter the labour market" (ESDC 2016a).

The three sub-programs contained under YES are designed to help different segments of the population. *Skills Link* is aimed at helping youth facing barriers to labour force entry, including "single parents, youth with disabilities, young newcomers and youth in rural and remote areas" (ESDC 2016). The program offers employers up to $25,000 per youth participant hired, with the expectation that the participant receive work experience and skills training. A study commissioned by the ESDC that measured the effectiveness of the programs found that five years after its *Skills Link* program start year, participants average annual earnings were approximately $14,000, falling well below the average Canadian youth (aged 15 to 24) who earned about $21,000 in 2012 (EDSC 2015). While the program is credited for successfully finding work for its target population (88 percent found employment after their program), these youth often lacked important foundations for continued and progressive employment such as "basic education and literary skills" (ibid). The recommendation for this program was increased departmental and agency monitoring for interventions that could increase economic returns for participants, and cost-effectiveness for the program. The *Career Focus* initiative is directed towards post-secondary graduates seeking to gain access to the labour market through paid internships. This initiative was highly successful in finding youth employment after their internships ended, with 97 percent of respondents finding subsequent work (ESDC 2015). Compared to the extremely low annual earnings in the *Skills Link* stream, the *Career Focus* participants saw their incomes rise to $36,314 five years after participation. Finally, the *Canada Summer Jobs* program, aimed at high school and post-secondary students, is designed to give wage subsidies to employers who create jobs for summer students (ESDC 2016a). The program offers funding to non-profit organizations, public-sector employers, and small businesses with 50 or fewer employees. The ESDC has claimed that the total number of summer jobs created under the program since 2005 is 391,000 (ibid). *Canada Summer Jobs* participants generally worked full-time for an average of 12 weeks (3 months), although placements ranged from 2 weeks to 28 weeks in length (ESDC 2015). A survey of the programs' participants found that work placements had helped facilitate occupation specific technical proficiencies (ibid).

At the federal level, the government has recently established an Expert Panel on Youth Employment that is designed to "assess the barriers faced by young people in Canada, including vulnerable youth, in finding and keeping jobs. The Panel will look at innovative practices used by other governments, NGOs, and employers, at home and abroad, to improve job opportunities for youth" (GC 2016b). In terms of funding, the Liberal government has committed to investing more into Youth Employment Strategy (and setting a new funding level at $385 million, a $50-million increase) with hopes of creating 40,000 youth jobs; doubling the Skills Link participants; offering employers of youth (18 to 24) hired into permanent positions between 2016–2018 a 12 months break in Employment Insurance premiums; and investing $40 million on co-op opportunities for students in STEM (science, technology, engineering, and mathematics) and business programs. The 2017 budget added to this commitment an additional $395.5 million over three years, starting in 2017–18, for the Youth Employment Strategy. It claimed that together with the Budget 2016 measures, these investments will help more than 33,000 vulnerable youth develop the skills they need to find work or go back to school; create 15,000 new green jobs for young Canadians; and provide over 1,600 new employment opportunities for youth in the heritage field (GC 2017, 59).

There are also many provincial programs. In general, as the following examples indicate, they correspond with or build upon federal measures. Thus in 2013 the Ontario government announced its *Youth Employment Strategy*, designed to help more young people find jobs as well as ensure that employers can find young workers with the requisite skills (OECD 2014). Starting in 2015, the *Strategy* invested $295 million over two years in an effort to connect 30,000 youth with the means to develop job-relevant skills, or to start their own business (Ontario Ministry of Advanced Education and Skills Development 2015). Quebec has implemented a number of initiatives including *Youth in Action (Jeunes en Action)*, or the *Youth Action Strategy*. This program is for young adults who wish to return to school or find employment. It involves intensive 20-hour a week workshops over 20–52 weeks and includes provisions for financial aid (OECD 2014). Eligibility criteria include those aged 18 to 24 who are not currently studying or working, and who have "a professional objective" (ibid). The program helps youth with professional development and job searching techniques including resumé preparation and interview tips, as well as building social skills and conflict resolution (Quebec 2016). New Brunswick ranks consistently as the province with the highest rates of youth unemployment in the nation (McHardie 2016). This is despite the fact that by 2012, "50 percent of persons in New Brunswick 45 years of age and older had a post-secondary certificate, diploma, or degree, whereas 67 percent of persons between the ages of 25 and 44 had one" (NB 2013). New Brunswick's *Growing Together, New Brunswick's Economic Development Action Plan 2012–2016* outlined a three pillar approach with some familiar themes: Support K-12 and postsecondary education Systems to Adequately Prepare Students for Labour Force Needs; Support Learning and Skills Development; Retention and Attraction of Highly Skilled Individuals. The government intended to focus its efforts on early education expansion, labour market information portals, and the facility to transfer post-secondary credits. There were some measures to increase demand for young workers. For post-secondary graduates employers will be provided with a "one-year (52-week) wage subsidy if they hire a recent post secondary graduate for a permanent full-time position (40-hours/week) at a minimum salary of $14/hour." The program would "reimburse employers for 70 percent of the salary to a maximum of $10/hour" (NB 2013).

However helpful some of these programs may be to individual participants the statistics cited earlier in this section show that their general impact on the overall conditions faced by the youth labour force is quite limited.

Conclusion

The general picture that has emerged in this book is of a tough and challenging labour market. Inequality and insecurity have increased. Within that context some groups—women, aboriginal people, the disabled, racialized immigrants, and youth—seem especially disadvantaged. This is particularly true in a period when social policy aims less at protecting individuals from the vagaries of the labour market than in integrating them into it on the basis that a job—any job, almost regardless of its fit with the skill-set of the individual—provides the best route to social security.

The gender gap in terms of incomes has improved, though slowly, some would say glacially, and it remains substantial. Unionized and public sector employment are often associated with greater gender parity but private sector union density is down and that in the public sector is constantly threatened either by direct legislation (see Chapter 9) or by the impact of austerity and privatization of various forms. Aboriginal people continue to face substantial deficits in income and earnings and experience much higher than average unemployment and poverty rates. The integration of disabled persons into the labour market depends on level of education, level of disability and gender. For those unable to attach themselves in the labour market the level of benefits in real terms has deteriorated, and receipt of benefits is increasingly subject to greater conditionality and discipline. Racialized immigrants face non-recognition of qualifications and discrimination which produces lower incomes, more lower incomes, more un- and underemployment, and exclusion than their human capital endowments would predict. And the labour market for young people, while fluctuating according to the business cyle, has deteriorated in many ways since the 1970s and 1980s and offers less economic security and opportunity than formerly.

References

Agócs, Carol and Catherine Burr. (1996). "Employment Equity, Affirmative Action, and Managing Diversity: Assessing the Differences." *International Journal of Manpower* 17(4/5): 30–45.

Alboim, Naomi and Elizabeth McIsaac. 2007. "Making the Connections: Ottawa's Role in Immigrant Employment. *IRPP Choices* 13(3):1–24.

Annis, R. 1987, "The Impact of the BC Government 'Restraint' Program on Provincial Employees, Social Services and Women," in Robert Argue, Charlie Gannage and D.W. Livingstone, eds., *Working People and Hard Times: Canadian Perspectives*. Toronto, Garamond.

Bauder, Harald. 2003. "'Brain Abuse', or the Devaluation of Immigrant Labour in Canada." *Antipode* 35(4): 699–717.

Berger, G.A. 1973. *Canadian Experience with Incomes Policy, 1969–70*. Ottawa: Prices and Incomes Commission.

Bernard, André. 2015. "Youth Labour Force Participation: 2008 to 2014", Statistics Canada. statcan.gc.ca/pub/11-626-x/11-626-x2015052-eng.htm.

Block, Sheila and Grace-Edward Galabuzi. 2011. "Canada's Colour Coded Labour Market: The Gap for Racialized Workers." The Wellesley Institute.

Caverley, Natasha. 2006. "What Works: Effective Policies and Programs for Aboriginal Peoples of Canada", Technical Report Presented to Human Resources and Social Development Canada by Turtle Island Consulting Services.

Campolieti, Michele. 2001. "Disability Insurance and the Labour Force Participation of Older Men and Women in Canada. *Canadian Public Policy/ Analyse de Politiques* 27(2): 179–194.

Campolieti, Michele and Chris Riddell. 2012. "Disability Policy and the Labor Market: Evidence from a Natural Experiment in Canada, 1998–2006." *Journal of Public Economics* 96(3): 306–316.

Canadian Human Rights Commission. 2013. "Report on Equality Rights of Aboriginal People." chrc-ccdp.gc.ca/sites/default/files/equality_aboriginal_report.pdf

Challinor, A.E. 2011. "Canada's Immigration Policy: A Focus on Human Capital." Migration Policy Institute. migrationpolicy.org/article/canadas-immigration-policy-focus-human-capital

Chang, Mariko Lin. 2000. "The evolution of sex segregation regimes." *American Journal of Sociology* 105(6): 1658–1701.

Chouinard, Vera. 2010. "Women with Disabilities' Experiences of Government Employment Assistance in Canada." *Disability & Rehabilitation* 32(2): 148–58.

CHRC. 2010. "Report on Equality Rights of Aboriginal People." Canadian Human Rights Commission.

Cohen, Marcy, Michael Goldberg, Nick Istvanffy, Tim Stainton, Adrienne Wasik, Karen-Marie Woods. 2008. "Removing Barriers at Work: Flexible Employment Options for People With Disabilities in BC." Canadian Centre for Policy Alternatives. policyalternatives.ca/sites/default/files/uploads/publications/BC_Office_Pubs/bc_2008/bc_removing_barriers_full.pdf.

CSLS. 2012. "Aboriginal Labour Market Performance in Canada: 2007-2011." Centre for the Study of Living Standards in Canada Report. Prepared for the Métis National Council. csls.ca/reports/csls2012-04.pdf

Department of Justice. 2015. "Cultural Diversity in Canada: The Social Construction of Racial Difference". Government of Canada: Reports and Publications. justice.gc.ca/eng/rp-pr/csj-sjc/jsp-sjp/rp02_8-dr02_8/p6.html

Drost, Helmar and John Richards. 2003. "Income On- and Off-Reserve: How Aboriginals are Faring." C.D. Howe Institute Commentary. cdhowe.org/sites/default/files/attachments/research_papers/mixed//commentary_175.pdf

Employment and Social Development Canada. 2016a. "Creating Jobs and Investment for Canadian Youth", Government of Canada Website. news.gc.ca/web/article-en.do?nid=1055809

Employment and Social Development Canada. 2016b. "Labour Market Development Agreements," Government of Canada Website. canada.ca/en/employment-social-development/programs/training-agreements/lmda.html

Employment and Social Development Canada. 2015. "Summative Evaluation of the Horizontal Youth Employment Strategy," Strategic Policy and Research Branch Employment and Social Development Canada. publications.gc.ca/collections/collection_2015/edsc-esdc/Em20-28-2015-eng.pdf

FAFIA. 2008. "Women's Inequality in Canada, Submission to the UN Committee on the Elimination of Discrimination against Women on the Occasion of the Committee's Review of Canada 6th and 7th reports." Feminist Alliance for International Action Report. socialrightscura.ca/documents/CEDAW/FAFIACanadaCEDAW2008.pdf

Fawcett, Gail. 2000. "Bringing Down the Barriers: The Labour Market and Women with Disabilities in Ontario." Canadian Council on Social Development. Ottawa.

Fortin, Nicole, David A. Green, Thomas Lemieux and Kevin Milligan. 2012. "Canadian Inequality: Recent Developments and Policy Options." *Canadian Public Policy* 38(2): 121–45.

Ferrao, Vincent. 2010. "Chapter 5: Paid Work" in "Women in Canada: A Gender-based Statistical Report." Component of Statistics Canada Catalogue no. 89-503-X. statcan.gc.ca/pub/89-503-x/2010001/article/11387-eng.pdf

Galarneau, Diane, René Morissette and Jeannine Usalcas. 2013. "What has changed for young people in Canada?." Statistics Canada. www.statcan.gc.ca/pub/75-006-x/2013001/article/11847-eng.pdf.

Gauvin, Michel, Nicole Marchand and Cal McKerral. 1975. *Collective Bargaining Legislation for Special Groups in Canada*. Ottawa: Labour Canada.

GC. 2016a. "Breaking Down Job Barriers: Expert Panel on Youth Established." Government of Canada News. news.gc.ca/web/article-en.do?nid=1138839

GC. 2016b. "Youth Employment Strategy." Government of Canada News. canada.ca/en/employment-social-development/services/funding/youth-employment-strategy.html

Houle, René and Lahouaria Yssaad. 2010. "Recognition of Newcomers' Foreign Credentials and Work Experience." Statistics Canada. statcan.gc.ca/pub/75-001-x/2010109/pdf/11342-eng.pdf

Hum, Derek and Wayne Simpson. 1996. "Canadians with Disabilities and the Labour Market." *Canadian Public Policy/Analyse de Politiques* 22(3): 285–299.

Human Resources and Social Development Canada. 2006. "Advancing the Inclusion of People with Disabilities." Human Resources and Skills Development Canada. Quebec.

Kaufman, Robert L. 2002. "Assessing alternative perspectives on race and sex employment segregation." *American Sociological Review* 67(4): 547–63.

Kustec, Stan. 2012. "The role of migrant labour supply in the Canadian labour market." Citizenship and Immigration Canada.

Lambert, Brittany and Kate McInturff. 2016. "Making Women Count: The Unequal Economics of Women's Work." Canadian Centre for Policy Alternatives and Oxfam Canada.

Lee, Marc and Marcy Cohen. 2005. *The Hidden Costs of Health Care Wage Cuts in BC.* Vancouver: Canadian Centre for Policy Alternatives.

Lee, Neil, Paul Sissons, Brhmie Balaram, Katy Jones, and Nye Cominetti. 2012. "Short-term Crisis - Long-term Problem? Addressing the Youth Employment Challenge." The Work Foundation: Part of Lancaster University.

Leung, Marlene. 2015. "Private Sector Workers Earn Less, Work More: Report." *CTV News* (23 March). Available online.

MacKinnon, Shauna. 2015. *Decolonizing Employment: Aboriginal Inclusion in Canada's Labour Market.* Winnipeg: University of Manitoba Press.

MacKinnon, Shauna. 2011. The Effectiveness of Neo-Liberal Labour Market Policy as a Response to the Poverty and Social Exclusion of Aboriginal Second-Chance Learners. Dissertation. University of Manitoba.

McHardie, Daniel. 2016. "New Brunswick's youth jobless rate highest in Canada as jobs disappear" *CBC News* (22 March). Available online.

McInturff, Kate. 2015. "The Best and Worst Places to be a Woman in Canada 2015: The Gender Gap in Canada's 25 Biggest Cites." Canadian Centre for Policy Alternatives. https://www.policyalternatives.ca/sites/default/files/uploads/publications/Nationalpercent20Office/2015/07/Best_and_Worst_Places_to_Be_a_Woman2015.pdf.

Mendelson, Michael. 2004. "Aboriginal People in Canada's Labour Market: Work and Unemployment, Today and Tomorrow." Caledon Institute of Social Policy. Ottawa.

NB. 2013. "New Brunswick's Labour Force and Skills Development Strategy 2013–2016." Province of New Brunswick.

Newman, Jacquetta and Linda A. White. 2006. *Women, Politics, and Public Policy: The Political Struggles of Canadian Women.* Don Mills: Oxford University Press.

Neysmith, Sheila, M. Reitsma-Street, Stephanie Baker Collins and Elaine Gertude Porter. 2009. "A Study of Women's Provisioning – Implications for

Social Provisions," in Marjorie Griffin Cohen and Jane Pulkingham, eds., *Public Policy for Women: The State, Income Security, and Labour Market Issues.* Toronto: University of Toronto Press.

ODSP Action Coalition. (n.d). "History, Issues, Strategies." odspaction.ca/page/history-issues-strategies.

ODSP Action Coalition. 2015. "Income Cut Coming for ODSP Recipients Who Work." Report. odspaction.ca/resource/odsp-recipients-who-work-lose-100-month

OECD. 2014. "Employment and Skills Strategies in Canada," OECD Publishing, Paris. DOI: http://dx.doi.org/10.1787/9789264209374-en.

Ontario. Ministry of Advanced Education and Skills Development. 2015. "Ontario Youth Jobs Strategy", Newsroom Ontario Website. https://news.ontario.ca/maesd/en/2015/01/ontario-youth-jobs-strategy.html

Owen, Timothy. 2003. "Immigrant Labour Market Policies, Programs and Outcomes.: City of Toronto." World Educations Services.

Pendakur, Krishna and Ravi Pendakur. 2011. "Aboriginal Income Disparity in Canada." *Canadian Public Policy* 37(1): 61–83.

Pennachini, Laura. 2017. "Citizens Work or Citizens Income." Social Europe. https://www.socialeurope.eu/2017/03/citizens-work-citizens-income/

Porter, Ann. 2003. *Gendered States: Women, Unemployment Insurance and the Political Economy of the Welfare State in Canada, 1945–1997.* Toronto: University of Toronto Press

Quebec. 2015. Secrétariat à la jeunesse du Québec. 2016a. "Incorporating Young People in Difficulty into the Labour Market and Young People not in Employment, nor in Education or Training." Secrétariat à la jeunesse du Québec Website. https://www.jeunes.gouv.qc.ca/strategie/travail-economie/employabilite.asp#contenuAxes

Richards, John and Aidan Vining. 2004. *Aboriginal Off-Reserve Education: Time for Action.* CD Howe Institute.

Schirle, Tammy. 2015. "The Gender Wage Gap in Canadian Provinces, 1997-2014." *Canadian Public Policy* 41(4):309–331.

Service Canada. 2016. "Youth Employment Strategy", Government of Canada Website. https://www.canada.ca/en/employment-social-development/services/funding/youth-employment-strategy.html?=undefined&wbdisable=true

Stasiulis, Daiva and Abigail Bakan. 2005. *Negotiating Citizenship: Migrant Women in Canada and the Global System.* Toronto: University of Toronto Press.

Statistics Canada. Nd. "Income Trends in Canada: Female to Male Earnings Ratios 1976-2007." Incomes Trends in Canada, 13F0022XCB.

Statistics Canada. 2017. "CANSIM Table 282-0002 - Labour Force Survey Estimates (LFS), by Sex and Detailed Age Group, Annual (Persons Unless

206

Otherwise Noted." Statistics Canada CANSIM Database. http://www5.statcan.gc.ca/cansim/a26?lang=eng&id=2820002

Supreme Court of Canada. 2016. Case Summary http://www.scc-csc.ca/case-dossier/info/sum-som-eng.aspx?cas=36500.

Turcotte, Martin. 2014. "Persons with Disabilities and Employment." Statistics Canada. statcan.gc.ca/pub/75-006-x/2014001/article/14115-eng.htm

Wilson, Daniel and David MacDonald. 2010. "The Income Gap between Aboriginal Peoples and the Rest of Canada." Canadian Centre for Policy Alternatives. policyalternatives.ca/sites/default/files/uploads/publications/reports/docs/Aboriginalpercent20Incomepercent20Gap.pdf/

Wilton, Robert and Stephanie Schuer. 2006. "Towards Socio-spatial Inclusion? Disabled People, Neoliberalism and the Contemporary Labour Market. *Area* 38(2): 186–95.

9

Dealing with Unions

Introduction

Trade unions developed to rectify the workplace power imbalance between employees and employers. In Standing's terms, they provide "representation security" or voice and input into the various decisions that have an impact on workers, including the other types of security that may or may not be provided either through the political system or through collective bargaining. At various times Canadian public policy was moderately encouraging in respect of efforts to unionize and bargain collectively on behalf of workers. At other times policy has been less supportive or even hostile to such efforts. Representation security through unionization was hard to achieve in Canada, slow to arrive, incomplete, and has proven hard to sustain in the neoliberal period. This chapter identifies such trends and seeks to explain the relatively hostile policy environment in which unions now function.

The state's involvement in regulating the relationship between labour and capital has its origins in labour's resistance to the unrestricted right of capital to manage its affairs, including its labour force. Trade unions are organizations of (typically) wage earners who combine together (into a "union") in order to collectively improve their working conditions and/or wages. The logic is simple: the power of the workers vis-à-vis an employer is greater when it is exercised collectively than when the individual stands alone. From the point of view of capital, labour has always constituted a problem. Pentland (1968, 2) characterized this labour problem as consisting of "how to make other people work effectively while turning over a good part of the fruits of their labour to the elite." For the employer, unions are to be opposed, avoided if possible, and coopted if formed. Employers have generally found it easier to deal with their employees as individuals rather than through a collective (and power-enhancing) intermediary.

In conflicts which arose between them, both labour and capital sought to make use of the state to bolster their own position. In capital's case such assistance would be additional to the legal structure which defended the rights of property in general. As a result of the regular or periodic conflict between capital and labour, the state became drawn into such matters as the regulation of their relationship, the specification of certain standards pertaining to the work process itself and, through its monopoly of legally sanctioned coercion, as arbiter of last resort. In this chapter, these aspects of state policy are dealt with under the general category of industrial relations policy.

The liberal state's relationship to the "labour problem" has been effectively described as follows:

> labour constitutes an indispensable factor of production with whose general availability, quality, discipline, and price the state may have to concern itself in the service of economic efficiency and growth. But the 'labour problem' is a problem of legitimation insofar as class conflict threatens the justificatory foundations of the liberal state in equity and community (Craven 1980, 160).

So the state's role, if not exactly a balancing act between rivals, does need to take into account the system's requirements for both economic growth and social stability.

Canadian industrial relations policy can be divided usefully into three substantive areas, the first of which—regulating the work process—is dealt with in Chapter 7 of this volume. The other two areas, the subject of this chapter, are regulation of the process of interaction between labour and capital; and the imposition of outcomes on the labour-capital interaction, either through coercively ending disputes, or through wage policies, which substitute a legislated settlement for a negotiated settlement of a given issue in dispute.

There are a number of distinct historical stages in the evolution of state activity in industrial relations policy that broadly correspond to periods in which particular economic paradigms were dominant. For this reason it makes some sense to conduct an analysis of each period while acknowledging a degree of overlap. The broad periods are the early period until the end of World War II, the Keynesian period from the war until the late 1970s in which union membership and influence expanded, and the neoliberal period from the early 1980s to the present. The imposition of outcomes on labour-capital disputes arguably becomes more important from the 1970s onward. Prior to this period—with the possible exception of wartime—the state could usually rely on the power imbalance between capital and labour to achieve the same results that, in later years, it would sometimes have to impose.

Unions themselves held different views about what their respective roles should be. To the extent that employers overcame their *absolute* opposition to trade unions, they favoured "responsible" unions which took account of their need to maintain profitability. On the union side were different conceptions of unionism and what tactics and strategies were likely to be effective. Those that have informed parts of the Canadian labour movement at some times and in some places are outlined briefly below.

The first is commonly described as "business unionism" (see Hoxie 1914). The organizational mode of these unions is based on job or occupation rather than any sense of being part of a working class with common interests. Business unionism accepts the economic system as is and seeks to achieve specific improvements for the benefit of union members. Goals are limited and largely economic in focus, and political action is eschewed entirely (or is confined to lobbying). There has been a strong tendency toward business unionism in Canada, especially in crafts-based unions, and so-called "international unions"—that is, unions that function as locals or districts of US-based unions.

A second type is "social reform" unionism. It has broader goals aimed at improving the conditions of all workers, not just those who belong to unions. Political action to achieve these goals has been an attractive option. In Canada this has typically taken the form of linking the unions with the social democratic party, the NDP and its predecessor, the Co-operative Commonwealth Federation (commonly known as the CCF). Traditionally this option was favoured by "industrial" unions organized on the basis of industrial sector (for example, the steelworkers) rather than by crafts-based unions. Thus there is a division of labour within the movement with the political arm, the NDP, seeking broad improvements, and the industrial arm, the trade unions, concentrating on economic issues of interest to their members through collective bargaining and some lobbying. Historically, the social democratic ideology offered its adherents a middle way between capitalism and communism. The Keynesian era was the high point of this approach, given that Keynesian economic management seemed to offer a relatively conflict-free way of meeting the goals of both capital and labour. The rise of neoliberalism has drastically narrowed the space for social democratic governance. As a result, Bryan Evans (2012, 94) has argued: "It is now virtually impossible to discover what sets an NDP government apart from those led by traditional parties of business."

This concept of unionism has become problematic, and there has been a trend toward "strategic voting," often expressed as voting for whatever party has the best chance of defeating the Conservative Party, on the part of some unions (see Savage 2012).

Radical and revolutionary unions have always been a minority tendency within Canada. However, two variants have had some impact historically. Both argued that permanent improvement in working-class living standards required the transformation of capitalism. The communist variant favoured class-based political action, including extra-parliamentary political activities, to achieve this end. The anarcho-syndicalist version relied on direct mass action, often in the form of the mass general strike to further its objectives.

This by no means exhausts the range of conceptions of the role of unions, but it does give an indication of how differently the basic goal of improving workers' conditions may be addressed. But as Stephanie Ross (2012) has reminded us with respect to business unionism and social unionism, the types may not be as counterposed in practice as they are as theoretically constructed ideal types. Unions play multiple roles. Even the most radical union will pay attention to the dull grind of collective bargaining, grievance arbitration and the like, as typified by business unions. Even the most narrowly focused business union is likely to pay some attention to influencing the political and legal context in which it must operate. Unions are engaged in a set of sometimes contradictory practices between which there may over time, or in response to circumstance, be some ebb and flow of emphasis. What is certain is that employers prefer to minimize unions' influence both in the workplace and in the broader sphere of politics.

Early Industrial Relations Policy: Process

Efforts to form unions have faced major obstacles. Looking at the early history of Canadian trade unionism we see a prolonged period of weakness, division, and uneven development between different sectors of the labour force. In the early years the size of the country, its sparse population and the difficulty posed by poor transport and communications all impeded organization. Despite this strikes occurred and organizations did emerge, sometimes from local societies and ethnic clubs, as with the Irish "navvies" who worked on canals (Russell 1990, 30–39). In any case it was not until the 1850–1870 period that industrial capitalism became established (Pentland 1968; Ryerson 1968). The emergent working class associated with this development was divided along ethnic lines (English versus Irish versus French), religion (Catholics versus Protestants), skill levels (crafts versus general labour), among others. Nevertheless a small labour movement, composed of generally small unions, did start to develop and clearly enjoyed a high degree of community or class support in certain locales. In the 1872 agitation for a Nine Hour Day, for example, demonstrations of 5,000 were held in Hamilton (out of a total population of 27,000) and 10,000 in Toronto (population 60,000) as well as in other centres (Langdon 1973, 19).

The first efforts at establishing central organizations of trade unions took place in this context with the Canadian Labour Protective Association, founded in Hamilton in 1872, followed by the Canadian Labour Union in Toronto the next year. Though the nine-hour day demand was only temporarily and incompletely achieved, the federal government did address union agitation with legislation removing its civil and criminal liability for conspiracy in restraint of trade. The development of a defined industrial relations system began with the federal 1872 Trade Unions Act under which unions were released from the threat of prosecution for criminal conspiracy. Later, legislation in 1875–76 legalized peaceful picketing. Helpful as this was for the unions, this type of legislation did not redress the power imbalance between labour and capital and in particular did nothing to compel employers to recognize and deal with unions as workers' representatives (Woods 1973, 39–42). Effectively, this legislation legalized trade unions. Notwithstanding their newfound legality, most unions and the labour centrals that had been established proved unable to withstand the economic depression of the 1870s and as a result disappeared from the scene.

As trade recovered so too did attempts to organize. However, in a nutshell, from the 1870s until World War II, trade unions were fragile and fragmented. This was partly a product of geographical dispersion, and the use of immigration and ethnic differences by employers to divide the workforce (Avery 1979; Bradwin 1972). Then, too, there were conscious efforts by political and economic elites to steer unions in moderate directions, and to forego radicalism and militancy. Where the latter did occur it was met with coercion (see Brown and Brown 1978).

In the 1870s some provinces, inspired by similar efforts in Australia, made attempts at establishing voluntary conciliation of worker-employer disputes. These, however, seem to have had little success, and were soon repealed (Smucker 1980, 242). Voluntary conciliation did feature as a part of the Canadian industrial relations system but this arrived later, in the early twentieth century, and at the federal level.

That approach involved either party being able to request state intervention in an actual or anticipated industrial dispute. Under the 1907 Industrial Disputes Investigation Act (IDIA) such a request resulted in compulsory investigation of the dispute during which suspensions of work were prohibited. The findings of a conciliation board were not binding on the parties, though there was provision for the publication of the board's findings. By this means it was assumed that the force of public opinion might influence the stance of the parties (Woods 1973, 56–64). As we noted in Chapter 2, following a 1925 judicial decision, labour jurisdiction became a largely provincial matter. However, with the exception of PEI, all provinces passed legislation enabling the Industrial Disputes Investigation Act to apply to them. Consequently the IDIA approach constituted the Canadian policy toward industrial disputes between 1907 and 1944. The Act did little to address the problem of employer refusal to recognize and negotiate with unions, a major issue for Canada's already fragile and fragmented labour movement in these years. Employers were compelled to participate with unions during the investigation of a dispute, but this "recognition" could prove merely tacit and temporary. The ban on work stoppages during an investigation also worked to hinder the exercise of labour's maximum sanction.

Early Industrial Relations Policy: Outcomes

The coercive apparatus of the Canadian state played a significant role in affecting the outcomes of labour-capital conflict. Examples included limiting workers' right to strike, picket, and boycott, while employers were able to fire and blacklist union members and hire strike-breakers (Csiernik 2009, 149; Palmer 2004, 336). In addition to dramatic events like the 1919 Winnipeg General Strike (see Masters 1956), repressive policies were routinely used against radical and militant workers' organizations, combined with a more conciliatory policy towards skilled workers and more moderate labour organizations (Cuneo 1980, 48–49; and, for a fuller account of the 1930s, Endicott 2012). The Royal Canadian Mounted Police and its predecessors carried out a labour control function (Brown and Brown 1978). Both the legislation and common law connected to industrial relations went "to great lengths to protect employers' property and freedom to use their property pretty much as they saw fit, while providing little or no protection of workers' freedom to protect their jobs and livelihoods" (Jamieson 1968, 471–72).

Canada's entry into World War II led to extensive state intervention into the economy, including regulation of wage levels (see Wood and Kumar 1976). After initially agreeing to them in the early years of the war, organized labour became increasingly hostile to wage controls (MacDowell 1978, 13). Associated with these criticisms was concern with labour's lack of input into government decisions, particularly those affecting workers. Dissatisfaction with wage controls helped to fuel labour's demands for reforms in the collective bargaining system that were conceded in 1944 with the Order-in-Council PC 1003. Wage controls were lifted in November 1946 and the issue faded from the scene until the late 1960s.

Industrial Relations in the Keynesian Era: Process

The full-employment conditions of World War II, and the labour militancy associated with it, enabled Canada's trade unions to win state support in establishing an ongoing bargaining relationship with employers (MacDowell 1978). The Keynesian paradigm—which saw in unions a partial mechanism for sustaining levels of aggregate demand—and served as a rationale for the state's concessions to the increased strength of organized labour may have helped. Essentially, however, the concessions were won through militancy in a context of full-employment and the need to keep labour on-side with the war effort. The initial response came in 1944 through a federal order-in-council (P.C. 1003) and this was later codified into law as the Industrial Relations and Disputes Investigation Act of 1948 (Smith 2008).

The Canadian legislation is often regarded as an imitation of the US Roosevelt New-Deal-era Wagner Act. Aspects of the Wagner Act's approach to labour-capital relationships were certainly included in the Canadian legislation. Such aspects consisted of the acceptance of trade unionism and collective bargaining as a right (provided there was evidence of a certain level of worker support) and the establishment of an enforcement machinery (Woods 1973, 64–70, 86–92). But Canada's post-war legislation also contained provisions for compulsory conciliation and mediation before strikes could occur, banned strikes during the duration of collective agreements, and placed a number of other restrictions on the way unions could operate (Godard 2013). In Canada, the focus on industrial peace meant more interventionism, constraining employers' ability to disregard workers' collective bargaining rights (even though, with time, several provinces enacted laws to protect employer free speech). However, Canadian labour law also denied unions access rights to the workplace, making it more difficult to organize (Godard 2013, 408).

The law set out to protect the ability of employers and unions to fairly bargain, prohibited anti-union behaviour, recognized the primacy of collective agreements, and acknowledged that the public needed to be protected during labour disputes. Organized labour received the right to bargain collectively, the legal right to strike, mandatory recognition, and trade union security, later expressed in an arbitration decision as the Rand Formula. Named after Mr. Justice Ivan Rand who, when arbitrating a case to resolve a Windsor strike, provided that the employer deduct union dues (known as "automatic checkoff") for all employees within a bargaining unit whether union members or not. This provided a degree of union security since "freeloaders" could no longer obtain the benefits of the union contract without having paid for them in the form of dues. On the other hand, unions were required to respect an employer's right to manage during the life of a negotiated settlement, ensuring stability in the workplace (Smith 2008).

Keynesian theories may have done something to reconcile Canada's political and economic establishments to an enhanced role for trade unions—unions could play a positive role in sustaining levels of aggregate demand. However, the legal concessions were driven by working class pressure, not economic theory. The industrial relations regime that emerged did represent major gains for labour. However, it was far from an unqualified victory for labour. The new industrial relations system was characterized by elaborate certification procedures, legally enforceable contracts, no-strike provisions for the duration of contracts, and liability of trade unions and their members if illegal strikes occurred. On the other hand, the legislation guaranteed the right to organize and to bargain collectively, forced employers to recognize unions once certain conditions were met, defined unfair labour practices, and provided remedies under the law for violations. Labour's pressure on the state to provide assistance in establishing a bargaining relationship ultimately proved successful. But the price for this assistance was extensive state regulation and the continuation of the compulsory conciliation and "work stoppage delay" features of earlier legislation (McBride 1983, 508–509). The cumulative effect of the restrictions was to curtail severely labour's right to strike (Woods 1973, 93) and perhaps encourage the adoption of a bureaucratic and legalistic approach amongst the labour leadership.

A Canada-wide system of collective bargaining continued to exist because most provinces adopted legislation patterned after P.C. 1003. That said, there were significant variations. One province deviated from the pattern in the direction of less restriction: public servants in Saskatchewan were granted the same right to trade unionism as other workers, and there were no compulsory conciliation procedures. Mostly, though, public sector union and bargaining rights came much later, in the 1960s and 1970s, and any deviations from the immediate post-war pattern were towards more restrictions on labour than the federal legislation contained. Examples included restrictions on picketing, secondary boycotts and sympathy strikes in BC, Newfoundland, and Alberta; prohibition of strikes in essential services in Alberta; government supervision of strike votes in BC and Manitoba; regulation of the internal affairs of trade unions in Ontario, Newfoundland, and BC; limits on the ability of unions to provide funds for political parties in BC, PEI, and Newfoundland; and decertification of allegedly communist-led unions in Quebec.

Public-sector collective bargaining became more widespread, after Quebec legislation in 1964, and passage of the federal Public Service Staff Relations Act in 1967. In terms of public sector bargaining, the Keynesian period saw the adoption of public sector bargaining laws which enabled bargaining over wages, and often provided a choice-of-procedures model, allowing unions to choose whether disputes would be settled through arbitration or work stoppages. This period—from roughly 1960 to 1982—saw rapid growth in federal and provincial public sectors, high wage settlements, and relatively high strike activity (Rose 2005, 520; Swimmer and Bartkiw 2003, 579). By the mid-1970s public service employees in all jurisdictions enjoyed some form of bargaining rights. There were differences between jurisdictions about the extent to which the right to strike applied to public servants, the scope of collective bargaining, and differential treatment of public sector workers.

Federal public servants, and those in BC, New Brunswick, Newfoundland, Quebec, and Saskatchewan, enjoyed the right to strike.

With the exception of Alberta, Ontario, and PEI, this right also applied to workers in the broader public sector. The scope of bargaining rights was generally narrower for public servants than for private sector workers, though there was considerable variation between jurisdictions (Gauvin et al 1976, 62–87). The economic crisis of the 1970s and the eventual displacement of Keynesianism by neoliberalism was reflected in attacks upon the collective bargaining rights of unions generally, and of public sector unions in particular (Ross and Savage 2013).

Industrial Relations in the Keynesian Era: Outcomes

The extension of concessions to labour took place in a context of developing international Cold War between the U.S. and its allies on the one hand, and the USSR on the other. Cold War coercion against radical unions and unionists also played a role in ushering in the new system. In a number of high-profile cases, such as that of the Canadian Seamen's Union (CSU), the state actively sought to remove radicals, mostly communists, from its leadership, ultimately preferring to see the CSU replaced by a union led by a notorious American gangster, Hal Banks (Green 1986). In other cases it tacitly encouraged more moderate unionists, in particular the social democrats belonging to the CCF, to oust radicals from the trade union movement (Lang n.d.; Green 1986; Abella 1973; Lembcke and Tattam 1984).

The end-result was that the Keynesian era was able to proceed with unions that were ideologically acceptable to capital on social and political issues, and while industrial conflict did take place it occurred within a legal framework that rendered its incidence predictable, even if some of the encounters were hard-fought. Over the post-war period a perception grew that labour was making gains at the bargaining table, and that wage increases were driving up inflation and prices, and therefore creating competitiveness issues for business. Compared to the immediate post-war period labour's share of national income had increased significantly by the mid-1960s, by between 14 percent and 18 percent, depending on the measure used (Kumar 1971, 12–13).

This triggered a response from the state in the direction of controlling wages. Initially, in 1969 the federal government established a Prices and Incomes Commission which, for the next several years, advocated the introduction of a voluntary program of prices and incomes restraint (Anton 1973). Clearly increased militancy on the part of organised labour, in conditions of relatively full-employment, was driving its increasing share of the national income (Wolfe 1977, 260–63). By 1972 the Prices and Incomes Commission had become inactive because of the "tensions (which) developed in the relations between (it and) the organized labour movements" (Berger, 15).

The other way of regulating the outcomes of labour-capital interaction—emergency back-to-work legislation—also mushroomed during the 1970s and 1980s. Even in the late 1960s, however, the increasing incidence of this type of legislation was apparent. Greater use of this policy instrument, by both federal and provincial levels of government, coincided with the extension of collective bargaining to public sector workers and, particularly in the later period, with deepening economic crisis and the perception that trade unions bore major responsibility for economic ills, such as inflation, afflicting the country.

In 1975 compulsory wage controls were introduced in the shape of the Anti-Inflation Program (Maslove and Swimmer 1980, 11). This program covered federal government and Crown corporation employees, public sector employees in participating provinces, workers in larger firms in the private sector, and professionals. Allowable wage increases varied according to a complex formula to which exceptions on certain grounds were theoretically possible. However, in general it can be said that between 1975 to 1978 the incomes of most Canadian workers were controlled and their collective bargaining correspondingly curtailed.

Subsequent rounds of wage controls in the 1980s and 1990s and beyond belong more to the neoliberal periodization adopted here. They tended to be aimed specifically at public sector workers, and were rationalized in terms of bringing budget deficits under control. These measures were taken in the federal and in most provincial jurisdictions. The specifics varied considerably in ways that need not detain us here—different categories of public sector employees were covered by restraint, and the wage limits to which they were subject also varied. The common feature, however, was that these policies severely undermined the collective bargaining rights achieved by public sector workers in the 1960s and early 1970s. With the exception of the 1975–78 period, and occasional exhortations to voluntary restraint, governments seemed content to allow rising unemployment to take care of wage bargaining in the private sector (McBride 1992). But some categories of private sector workers, along with many in the public sector, continued to be affected by the second major type of intervention in the outcomes of collective bargaining: the use of ad hoc emergency legislation to end disputes.

Industrial Relations in the Neoliberal Era: Process

Public sector workers, having gradually achieved collective bargaining rights by the 1970s, have witnessed their erosion and restriction since then. Bargaining rights were further expanded in some areas, especially in the early 1970s, but since then the general trend has been towards restriction. In addition to wage controls and ad hoc emergency legislation, there has been a determined effort in some provinces to dramatically roll back collective bargaining rights and union security. These efforts have been especially visible in the public sector but have not been confined to it—there have been restrictions on private sector bargaining rights as well.

Chart 25 presents a summary of activity in these areas. Given the abundance of legislation no thorough summary of it is possible here. But some of the main trends will be touched upon.

About two thirds of these interventions (140 out of 218) deal with "outcomes" through enactment of back to work legislation or imposed wage freezes or roll-backs. The remainder (78/218) affect the way labour and capital interact or what I have termed "process." These are grouped into regulations concerning: how unions get certified (a process that compels employers to recognise and bargain with them), who may belong to a union, and the scope of bargaining or of union behaviour more broadly. Summarizing the evidence, the Canadian Foundation for Labour Rights noted that: "Restrictions have been placed on the right of unions to organize. Collective agreements have been torn up. Freely negotiated wages and benefits have been taken away. Employers' proposals have been legislatively imposed on workers and the right to strike removed. Both the private and the public sectors have been hit by this phenomenon" (Canadian Foundation for Labour Rights 2015).

Chart 25: Summary of Labour Laws Restricting Collective Bargaining and Trade Union Rights, 1982 to 2016

Legislation	Jurisdiction											
	Fed	BC	AB	SK	MB	ON	QC	NB	PE	NS	NL	Total
Back to work—dispute sent to arbitration	11	4		3		15	3	2		2		40
Back to work—settlement imposed	8	5	4	3		5	17	4		1	3	50
Suspension of bargaining rights—wage freeze or rollback imposed	6	12	1	1	2	7	6	2	2	8	3	50
Restrictions on certification process	1	1			1	2	1				2	8
Denial of workers' rights to join a union		1	2			3	3					9
Restrictions on scope of bargaining and other union activities	7	16	5	7	4	6	3	4	1	5	3	61
Total	33	39	12	14	7	38	33	12	3	16	11	218

Source: Canadian Foundation for Labour Rights (labourrights.ca/issues/restrictive-labour-laws-canada).

A partial list of federal and provincial incursions into established rights would include the following: (1) increasing the number of jobs which are designated "essential to the safety and security" of the public and consequently removing the right to strike from occupants of these jobs; (2) back-to-work legislation which contained increasingly draconian penalties for violators (Panitch and Swartz 1988, 70–77); (3) using arguments of fiscal restraint to alter or abrogate existing contractual provisions in staff contracts, eliminate job security for public sector employees; declaring political strikes to be illegal; (4) making union certification more difficult and decertification easier; (5) restrictions on secondary picketing; and forcing union workers to work alongside non-union workers on union work sites (Annis 1987, 138); (6) provisions which weakened union shops and allowed the circumvention of union hiring halls; (7) easing the conditions under which unionized companies could set up non-union firms; (8) increasing opportunities for individuals to opt out of unions and to have unions decertified; and forced unions to hold votes on company "final offers"; (9) banning strikes by nurses and hospital workers and substituting compulsory arbitration which had to take into account such factors as ability to pay, government guidelines and general fiscal policy; (10) rewriting public sector collective agreements' provisions regarding job security and working conditions; (11) measures to grant employers greater latitude in opposing unionization drives; (12) and increasing the majorities necessary for certification or strike votes. Of course, not all of these provisions are in place in all jurisdictions or at all times. But the list is indicative of a widespread effort to whittle away at labour rights and, in some cases, alter them dramatically.

There are examples of legislative changes more favourable to labour. These include: check-off of union dues on demand; prohibition on the use of professional strikebreakers; legislation to impose first contracts and thus overcome employer resistance; easing restrictions on union certification; and improving grievance arbitration procedures. But the list is shorter, and measures were often revoked by incoming governments of a different persuasion to that which enacted them.

Many of the changes seem quite technical but can carry major implications for unionization. An example is how unions get certified. One option is for them to sign up a specified percentage of workers in the bargaining unit, after which certification becomes automatic. An alternative is to have the signatures trigger a mandatory vote, a device which arguably gives employers the option of making their opposition known or otherwise influence the workforce. Much labour legislation has shifted from card check to secret ballot/mandatory vote (Dickie 2005, 3). Mandatory vote correlates with much weaker union organizing success than card check. In BC and Ontario—which together account for about 50 percent of the Canadian workforce—the delay inherent in mandatory elections had a significant negative effect on union wins in certification campaigns (Warner 2013, 120). In a study of Ontario from 1993 to 1998, the first three years were card check and the last three followed the principle of mandatory elections. Controlling for bargaining unit size, type of employment, and initial level of support, unionization attempts under mandatory vote were 21 percent less likely to be successful than under card check (Warner 2013, 120). A study of all provinces found that from 1978 to 1996, mandatory elections reduced union success rates in certification by 9 percent (121). British Columbia went back and forth between the two options from 1984 onwards. Certifications decreased in every period of mandatory vote and increased in every period of card check (Dickie 2005, 4).

As negative as such restrictions are from a union perspective, there is always the fear that worse may be on the horizon. An example of a potential shift is "right to work" legislation, which undermines union security. Union security arrangements are rules that ensure unions can continue to consistently represent workers in a workplace; may require workers in a legally constituted bargaining unit to be union members and/or to pay union dues (Sinclair-Waters 2014, 6).

In 2012 one of the opposition parties in Ontario, the Ontario Progressive Conservative party, produced a white paper entitled "Paths to Prosperity: Flexible Labour Markets" which, among other provisions, sought to outlaw "fair share" union dues (in other words, to prohibit the Rand formula), ban arrangements that make union membership a condition of employment, make union leaders collect dues instead of employers, place limits on union funded advocacy and political action, and impose extensive financial reporting requirements on unions (9). These provisions are similar to those found in many parts of the US where individual states have the ability to adopt laws that prohibit union security arrangements, thus giving rise to "Right to Work" (RTW) laws that block the equivalent of the Rand formula in the US (10). In 2016, 24 states, mostly in the south, have adopted RTW laws, most recently in Indiana, Wisconsin, and Michigan. Michigan in particular is a competitor state to the central Canadian industrial provinces. Unsurprisingly right to work states feature substantially lower union density and lower wages (average annual wages were $5,766 lower in RTW states than the rest of the US), 18 out of 22 RTW states had median incomes below the national average; and a 2011 Economic Policy Institute study, controlling for 42 economic, demographic, and geographic policy factors, isolated the effect of RTW legislation to reduce real wages by 3.2 percent. This is a very conservative measure that ignores indirect impacts of unionization on wages (e.g. threat of employer relocation in RTW states also suppresses wages) (12). The Ontario Progressive Conservatives were unsuccessful in the election but the issue of right to work was put on the political table.

Two pieces of federal legislation raised concerns about the direction of the Canadian labour relations regime, had the Harper government been re-elected. These were Bill C-525 "The Employees' Voting Rights Act" which made it more difficult for workers to join a union at the federal level and easier to decertify one (Canadian Foundation for Labour Rights 2015). The Act shifts certification to mandatory vote, such that once 40 percent of workers sign a union card, a vote can take place, regardless of what percentage of workers sign union cards. Decertification is possible once 40 percent of a bargaining unit's members wish to do so. Another example is Bill C-377 an "Amendment to the Income Tax Act," which passed on June 30, 2015 (Canadian Foundation for Labour Rights 2015). The Act went through various iterations utilizing the language of transparency and accountability in an effort to mobilize public support for imposition of onerous accounting costs on unions. Labour organizations would be required to post all financial statements and transactions over $5,000 on a government website on the grounds that union dues are tax deductible. There were no reciprocal obligations on corporations and professional societies who benefit from similar tax credits. The extensive reporting requirements would be overwhelming for small union locals, disproportionately increasing the cost of representing small units (Godard 2013, 411). The Act received support from some of Canada's leading anti-union organizations and was presented as a private member's bill, albeit one that passed as a result of government support (Stevens and Nesbitt 2014). Early in 2016 the new Liberal government announced it would repeal both pieces of legislation (Press 2016).

Industrial Relations in the Neoliberal Era: Outcomes

Chart 25, above, depicts the general pattern of legislation to affect and often nullify the outcome of collective bargaining with 140 legislative actions to impose back to work legislation or wage freezes or roll-backs. In combination with the process changes outlined above, the environment of labour action has become debilitating, notwithstanding moments of, sometimes, successful resistance. In the 1990s the Conservative Harris government in Ontario enacted cuts to the welfare state and amended labour legislation in a pro-management direction provoking major opposition despite splits in the labour movement about the tactics—direct action or parliamentary-electoral—to be followed.

The Days of Action in Ontario were city-wide mobilizations. The first took place in London, Ontario, on December 11, 1995, as over 20,000 workers and citizens took to the streets to protest the policies of the Harris government. A few months later in Hamilton, there were two more days of action. On February 23, 1996, almost 30,000 workers struck on the first day of action. On the following day, February 24, between 100,000 and 120,000 thousand people turned out, making it one of the largest protests in Canadian history.

A week after the Hamilton days of action, Ontario government workers represented by the Ontario Public Sector Employees Union (OPSEU) began a five-week strike, and labour-led protests were undertaken in Waterloo-Kitchener (30,000 people) and Peterborough. These demonstrations set the groundwork for the Toronto day of action on October 25, 1996. Public sector workers, including transport workers from the TTC (that is, the Toronto Transit Commission), struck illegally, essentially shutting down the city, and the following day approximately 250,000 people demonstrated at Queen's Park.

Despite these strong shows of solidarity, the movement eventually lost momentum (account based on rankandfile.ca/2014/11/06/the-ontario-days-of-action-a-graphic-history). Whether it failed to reverse the government's policies or succeeded in preventing even more drastic cuts continues to be debated.

Other actions enjoyed some limited success. For example, in a 2002 public sector strike, OPSEU won significant wage increases and greater job security for contract employees. The government gained the right to pay for performance bonuses, but lost the attempt to take full control of the pension plan surplus.

In BC a 2004 dispute between the BC Hospital Employees' Union (HEU) and the government of BC saw 40,000 union members participate in an illegal strike. The strike action was taken in response to threats to privatize jobs and health services throughout the province. As the BC government attempted to implement "leaner" health services, contention arose surrounding job security and pay as 2,500 workers were laid off after a notice to bargain was given. Furthermore, the BC government proposed to cut wages by 15 percent, increase work hours for the lowest-paid workers, and place very few limits on contracting out (Lee and Cohen 2005, 7–8).

The argument for the wage cut was to achieve a reduction of $200 million per year in operating costs, during a time when the health care budget was expanding and doctors and nurses were receiving pay increases (Lee and Cohen 2005, 8). This was part of a larger project of public sector restructuring by the BC Liberals who came to power in 2001. In January 2002, the BC government passed Bill 29, removing security protections, contracting out protections and allowing employers to avoid union succession rights by firing and re-hiring workforces between contracts (Lee and Cohen 2005, 9).

After conciliation and mediation failed, the BC HEU issued a 72-hour strike notice on April 22, and set up pickets at every hospital and long-term care facility on April 25. On April 28, the government tabled Bill 37—back to work legislation that included retroactive concessions and no employment security. After the passing of Bill 37 the following morning, over 30,000 union members from across the public and private sector walked off the job in support. The HEU and sympathy strike eventually ended on May 2, 2004, as the BC Federation of Labour and the HEU signed a memorandum with government limiting the severity of the collective agreement as it directed its members to stand down and return to work.

The union won restrictions on contracting out, but accepted the 15 percent rollback on wages. Furthermore, existing contracts covering housekeeping, food, and laundry services were retained by private health corporations (Isitt and Moroz 2006, 91).

Another BC case shows the longevity of labour disputes and also the mixture of tactics employed by labour—in this case traditional strike actions augmented by appeals to the courts that were ultimately successful. In 2002, the BC Liberals passed two laws governing collective bargaining between the British Columbia Teachers' Federation (BCTF) and the British Columbia Public School Employees Association. The legislation imposed a three-year collective agreement on approximately 45,000 teachers in the BCTF, and prohibited future bargaining on certain issues such as class size, staffing (contracting out), and integration of special needs students (The Supreme Court of Canada 2016).

The dispute eventually came to the Supreme Court of Canada through the Supreme Court of British Columbia. In 2011 the Supreme Court of British Columbia had found that the legislation was unconstitutional due to its infringement upon s. 2(d)—freedom of association—of the Canadian Charter of Rights and Freedoms. In 2012, to address the decision, the BC government enacted another piece of legislation—the Education Improvement Act—that contained sections "virtually identical," to the earlier legislation. BC Supreme Court Justice Susan Griffin ruled that the Education Improvement Act was also unconstitutional (The Supreme Court of Canada 2016).

The government took the case to the British Columbia Court of appeal which ruled in its favour. In response, the BCTF took the case to the Supreme Court, which ruled in favour of the teachers in a 7-2 decision, reinstating the 2014 ruling by BC Justice Griffin (*The Huffington Post* 2016).

Throughout the dispute the BCTF combined legal avenues through the various courts, and also engaged in several strikes. These direct actions involved a three-day strike in 2012, and a 2014 strike that was the longest in BC teacher's history (*Vancouver Sun* 2016). Collective bargaining in 2014 eventually led to a six-year deal (expiring in 2019), but did not address the issues that were moving through the courts at the time. Both parties agreed to negotiate those points of the deal subsequent to the respective court decisions.

The implications of this decision could have far reaching consequences, not only for the public sector in BC, but also across the country. The fact the case eventually went to the Supreme Court of Canada may help establish a precedent for the constitutionality of collective bargaining in the public sector, in the face of numerous attempts by various governments across the country to restrict or suspend the scope of collective bargaining.

On the other hand, the previous history of recourse to the courts, even since the 1982 Charter of Rights and Freedoms, is not altogether encouraging. Reviewing the thirty year period after the Charter, Charles W. Smith (2012, 196) concluded that:

> court decisions have been mixed, and labour's legal strategies
> have served as defensive efforts to preserve a small component

of the post-war labour regime. To be sure these decisions have opened small spaces of resistance, giving labour tools to extend spaces of legimation. Yet … judicial interpretation of existing laws have limitations as well as opportunities.

Of course, legislative erosion of labour rights is only one factor in weakening labour. Structural and political factors such as competition induced by globalization and trade agreements and government tolerance of high unemployment, and stripping of the system of social supports, all have a major impact on union strength.

Federally the effects of these factors in containing wage rates were supplemented by statutory income policies, beginning in the Keynesian period with the implementation of compulsory wage and price controls in 1975, a move which led to massive but ultimately unsuccessful worker protests (Briskin 2006, 7). Incomes policies in the form of wage restraints or freezes were continued into the neoliberal period, especially with regard to public sector workers. In 1982, the "Public Sector Compensation Restraint Act (C-124)" imposed a two-year wage restraint on public employees and suppressed their right to bargain and strike, with most provinces following suit and leading to a drop in strike frequency. Public sector workers were increasingly designated as "essential," thereby removing their right to strike and in other cases, were faced with "back to work" legislation (7). Bryan Evans (2013) has tracked the incidence and impact of public sector wage restraint at both federal and provincial levels and depicts it as having become a permanent feature of fiscal policy.

At the federal level alone there were at least ten pieces of legislation that variously designated essential workers, imposed or removed arbitration as an option in settling disputes, instructed arbitrators to take into account the government's fiscal circumstances in awards, imposed caps on salary increases, or wage freezes, excluded some issues such as staffing and job classification from collective bargaining, terminated disputes through back to work legislation, and allowed governments to impose terms and conditions.

Notwithstanding impressive examples of resistance to legislative erosion of labour rights and austerity policies, the strike (Chart 26) and union density statistics (Chart 27) tell their own tale of the impact on trade union organization and practices.

Chart 26: Person Days Lost Through Strikes and Lockouts, 1976 to 2014

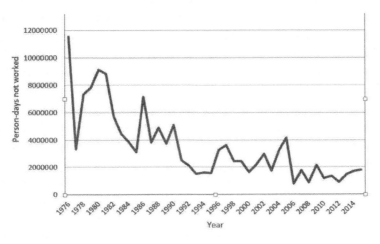

Source: Table 278-0013 - Work stoppages in Canada, by jurisdiction and industry based on the North American Industry Classification System (NAICS), Employment and Social Development Canada - Labour Program

Chart 27: Union Density: Change in Unionization in Canada

Jurisdiction	1981 (%)	2015 (%)	% Change
Canada	38	30.6	-19.5
Newfoundland	45	37.3	-17.1
PEI	39	34.1	-12.6
Nova Scotia	34	31.0	-8.8
New Brunswick	41	29.3	-28.5
Quebec	45	39.4	-12.4
Ontario	37	26.8	-27.6
Manitoba	38	35.9	-5.5
Saskatchewan	38	33.2	-12.6
Alberta	28	23.5	-16.1
BC	45	30.3	-32.7

Source: CANSIM Table 282-0078 Labour Force Survey Estimates (LFS)

Erosion of union coverage since the 1970s in Canada has meant wage stagnation and heightened income inequality (Brennan 2014, 7). Union density (total private and public sector coverage as a percentage of the workforce) was 38 percent in 1981 and just over 30 percent in 2015 (Galarneau and Sohn 2013). The decline was observed more among men than women, as the percentage of men in unionized jobs fell from 42 percent in 1981 to 29 percent in 2012, while women's unionization rate stayed around 30 percent during the same period (Galarneau and Sohn 2013, 3). From 1999 to 2012, union coverage in all industries dropped from 30.4 percent to 29.9 percent, the public sector increased from 70.8 percent to 71.3 percent while the private sector dropped from 18.4 percent to 16.4 percent (again indicating that the bulk of decline in union density occurred during the 1980s and 1990s) (Galarneau and Sohn 2013, 6).

The impact of declining union density on incomes was significant. Families with one or more full-time unionized worker were 1.75 times more likely to have incomes at the upper end of the income scale (deciles 5 to 9) (Mackenzie and Shillington 2015, 3). In each recessionary period, workers who entered it with union coverage and exited without it dropped on the income ladder, often by two or more deciles (e.g. from 2006 to 2011, 39 percent of those who lost union jobs declined two or more deciles; median income dropped by 9 percent) (3). Comparing them to those who gained union representation during the course of a crisis, 35 percent of whom moved up two or more deciles, with their median incomes increasing by 39 percent (3), illustrates the point that unions are a mechanism of socio-economic mobility and insurance against economic difficulty (4).

The contrast with the postwar Keynesian era is dramatic. From 1945 to the late 1970s and early 1980s, the gap between the rich and the rest narrowed while the economy grew: the income share of the richest 5 percent of Canadians dropped from 24.6 percent of all income in 1945 to 22.1 percent in 1979; the income share of the richest 1 percent dropped from 10.1 percent in 1945 to 7.7 percent in 1979 (Mackenzie and Shillington 2015, 5). During that same period, the real average weekly earnings of working Canadians more than doubled, increasing by 114 percent after inflation (5). From the early 1990s to today, coinciding with a period of stagnation in median real incomes, the richest 10 percent collected 48 percent of all inflation adjusted income *growth* in the country; the richest 5 percent accrued 35 percent of all income growth; the richest 1 percent received 18 percent of all growth; whilst the bottom 50 percent received 7 percent (6).

Conclusions

Founded to moderate power imbalances between capital and labour, unions endured long periods of fragmentation and weakness before emerging at the end of World War II and into the post-war era as more powerful actors. Even then their power was circumscribed in comparison to unions in western Europe, but sustained by relatively full-employment and a degree of legal support, they were able to exert influence on pay and conditions.

The replacement of the Keynesian period by neoliberalism and globalization meant the end of full-employment, a transition to a flexible labour market characterized by insecurity, and increased state intervention into the outcomes and processes of collective bargaining by which means unions had attempted to improve wages and working conditions. Clearly state action contributed to weakening unions and their ability to foster various kinds of security: union density declined especially in the private sector, and use of strikes declined as workers calculated the diminished odds of winning under the new conditions in the political economy. The decline of the organizations best able to protect workers' interests in turn facilitated the implementation of neoliberal policies of flexibility and insecurity.

References

Annis, R. 1987. "The Impact of the BC Government 'Restraint' Program on Provincial Employees, Social Services and Women," in R. Argue, C. Gannage, and D.W. Livingstone, eds., 1987, *Working People and Hard Times: Canadian Perspectives*. Toronto, Garamond.

Avery, Donald. 1979. *"Dangerous Foreigners": European Immigrant Workers and Labour Radicalism in Canada, 1896-1932*. Toronto: McClelland and Stewart.

Berger, G.A. 1973. *Canadian Experience with Incomes Policy, 1969–70*. Ottawa: Prices and Incomes Commission.

Bradwin, Edmund. 1972. *Bunkhouse Man: A Study of Work and Pay in the Camps of Canada 1903-1914*. Toronto: University of Toronto Press.

Brennan, Jordan. 2014. "The Creation of Shared Prosperity in Canada: Unions, Corporations and Countervailing Power." Ottawa: Canadian Centre for Policy Alternatives.

Briskin, Linda. 2006. "Worker Militancies Revealed: Interrogating the Statistical Data." Paper Prepared for the Union Module of the Gender and Work Database.

Brown, Lorne and Caroline Brown. 1978. *An Unauthorized History of the RCMP*. Toronto: James Lorimer.

Canadian Foundation for Labour Rights. 2015. "Restrictive Labour Laws in Canada."

Craven, Paul. 1980. '*An Impartial Umpire*': *Industrial Relations and the Canadian State 1900–1911*. Toronto: University of Toronto Press.

Csiernik, Rick. 2009. "Labour Welfare in Canada: An Examination of Occupational Assistance." *Journal of Workplace Behavioural Health* 24(1/2): 147–64.

Cuneo, Carl. 1980. "State Mediation of Class Contradictions in Canadian Unemployment Insurance, 1930-1935." *Studies in Political Economy* 3(1): 37–65.

Dickie, Patrick. 2005. "The Crisis in Union Organizing under the BC Liberals." Hastings Labour Law Office.

Endicott, Stephen L. 2012. *Raising the Workers' Flag: The Workers Unity League of Canada, 1930-36*. Toronto: University of Toronto Press.

Evans, Bryan. 2012 "From Protest Movement to neoliberal management" in Bryan Evans and Ingo Schmidt, eds., *Social Democracy After the Cold War*. Edmonton: Athabasca University Press.

Evans, Bryan. 2013. "When Your Boss is the State: The Paradoxes of Public Sector Work" in Stephanie Ross and Larry Savage, eds., *Public Sector Unions in the Age of Austerity*. Halifax: Fernwood.

Galarneau, Diane and Thao Sohn. 2013. Long-term Trends in Unionization. Statistics Canada.

Gauvin, Michel; Marchand, Nicole, and McKerral, Cal.1975. *Collective Bargaining Legislation for Special Groups in Canada*. Ottawa: Labour Canada.

Godard, John. 2013. "Labour Law and Union Recognition in Canada: A Historical-Institutionalist Perspective." *Queen's Law Journal* 38(2): 391–418.

Green, Jim. 1986. *Against the Tide: The Story of the Canadian Seamen's Union*. Toronto: Progress Books.

Hoxie, Robert F. 1914. "Trade Unionism in the United States." *The Journal of Political Economy* 22(3): 201–17.

Isitt, B. and Moroz, M. 2007. "The Hospital Employees' Union Strike and the Privatization of Medicare in British Columbia, Canada." *International Labor and Working-Class History* 70.

Jamieson, Stuart. 1968. "Times of Trouble: Labour Unrest and Industrial Conflict in Canada, 1900-1966." Ottawa: Study No.22 for the Task Force on Labour Relations.

Kumar, Pradeep. 1971. *Long-run Changes in the Labour Share of National Income in Canada, 1926–1966.* Kingston: Industrial Relations Centre, Queen's University.

Lang, John. N.d. "A Lion in a Den of Daniels: A History of the International Union of Mine-Mill and Smelter Workers in Sudbury, Ontario, 1942–62." Unpublished M.A. Thesis, University of Guelph.

Langdon, Steven. 1973. *The Emergence of the Canadian Working Class Movement.* Toronto: New Hogtown Press.

Lee, M. and Cohen, M. 2005. *The Hidden Costs of Health Care Wage Cuts in BC.* Vancouver: Canadian Centre for Policy Alternatives

Lembke, Jerry and Tattam, William M. 1984. *One Union in Wood: A Political History of the International Woodworkers of America.* New York: International Publishers.

MacDowell, Laura Sefton. 1978. "The Formation of the Canadian Industrial Relations System During World War II." *Labour: Journal of Canadian Labour Studies* 3, 175–96.

Mackenzie, Hugh and Richard Shillington. 2015. "The Union Card: A Ticket Into Middle Class Stability." Ottawa: Canadian Centre for Policy Alternatives.

Masters, D. C. 1950. *The Winnipeg General Strike.* Toronto: University of Toronto Press.

Maslove, A. M. and Swimmer, G. 1980. *Wage Controls in Canada, 1975–78: A Study of Public Decision Making.* Montreal: Institute for Research on Public Policy.

McBride, S. 1992. *Not Working: State, Unemployment, and Neo-conservatism in Canada.* Toronto: University of Toronto Press.

Palmer, Bryan P. 2004. "System Failure: The Breakdown of the Post-War Settlement and the Politics of Labour in our Time." *Labour/Le Travail* 55, 334–46.

Panitch, L. and Swartz, D. 1988. *The Assault on Trade Union Freedoms: From Consent to Coercion Revisited.* Toronto: Garamond

Pentland, H. Clare. 1968. "A Study of the Changing Social, Economic and Political Background of the Canadian System of Industrial Relations." Draft Study Prepared for the Task Force on Labour Relations. Ottawa: Privy Council Office.

PressProgress. 2015. "Canada creates auto sector jobs in US and Mexico as 1,000 GM workers laid off in Canada." (30 April). Available online.

Press, Jordan. 2016. "Liberals To Repeal Controversial Tory Union Bills C-377, C-525." *Huffingtonpost* (28 January). Available online.

Rose, Joseph B. 2005. "Unions in the Time of Revolution: Government Restructuring in Alberta and Ontario—A Review Article." *Journal of Labor Research* 26(3): 519–31.

Ross, Stephanie and Larry Savage (eds.). 2013. *Public Sector Unions in the Age of Austerity*. Halifax: Fernwood.

Ross, S. 2012. "Business Unionism and Social Unionism in Theory and Practice," in S. Ross and L. Savage, eds., *Rethinking the Politics of Labour in Canada*. Halifax: Fernwood.

Russell, Bob. 1990. *Back to Work? Labour State and Industrial Relations in Canada*. Scarborough: Nelson Canada.

Ryerson, Stanley. 1968. *Unequal Union Confederation and the Roots of Conflict in Canada 1815-1873*. Toronto: Progress Books.

Savage, L. 2012. "Organized Labour and the Politics of Strategic Voting," in S. Ross and L. Savage, eds., *Rethinking the Politics of Labour in Canada*.

Sinclair-Waters, Brynne. 2014. "Understanding Union Security and its Effects." Ottawa: Canadian Centre for Policy Alternatives.

Smith, Charles W. 2008. "The Politics of the Ontario Labour Relations Act: Business, Labour, and Government in the Consolidation of Post-War Industrial Relations, 1949-1961." *Labour/Le Travail* 62, 109–51.

Smucker, Joseph. 1980. *Industrialization in Canada*. Scarborough, Prentice-Hall.

Statistics Canada. 2014. "Union Coverage in Canada, 2013."

Stevens, Andrew and Dough Nesbitt. 2014. "Working in the shadows for transparency: Bills C-377 and C-525." Rank and File.

Supreme Court of Canada. 2016. Case Summary http://www.scc-csc.ca/case-dossier/info/sum-som-eng.aspx?cas=36500.

Swimmer, Gene and Tim Bartkiw. 2003. "The Future of Public Sector Collective Bargaining in Canada." *Journal of Labor Research* 24(4): 579–95.

Warner, Kris. 2013. "The Decline in Unionization in the United States: Some Lessons from Canada." *Labor Studies Journal* 38(2): 110–38.

Wolfe, David. 1977. "The State and Economic Policy in Canada, 1968-75", in Leo Panitch, ed., *The Canadian State*. Toronto: University of Toronto Press.

Wolfe, David. 1984. "The Rise and Demise of the Keynesian Era in Canada 1930-82," in Michael S. Cross and Gregory S. Kealey, eds., *Readings in Canadian Social History of Canada, vol. 5: Modern Canada, 1930–1980s*. Toronto: McClelland and Stewart.

Wood, W.D. and Pradeep K. (eds.). 1976. *Canadian perspectives on Wage and Price Guidelines*. Kingston: Queens University Center for Industrial Relations.

Woods, Harry D. 1973. *Labour Policy in Canada*. 2nd edition. Toronto: Macmillan.

10
Conclusions: Restoring and Refocusing the State

In the opening chapter of the book I described a labour market that has become dysfunctional. This is particularly true for those employed in the precarious, low-waged sectors of the labour market, and for those trying to gain entry to the labour market on terms and conditions that would provide a reasonable standard of living. Compared to the post-World War II era, workers are less likely to be in full-year, full-time employment, to be covered by a union contract, to receive benefits if they become unemployed, and are more likely to be in a precarious, part-time or temporary working situation, in receipt of low pay and, as a result, less likely to have any sort of benefits package beyond that provided by the state.

The trends noted are by no means limited to Canada. Neoliberalism and the flexibility agenda are international phenomena. Especially since the economic crisis of 2007/8 there has been sporadic opposition but without an overall pattern or alternative emerging. Amidst the anti-austerity demonstrations and electoral results showing a rise in left parties in some countries, and right wing populist parties in others, two events deserve mention. The Brexit vote, ostensibly on whether Britain should remain in or leave the European Union, and the election of Donald Trump as President of the United States, are undoubtedly complex events that will receive much analysis in coming years. However, an undercurrent in both of them seems to have been extreme dissatisfaction by sizeable sections of the population who feel they have been "left behind" and that their economic present and future, shaped by the kind of labour market we have identified, seems bleak. How important the labour market factor is compared to others is beyond the scope of this work, but it can hardly be doubted that employment conditions have generated significant dissatisfaction with the performance of the system. Of course, how that real dissatisfaction is framed in political terms is the stuff of ideological contestation. Settling on the causes and the range of solutions are the subject of wide and different interpretations. For example, the extent to which the repudiation of trade agreements would deliver jobs, after several decades of integration of national economies and international supply chains within firms: this is an area of ongoing debate.

In Canada, as elsewhere, new forms of precarious employment continue to emerge. Examples include unpaid internships in which participants work for nothing in the hope or expectation, frequently dashed, that they will gain the experience necessary to be hired by the firm providing the internship. Then there are jobs in the "gig" economy such as drivers for Uber, who can be designated as "self-employed," thereby allowing de facto employers of de facto workers to escape employment standards provisions. Older forms of precarious employment, such as that in temporary employment agencies, have enjoyed a revival in this period as well. Precarious employment has broader social implications. Those employed precariously are often excluded from community involvement and more likely to suffer negative health effects.

The labour market is an increasingly unequal place and the social supports and benefits for those who fail to prosper in it are inadequate to sustain a decent standard of living and quality of life. The social determinants of health literature refers to social and economic conditions that have an effect on the health of both individuals and communities. Pertinent resources under a social determinants of health framework include income, education, health services, housing, and nutrition. Society's members do not have an equal ability to access these resources that, as research shows, influence their health outcomes in significant ways (Raphael 2009). Moreover, as the well-documented volume by Wilkinson and Pickett (2010) demonstrates, the effects of inequality contaminate whole societies, not just those who are at the bottom of the hierarchy.

Nor is the outlook for the future encouraging. New technology, such as automation in general, artifical intelligence (AI), "cashless" banking (cbsnews.com/news/stores-to-customers-cash-not-welcome-here/), automated customer service, and computerization predict major job losses in sectors of the economy. These sectors have generated full-time employment for hundreds of thousands of lesser-skilled workers and now are under threat. Take, for example, truck driving, which is the largest employer of male workers in North America. Indeed, it is the most common job in 29 of the 50 states in the US (npr.org/sections/money/2015/02/05/382664837/map-the-most-common-job-in-every-state). Automation in this sector will have serious consequences. More generally, Sunil Johal, policy director of the Mowat Centre in Toronto, predicted that between 1.5 and 7.5 million Canadian workers could be displaced by technological changes such as artificial intelligence and robotics over the coming decade (cited in Hennessy 2017).

Complaints of dysfunctionality from the employers' side surface less frequently. The labour market has, after all, been restructured in their general interest by providing them with flexibility to manage their employees in a less regulated way. Most of their complaints have to do with skill-shortages in specific occupations or professions, or the unavailability of cheap temporary workers at prevailing wages and conditions, a gap frequently filled by resorting to temporary migrant workers rather than improving wages and conditions. But for the most part the labour market is a buyers' market so employer complaints are muted. And the logic of competitiveness leads employers to deploy strategies which suppress wages and employment security.

Dissatisfaction with neoliberal austerity has found electoral expression in Canada. Many factors beyond the labour market fed into the defeat of the Conservative Harper government in 2015 and its replacement by a Liberal government, led by Justin Trudeau. Both the governing Conservatives and the opposition NDP espoused a continuation of fiscal conservativism through balanced budgets. However, the Liberals' election campaign had sounded the need for change. In particular their campaign seemed to promise an end to, or at least an easing of, austerity measures.

Having won the election, the reality may turn out to be different. Investment in infrastructure and acceptance of modest budget deficits made an attractive link to more jobs and better opportunities. However, the chosen vehicle, the Infrastructure Bank, may serve a different agenda. Its structure seems intended to grant equity ownership rights to private capital through investment entities like public-private partnerships: "the same model tagged with adding $8-billion unnecessarily to Ontario's long-run debt, or where borrowing through partnerships, is doubling long-run costs for British Columbia taxpayers" (Whiteside 2016).

The new government has allowed the deficit to rise but, disappointingly, has also signalled that experiences in the labour market may not be all that different to those prevailing to this point in time. In late 2016 Finance Minister Bill Morneau warned that Canadians should get used to so-called "job churn"—short-term employment and a number of career changes in a person's life—and went on to say that high employee turnover and short-term contract work will continue to be features of young people's working lives (*National Post*, 22 October 2106). While the ratio of part-time to full-time jobs varies from year to year in 2016 there were 153,700 net new part-time jobs and just 60,400 full-time positions (*The Star*, January 6 2017), figures that suggest Morneau's prediction might not be off the mark.

Such comments imply that even if ameliorated the substance of the shift from full-employment to flexible employment will remain and current policy-makers and policies offer no solution. In Chapters 4 to 9 of this book, we have looked at specific policies central to employment and noted the pre-occupation with supply of labour, rather than demand for it, which is taken to be given, or established by market forces with minimal state interference. The demand-side focus of the Keynesian era is long gone. Here, I reprise some of what the supply-side chapters have to say about how the labour market has been structured into its present form. The overall conclusion must be that these policies have not worked. On the contrary, they have produced, or contributed to producing, the insecure and problematic labour market described in this book.

In Chapter 4 the evolution of the Canadian training regime was outlined. Above all, training has to do with the quality of the workforce that will be available to employers, and the type of opportunities that will be available to prospective employees. For employers, the training regime can provide suitably trained workers, either with generic skills through the regular education system, or more specific ones through training programs. For workers, training represents what Standing (1999) referred to as "skill reproduction security," that is the opportunity to gain, retain, or upgrade skill sets and achieve employment as a result. There is an equity component as well as an efficiency one. Other things being equal, better-skilled workers will enhance economic efficiency, and skill acquisition can provide a route out of poverty and towards economic security for variously disadvantaged workers. Whilst not absent from the training portfolio equity considerations can hardly be said to have been of primary importance in the development of training policy

Until the 1960s, the Canadian state was not heavily invested in the provision of training. Thereafter, greater priority was accorded to this policy area, though implementation was difficult due to the jurisdictional issues covered in Chapter 2. One of the big issues in training policy—and intimately linked to its theoretical underpinnings in human capital theory—is the development of a highly skilled labour force. Should this be a social asset with general benefits, with all the funding and collective responsibility that this implies, or should training and acquisition of human capital assets be individual responsibilities, the successful performance of which will enhance individual rewards in the labour market? The funding and potential responsibilities of government are quite different in the two models.

For much of its history Canadian training policy focused on education, and hence incidental acquisition of generic skills, leaving the rest to the market and individuals. In the 1980s and 1990s there was a serious effort to build an active labour market policy featuring a high-skill, high-wage, competitive economy. It foundered on the reluctance of Canadian business to engage in the type of corporatist planning and power-sharing with labour that would be required. Since the mid-1990s there has been increased emphasis on the second approach, labour market deregulation that encourages individual adaptation to whatever the labour market is offering. In this approach, active labour market policy refers more to the "activation" of individuals to adapt to the market, even if that means provision of low-skills, life-skills appropriate for a low-wage economy.

In terms of the immigration file the supply of quantities of labour and the qualitative characteristics of this labour are both present. There have, of course, been other motives at work in immigration policy. These include nation-building, overcoming adverse demographic trends, attracting investors, humanitarian concerns as with refugees or family re-unification, and so forth. However, an economic focus has played a major part. To say there are economic motivations behind immigration policy, however, does not preclude considerable debate about what types of immigration best serves economic needs. One view has focused on the contribution of immigration to population growth and, through it, economic growth and expanded demand. This view has been relatively insensitive to the state of the economic cycle, and its advocates have supported significant immigrant flows even when unemployment was high. As well, this approach is less concerned with the specific skills that immigrants might possess and, at least in the contemporary period, favours generic skills conferred by education on the grounds that these promote adaptation on the part of workers.

Others, operating from a narrower construction of business interests emphasize the short-term interests of businesses requiring a certain volume of immigration possessed of in-demand skills. Thus, suitably skilled immigrants can function as a "just-in-time" labour force. Similarly, from a labour perspective there has often been oppositicon to the importation of labour, especially in economically challenging times, on the grounds that the increased supply would serve to depress wage levels in such a context. Thus the notion of the "absorptive capacity" of the economy served to calibrate levels of immigration with the economic cycle and tended to enjoy labour's support.

In recent years there has been an expansion of the role of temporary foreign workers—that is, workers who generally have no entitlement to, or even possibility of applying for, permanent residency, who migrate (temporarily for work purposes) but are not able to immigrate.

Apart from physically adding people to the labour force through immigration, the size of the labour force can also be adjusted by defining certain categories of people into it or out of it, and by providing generous social programs that could reduce its size by creating opportunities for survival outside the labour force or, alternatively, less generous ones that increase participation in the labour force by making receipt of social benefits difficult to obtain or conditional on achieving rapid labour force re-attachment. Direct measures include imposing minimum ages for child employment and maximum ages for retirement. Less direct measures could include stipulating years of compulsory schooling, which would reduce children's ability to participate in the labour force, and abolishing mandatory retirement, which will increase the working life of at least some labour force participants. As we saw in Chapter 6 the general trend has been to increase labour supply by reducing decommodification opportunities under a more stringent system of employment insurance and associated social policies. Similarly, we saw in Chapter 7 that restrictions on employment of children have been eased, and noted the abolition of mandatory retirement provisions.

Also in Chapter 7 we observed that while the regulation of employment standards could be an instrument to defend or extend workers' rights, their design and implementation has always been moderated by a countervailing recognition that employers' cost stuctures must be protected. In the neoliberal period this imperative has loomed ever larger and many standards have declined or their enforcement has gradually diminished. In terms of Standing's categorization of security, these chapters show adverse effects on employment security, work security, and income security.

Within a general context of a flexible, insecure, and unequal labour market there have been special measures to address the plight of designated vulnerable groups—women, the disabled, indigenous Canadians, racial minorities and young people. Programs for these groups have had some impact but are generally viewed as insufficient to overcome their disadvantages. As a result, not only are their potential labour-force contributions underutilized, but their life experiences and life chances are circumscribed.

Finally, Chapter 9 described how representation security, achieved by workers having a voice through their trade unions, had declined along with union density, especially in the private sector. This factor, along with the hostile legislative environment and the impact of globalization, meant that the power of workers to bargain collectively was undermined. Those outside unions faced a situation of individual negotiations with employers in an inhospitable context. In the neoliberal period, a combination of structural factors unleashed by globalization and political initiatives reflecting the anti-union bias of neoliberalism have combined to weaken unions and representational security, and particularly so in the private sector. The decline in private sector union membership has resulted in a marked shift in the profile of union members. A majority of Canadian union members are employed in the public sector and are female. In an era of permanent public sector austerity, this dramatically shifts the focal point of struggle to the state sector; this has implications for the relatively "privileged" employment contract in the public sector and the adoption by public sector employers of strategies to flexibilize their workforces through short-term contracting and the use of third party contractors to deliver programs.

Looked at in the long-term, today's employer-friendly labour market and Canada's employment policy might be seen as a product of path-dependency. In terms of the "variety of capitalism" literature, Canada has always been, and remains, a liberal market economy (albeit one with a degree of "statism" that might be more highly developed than is generally found within that category). Path dependence describes a phenomenon wherein moves in a direction elicit further moves in that same direction ("continuity") partly because they are based on the idea that early conditions continue to matter. This means that a particular policy "path" becomes "locked-in," making shifts away from it increasingly difficult. The pattern of continuity would include the deep roots of the state's concern with the supply of labour and, within certain limits, allowing the relative power of capital and labour to shape the labour market, mostly to capital's advantage. From this historical perspective, it is the period between roughly 1945 and 1975 that is exceptional and in need of explanation. The rest is normal.

However, such a view tends to downplay the significance of that exceptional period and of the processes that led to its dismantling. Those processes were protracted and, in some respects, are ongoing, and have contributed to the creation of a quite different labour market than that which existed in the post-war era. Then, and without indulging in any kind of golden-age nostalgia, jobs were easier to find because of relatively full employment; also conditions, including greater equality of outcomes, were better. The various types of security referred to in the first chapter were all more highly developed than they are now. The dysfunctional, supply-side labour market (for workers) that has developed since the mid-1970s is not an expression of a pre-Keynesian path dependency. The conditions which gave rise to Keynesian policies in the post-war period have either faded or disappeared. These included memories of the hardships of the Great Depression, a sense of national unity and faith in the state forged during World War II, the existence of an ideological rival in the shape of the USSR and its alternative model, working class strength developed during the wartime years of full-employment, the determination of returning veterans to avoid a repeat of the aftermath of the previous war when unemployment quickly resurfaced, and a theoretical account of how this might be averted (McBride 2005, 4–7; Stanford 2008, 45–51, 326–28). Though today's labour market may share some characteristics, including insecurity with that distant pre-Keynesian past, it is something new, forged in the battle of neoliberalism against Keynesianism, and in the transition from nationally based, albeit internationally linked economies, to globalization. The "credit" for today's labour market rests firmly with the neoliberal governments and their policies that have ruled in Canada and elsewhere, since the 1970s.

In short we need to return to the question "what happened?" And perhaps more importantly in terms of considering alternatives, to the question "why did it happen?" To the extent that today's labour market is the result of unstoppable structural forces on the one hand, and some iron law of path dependency on the other, it may be that there is little to be done except, as Finance Minister Bill Morneau advised young Canadians, to "get used to it." This would be a contemporary expression of Mrs. Thatcher's famous aphorism: "There is no alternative." Consciously or not this approach does seem to have informed public policy towards employment. On the other hand, to the extent that today's labour market occurs "by design," either by capital or the state, then possibilities for changing it and escaping its insecurities and sparse opportunities may be achievable by political means.

In the mid-1970s the Keynesian paradigm and its post war construction—the welfare state—experienced a crisis. In Canada the political consensus and class compromise surrounding Keynesian policy began to unravel with the Bank of Canada's 1975 conversion to monetarism, a technical monetary policy doctrine that held that control of inflation was of higher priority than attempting to deliver full-employment. By the time of the 1995 federal budget the Keynesian era was definitively over.

The great unravelling was crisis-driven but, like any crisis, its interpretation was contested. Ideas about the crisis, and what to do about it, mattered. Ultimately the ideas that prevailed were those that responded to concerns among Canadian capital, and its counterparts elsewhere, about how capital accumulation processes could be maintained and potential threats to capital's hegemony from labour and potentially from the state itself, could be averted. After the United States removed the dollar from gold convertibility in 1972 the international monetary system became unpredictable, capital searched more energetically for cheaper production sites, and a process of "de-industrialization" began in the advanced industrial states. This was compounded by the oil crisis and inflation. Unemployment began to drift upwards and, with it, a "fiscal crisis" of the state was proclaimed (O'Connor 1973) as state revenues and expenditures (at existing tax rates) were declared incompatible.

The solution that found favour with capital and political forces on the right involved a reduced and redefined role for the state. Pushing an agenda of balanced budgets, suppressing inflation even at the cost of high unemployment, privatization, and deregulation, and mobility for capital internationally along with free trade, the most powerful business organizations in Canada initiated a reorganization of the structure of business representation and used it first to win over virtually the entire business community (which, in the mid 1970s, was still somewhat divided), and then to extend their reach to the broader society. In 1976 the Business Council on National Issues (BCNI) was founded[6] comprising the CEOs of the top 150 companies in Canada and including, as ex-officio members, the heads of the other main peak business organizations, the Chamber of Commerce and the Canadian Manufacturers Association. The BCNI spearheaded an "attitude adjustment" in the ranks of business (Bradford 1998) and both directly, and through corporate financed think-tanks, did the same in the broader political culture.

Ideationally, Keynesianism was declared a failure, partly because it was seen as too tolerant of budget deficits that had now seemed counter-productive. Keynesianism was also dismissed because it failed to anticipate the simultaneous appearance of inflation *and* unemployment. According to some versions of Keynesianism, which reference the Phillips curve, a country might expect one or the other but not both at the same time. Given the inability of governments to escape this awkward combination of economic problems, new alternatives began to be posed. In practice control of inflation was privileged and unemployment was left to find its own "natural" level.

With the benefit of hindsight the transition amounts to a twenty-year period of sustained pressure in a neoliberal direction punctuated by efforts to find alternatives.[7] Canadians were reluctant converts to the tenets of neoliberalism and the state's gradual orchestration of the change was a necessary feature.

Faced with the economic crisis of the mid-1970s, fissures emerged or deepened between and within political parties, and between different state institutions. Canadian capital had come to define its interests in continental, or even global terms, and gradually political parties the media and public discourse came to reflect these priorities. Rather than rely on a relatively small internal market big players in Canadian business increasingly favoured an export-led growth strategy (Coher 1991). Rather than being sustained by high wages, domestic demand would be supported by increased levels of consumer debt. In Canada, for example, consumer debt as a percentage of disposable income

6 It later became known as the Canadian Council of Chief Executives (CCCE) and, in 2016 changed its name once more to the Business Council of Canada.

7 Such alternatives included trying to alleviate inflation through wage controls in the mid-1970 rather than interest-rate induced recessions and high unemployment; and a nationalist industria policy, as with the National Energy Program, seen as an alternative to continentalism and lettin market forces work their way, as represented by free trade with the United States.

increased from levels in the 60 to 80 percent range in the 1960s and 1970s, to 110 percent in 2000, and 165 percent in 2015.[8] Underpinning this trend were policies to make mortgage borrowing easier with a resultant rise in home ownership and rising property values—a process found in many countries and described by Colin Crouch (2011, Chapter 5) as "privatized Keynesianism," signifying the substitution of private debt for public spending in sustaining consumption. The term is really a misnomer as there was nothing Keynesian about the goals; even if debt did sustain demand to some degree, it did so in a context of downward pressure on wages, less than full-employment, and increasing precarity and insecurity within the labour market. This was one aspect of what has come to be described as "financialization." Another side of financialization was the deregulation of the financial sector, increased risk-taking and speculation, and asset bubbles. Large fortunes were to be made in the financial economy and in conjunction with flatlined wages, and reduced taxes, produced widening inequality in society. Ultimately, of course, these processes culminated in the great financial crisis of 2007–2008 (see Teeple 2011).

In the neoliberal economic strategy the price of access to large external markets involved opening up the Canadian market to increased foreign competition. Both the pressure to export and the pressure to be competitive with cheaply produced imports exerted downward pressure on wages. An additional perceived benefit of free trade was that the rules embodied in free trade agreements would constrain state activism.

The means of ensuring accumulation changed from the light interventionism of the Keynesian state, predicated on sustaining adequate domestic demand and a high wage, full-employment economy, to an export-led strategy in the "real economy," but driven by financialization—the growing size, importance, and profitability of an increasingly deregulated finance sector which has prospered at the expense of the rest of the economy and led to greater inequality. In these conditions, good domestic labour conditions were seen as obstacles to competitiveness, rather than contributors to national economic growth. The drive to make labour markets more flexible (for employers) was a key part of the neoliberal package. In that context the state focused on opening foreign markets for Canadian exporters and investors through free

8 publications.gc.ca/collections/collection_2012/banque-bank-canada/FB4-11-2010-eng.pdf, Chart 13; livingwagecanada.ca/index.php/blog/income-trends-and-canadian-consumer-debt/

trade agreements and constraints on domestic labour to contain labour costs. Free trade made possible cheap imports that reduced upward pressure for wages, and capital mobility—the ability to move or plausibly threaten to move production to cheaper locations—strengthened the hand of capital in dealing with labour. Thus the problems observed in the labour market are partly attributable to the overall neoliberal policy paradigm and accumulation strategy being pursued. One indicator of the outcomes is the share of wages in national income. A joint report by the International Labour Organization and the OECD (ILO/ OECD 2015) for the G20 Employment Working Group reported significant declines in the share of national income going to labour between 1990 and 2011 for the EU 28 countries plus 11 others including Canada. Between 1970 and 2014 the share of labour in Canada declined by around 7 percent. In the US, UK, and France, for whom longer-term data is available, labour's share of national income has gone back to pre-World War II levels.

Notwithstanding, or perhaps because of such results, key actors and elites remain committed to the neoliberal approach and this ideological consensus constitutes an obstacle to the development of alternatives. A further obstacle lies in the "constitutionalization" of important economic powers through international agreements. This involves the removal of some policy instruments from the discretion of nation-states. This is all the more important as employment policy is essentially a derivative of some of these other policy instruments.

In the most developed of these arrangements, the European Union, broad areas of economic policy-making are either removed from national control, subject to co-determination between national or supranational institutions, or left in the hands of national governments operating under constraints orchestrated by Brussels (see McBride 2016). For countries like Canada a sort of international or external constitution (Clarkson 2003) operates to constrain its national policy capacity, but in a context where supra-national institutions are hardly developed. Rather, rules are imposed through trade and investment agreements. These newer agreements reach far further beyond national borders than did their equivalents negotiated in the post-war period. Enforcement is sometimes through state-to-state dispute settlement adjudicated by an international body such as the World Trade Organization (WTO). Increasingly common, at least at the level of obtaining financial damages for adverse regulation, investor state dispute settlement mechanisms are used. These give foreign investors the right to launch cases against states and have them adjudicated under the rules of international commercial arbitration. Such procedures have been widely criticized as inducing "regulatory chill" on states (see Van Harten 2009, 2–3). Critics and protestors against this transfer of public to private authority have not been entirely ineffective. Negotiations over the TransPacific Partnership (TPP), involving a dozen Pacific-rim countries, and the Comprehensive Economic and Trade Agreement (CETA) between Canada and the EU, ran into ratification difficulties partly based on opposition to the inclusion of such procedures.

If industrial policy instruments like trade and investment policy are circumscribed by international agreements, in Canada it is largely domestic pressures that restrict monetary policy and fiscal policy options—though even here the influence of the international neoliberal consensus exerts its influence. That said, such ideational influences are weaker than the institutionally embedded constraints imposed on members of the Eurozone or Fiscal Compact in Europe, which seeks to automatically adjust budgets and public debt to predetermined levels and thus remove fiscal policy from everyday politics.

Against this background, and recognising that in many ways employment policy is derived from or conditioned by these other policy areas, what can be done about the labour market that has been constructed in recent decades? We have noted that the issues in Canada's labour market are far from unique. International variations do exist but to various degrees all the industrialized countries suffer from the effects of precarity and insecurity, rising inequality, and diminishing opportunities and security.

Could different political choices make a difference to the outcomes and reverse or improve the labour market experiences of the recent period? One often meets the argument that there is "no going back" to the days of Keynesian full-employment as the conditions that promoted that political economy no longer exist. The power of this argument can be readily conceded. The specific historical conditions that ushered in that period have passed and could not be re-created.

However, it hardly follows that we are therefore stuck forever with the type of neoliberal global economy and the labour market it has created, which have been described in this book. Of course, just as Rome was not built in a day, neither was the flexible and insecure neoliberal labour market. Equally, even if possible, its undoing and replacement will prove a lengthy and complex affair. And with the neoliberal components—flexibilization, deregulation, privatization, the austerity state, and international capital mobility—being intertwined and interconnected, the development of alternatives is rendered difficult. Still, it seems unduly pessimistic and passive to conclude that nothing can be done about our unequal and dismal labour market.

Reviewing the details of previous chapters it is not difficult to compose a list of measures that could alleviate the difficulties many face in the labour market, and that in some cases could increase aggregate demand in the economy and thus demand for labour. Examples might include decreasing the incentives given to employers to use flexible, insecure, and precarious workers by providing more stringent regulation of employment conditions, extending benefits to such workers on a pro-rated basis, and providing them with greater certainty about matters such as scheduling and increased call-out guarantees. Minimum wages might be increased to living wage levels. Training programs could be expanded based not just on employer demands but on the need or desire of workers to acquire new skills and hence better their economic opportunities. Labour legislation might be reformed to make it easier to organize and to bargain effectively. Employment standards could be strengthened for all workers and, above all, strictly enforced to end widespread employer violations of whatever standards are decided on. So called gig economy workers should be recognized as employees and have all employment standards extended to them. The (un-)employment insurance system needs reform and to be restored to former levels in terms of its coverage of those who become unemployed. Programs addressing the employment needs of vulnerable groups should be expanded. Use of temporary foreign workers (TFWs) should be reduced. If positions are more or less permanent, even if the occupants are temporary, and cannot be filled by local workers, then levels of permanent immigration should be adjusted upwards to fill the gap. Rights including the right to apply for permanent status, should be extended to the remaining complement of TFWs. The welfare state should be reformed to concentrate on meeting actual needs rather than serving as is the case with some of its programs, as an adjunct to conditioning labour force attachment. Huge and already identifiable needs in areas like long-term care should be the subject of public investment and increased public sector employment. An industrial policy, including filling infrastucture deficits, should be deployed. On grounds of greater efficiency these will likely be public ventures rather than private or P3 collaborations. Clearly the list could be extended.

Equally clearly, implementing such a program, or even significant parts of it, would run into objections from the beneficiaries of the neoliberal ideology that has dominated public discourse for decades. The improvements in labour market conditions would be costly. Some of the costs would be borne by consumers who would have to pay more for goods and services than they do now. (Offsetting that effect, many of these consumers would benefit from the improved labour market conditions created.) Public expenditure would also increase and with it taxation. Some tax implications could be offset by closing tax loopholes (Macdonald 2017) that benefit the affluent and by creating a fairer tax system, but there is no getting away from the fact that societies get what they pay for, and tax levels would need to increase to meet the objectives of a more equal society, and decent living and working standards for all.

All the ingredients of the neoliberal package—labour market flexibility and insecurity, the unequal society, austerity, a reduced and constrained state, deregulation, privatization, free trade, and capital mobility—would be challenged. It would require a real paradigm shift of similar scope to that which occurred between 1975 and 1995. The new paradigm would need to prioritize security over flexibility, greater equality rather than inequality, public and state over private and market, and national obligations to citizens over international ones to capital. And, like any rising paradigm it would need organizations and social forces prepared to wage a political battle for its implementation.

There are some signs that the twin edifices of neoliberalism and globalization are under challenge, though mostly not in the way posited above. In fact, the failure of the left to mount a challenge to structures of neoliberalism (Evans 2014)[9] has opened the way for right wing authoritarian movements to reap the political benefits of growing discontent with neoliberal globalization. The crisis of 2008 posed significant difficulties for neoliberal global elites in managing the system their policies had created. For a time the entire system seemed on the verge of melt-down and collapse. Although that was averted the years since have not been encouraging. Economic recovery has been incomplete, slow, and fragile. And 2016 is widely seen as the year in which some of the system's political chickens came home to roost. Elite responses to events such as the Brexit referendum and the US Presidential

---

9 Although there are exceptions, Podemos in Spain, and in the June 2017 UK elections, the relative success of the Labour Party, led by Jeremy Corbyn and running on a left manifesto.

election show denial and incomprehension at the outcomes. In the UK a majority of voters opted to leave the European Union. In the US, although Donald Trump lost the popular vote, under that country's electoral college system he was a comfortable winner of the election. The sheer nastiness of the Trump campaign in the US, and of some of those involved in the "Leave" campaign in the UK, often taking overtly racist and misogynist forms, help account for the negative reactions to the results.

But equally obviously, (neo-) liberal elites of all political affiliations seem unable to comprehend any rationality lying behind the rejection of neoliberal globalization and its policies and institutions (like the EU). Large numbers of people indicated their alienation from the existing economic and political system. At some level they consider, correctly, that they have been left behind economically and their views and opinions are ignored politically. In some way, not always clearly articulated, and often expressed unattractively, they attribute this situation to globalization and the remote and cosmopolitan elites in charge. Invited, honestly or not, to vote to "take back control of the country" or to "make America great again," large numbers of people accepted the invitation. In doing so they delivered a verdict that poses a widely recognized challenge to the certainties of neoliberal globalization. They have noticed that the neoliberal emperor has no clothes. The politics surrounding globalization are therefore much more fluid than formerly. Opportunities may exist to challenge components of the neoliberal consensus and devise and implement progressive alternatives that are quite different from the inchoate expressions of rage represented by right wing populism. This raises the issue of which spatial level such challenges are likely to emerge.

In a year-end review, BBC journalist Gavin Hewitt (2016) looked ahead to 2017 as the year which would see a "battle of ideas" between nationalism and internationalism. Would solutions to the on-going crisis of neoliberal globalization be found through further internationalization, or through attempting to return to greater power or autonomy for nation-states?

Most liberals and many on the political left would prefer an internationalist solution. More international decision-making and coordination is seen as necessary to steer the global economy. Partly this is driven by the argument that international capital can no longer be controlled by any nation-state (though many of the people making this argument do not, in truth, favour controlling international capital anyway). Partly it is driven by the ugliness of the revived nationalism on display in parts of the European Union and in the United States. Yet the history of creating international institutions shows little evidence of controlling capital. Rather the purpose of the international institutions created has been to liberate capital from controls and confer greater rights upon it. As income and wealth inequality statistics show, the result has been the further enrichment of the already rich. Democratic accountability through national governments has been sacrificed and there are virtually no supranational accountability mechanisms. Given the post-crisis posture of the European Union, for example, and the on-going efforts to constitutionalize neoliberal principles in its institutions (McBride 2016) it is unclear why anyone would expect anything except more of the same from further internationalization. Again, taking the European Union as an example of regional integration it is clear that whatever it might once have represented, what it actually has become is a thoroughly neoliberal institution. None of the established elites—economic, political, or media—would consider changing those characteristics which are seen as natural, valid, and beyond dispute. For those favouring greater equality, and greater security, the evidence points to the international option as being a complete dead end.

That leaves the national level. Canada, of course, is not as implicated in regional entities as the members of the EU and on paper has more freedom of action. NAFTA, for example, is a rules-based agreement with very weak institutions, and its continued existence has been questioned by the United States. However, a number of factors including its modest population size, and the way the country is located in the international political economy, as a relatively open economy with a high degree of trade dependency overwhelmingly concentrated on the United States market, significantly constrain Canada's autonomy. How might a country with this profile improve the characteristics of its labour market and, by doing so, improve the conditions of life and the economic prospects of its citizens?

The 2015 federal election hinted at a rethink of some of the fundamentals of the austerity approach favoured by the Conservative government. Liberal leader Justin Trudeau expressed less concern about budget deficits than his competitors and this anti-austerity stance won him a majority government. And the Liberal government has kept its promise to run a significant (albeit still modest) budget deficit in the name of stimulating the economy. Even by the standards of neoliber-

alism this is a policy position that Canada can easily afford as it has by
far the lowest public debt ratio of any of the G7 countries. The manner
that public spending on infrastructure is to be structured, however,
raises concerns that the budget deficit is not really a departure from
the tenets of the orthodox doctrine. Spending will be financed primarily from private capital markets using public private partnerships
(P3s)—a policy device with long-term costs likely to intensify demands
for austerity in the future (Whiteside 2015). We have already noted
Finance Minister Bill Morneau's advice to young Canadians that they
can expect no respite from the flexible/insecure labour market that
exists. Similarly, then International Trade Minister Chrystia Freeland
told a Toronto Board of Trade meeting that the government was more
enthusiastic than ever about free trade agreements.[10] The Comprehensive Economic and Trade Agreement (CETA) with the EU, which
amongst its many provisions contains an investor – state dispute settlement mechanism, and opens up government procurement to European competition, remains a priority of the government. It seems
then that the rethink is very limited and that the main elements of
neoliberalism remain intact. Thus the Trudeau government, like its
predecessor, is locked into a market first economic strategy, with some
tinkering around the margins, and equally importantly is committed
to expanding the international trade and investment agreements that
constrain any alternative based on a larger and more pro-active role for
the state.

The failure of this strategy to deliver is increasingly apparent. However, the domestic obstacles to change in the form of a bloc of elite
interests and an ideological consensus based on them are formidable
and the institutional constraints imposed by the architecture of international economic agreements reinforce that situation. Yet the current
international mood of disaffection with the effects of neoliberal globalization provides an opportunity to challenge this architecture—in the
first place by refusing to extend it through new agreements, and subsequently to begin disentangling the network of prohibitions and inhi-
bitions that they impose on nation-states. Were it to gain momentum
such a process would also help challenge the postulates of neoliberal
orthodoxy domestically.

That said, the economic and political situation is not conducive
except insofar as a deep crisis clearly demonstrates the failure of the

---

10 cbc.ca/news/business/chrystia-freeland-trade-1.3882032 (December 5, 2016).

old neoliberal paradigm. That paradigm may have been implemented in the late twentieth century but its ideational base is from the (early) nineteenth century. We are ruled by pre-industrial revolution ideas. Moreover, it is increasingly apparent that the four-decade-long experiment with neoliberalism that promised "higher growth rates, higher investment rates, higher productivity rates and a trickle down of income from rich to poor" is broken because it "has delivered none of these things" (Elliott 2017).

A crisis, of course, does not guarantee that change will occur. Many observers are quite pessimistic. Wolfgang Streeck (2014) noted three long-term tendencies: declining rates of economic growth; increased indebtedness, both public and private; and rising inequality of both income and wealth (in which the deregulation of labour markets as examined in this book plays an important role). In his view these trends lead to a "long and painful period of cumulative decay" in which the association between capitalism and democracy may be broken (Streeck 2014, 64).

This is a rather bleak vision. To the extent that we recognize such a bleak future in the absence of political action, it might serve as a call to action. The labour market and employment policy is a good place to begin the pushback against the dominant neoliberal paradigm because a majority of the working age population depend on income earned in the labour market and know, or can sense, that the market and the policies that structure it are not working.

References

Bradford, Neil. 1998. Commissioning Ideas: Canadian National Policy Innovation in Comparative Perspective. Toronto: Oxford University Press.

Clarkson, Stephen. 2003. "Locked In? Canada's External Constitution under Global Trade Governance." *American Review of Canadian Studies* 39(1): 66–76.

Cohen, Marjorie. 1991. "Exports, Unemployment and Regional Inequality: Economic Policy and Trade Theory," in Daniel Drache and Meric S. Gertler, eds., *The New Era of Global Competition: State Policy and Market Power*. Montreal: McGill-Queens University Press.

Crouch, Colin. 2011. *The Strange Non-Death of Neoliberalism*. Cambridge: Polity Press.

Elliott, Larry. 2017. "Populism is the Result of Global Economic Failure." *The*

Guardian (26 March). Available online.

Evans, Bryan. 2014. "Social Democracy in the New Age of Austerity," in Donna Baines and Stephen McBride, eds., *Orchestrating Austerity: Impacts and Resistance*. Halifax: Fernwood.

Hennessy, Angela. 2017. "'As Well or Better than Humans': Automation Set for Big Promotions in White-Collar Job Market." CBC News (28 February). Available online.

Hewitt, Gavin. 2016. "The World in 2017: The Battle of Ideas." BBC News (27 December). Available online.

ILO/OECD. 2015. "The Labour Share in G20 Economies." Report Prepared for the G20 Employment Working Group. Antalya, Turkey.

Macdonald, David. 2017. "Out of the Shadows: Shining a Light on Canada's Unequal Distribution of Federal Tax Expenditures." Ottawa: Canadian Centre for Policy Alternatives.

McBride, Stephen. 2016. "Constitutionalizing Austerity: Taking the Public out of Public Policy." *Global Policy* 5–14

McBride, Stephen. 2005. *Paradigm Shift: Globalization and the Canadian State*. Halifax: Fernwood.

O'Connor, James. 1973. *The Fiscal Crisis of the State*. New York: St Martin's Press.

Raphael, Dennis. 2009. "Social Determinants of Health: An Overview of Concepts and Issues." In *Social Determinants of Health*, 2nd edition. Toronto: Canadian Scholars Press Inc, pp. 2–19.

Standing, Guy. 1999. *Global Labour Flexibility: Seeking Distributive Justice*. Basingstoke: Palgrave.

Stanford, Jim. 2008. *Economics for Everyone: A Short Guide to the Economics of Capitalism*. Halifax: Fernwood.

Streeck, Wolfgang. 2014. "How will capitalism end?" *New Left Review* 87: 35–64.

Teeple, Gary. 2011. "Notes on the Continuing Economic Crisis," in Gary Teeple and Stephen McBride, eds., *Relations of Global Power: Neoliberal Order and Disorder*. Toronto: University of Toronto Press.

Van Harten, Gus. 2009. "Reforming the NAFTA Investment Regime." In Kevin Gallaghar, Enrique Dussel Peters and Timothy Wise, eds., *The Future of North American Trade Policy: Lessons from NAFTA*. A Pardee Center Task Force Report.

Whiteside, Heather. 2016. "Canada Infrastructure Bank: Theft by Deception." *Hill Times* (7 December). Available online.

Whiteside, Heather. 2015. *Purchase for Profit: Public-Private Partnerships and Canada's Public Health Care System*. Toronto: University of Toronto Press.

Wilkinson, Richard and Kate Pickett. 2010. *The Spirit Level: Why Equality is Better for Everyone*. London: Penguin.

Index